Writing Gender History

Also in the *Writing History* series

Published:

Writing History: Theory and Practice, 2nd edition
Edited by Stefan Berger, Heiko Feldner and Kevin Passmore

Writing Contemporary History
Edited by Robert Gildea and Anne Simonin

Writing Medieval History
Nancy Partner

Writing Early Modern History
Garthine Walker

Forthcoming:

Writing Postcolonial History
Rochona Majumdar

Writing the Holocaust
Edited by Jean-Marc Dreyfus and Daniel Langton

Writing the History of Memory
Edited by Stefan Berger and Bill Niven

Writing Gender History

Second edition

Laura Lee Downs

BLOOMSBURY
NEW DELHI • LONDON • OXFORD • NEW YORK • SYDNEY

First Published in India 2017

Bloomsbury Academic
An imprint of Bloomsbury Publishing Plc
Bloomsbury is a registered trade mark of Bloomsbury Publishing Plc

This edition published with permission from Bloomsbury Publishing Plc
50, Bedford Square, London, WC1B3DP

British Library Cataloguing-in-Publication Data
A catalogue record for this book is available from the British Library.

ISBN: 978-9386643-18-6
10 9 8 7 6 5 4 3 2 1
For sale in the Indian subcontinent only

Bloomsbury Publishing India Pvt. Ltd
Second Floor, Building No. 4
DDA Complex LSC, Pocket C – 6 & 7
Vasant Kunj, New Delhi 110070
www.bloomsbury.com

Exclusively Distributed in India by:
Manohar Publishers & Distributors
4753/23, Ansari Road
Darya Ganj, New Delhi 110002
Tel.: 23284848, 23289100
Email: sales@manoharbooks.com, manoharbooks@gmail.com

Series: Writing History
Printed and bound in India

Contents

Acknowledgements vi

Introduction: Writing gender history 1

1 Prologue: Before the second wave: scholarship on women from the early twentieth century into the 1960s 9

2 Second-wave feminism and the rediscovery of women's history, 1968–1975 20

3 Feminist historians and the 'new' social history, 1968–1995 30

4 Is female to male as nature is to culture? Feminist anthropology and the search for a key to all misogynist mythologies 43

5 Beyond separate spheres: from women's history to gender history 55

6 Gender history, cultural history and the history of masculinity 73

7 Gender, poststructuralism and the 'cultural/linguistic turn' in history 88

8 Gender and history in a postcolonial world 106

9 From separate spheres to the public sphere: gender and the sexual politics of citizenship 147

10 Gender and history in a post-poststructuralist world 165

Conclusion: Women's and gender history as a work-in-progress 182

Suggestions for further reading 198

Bibliography 201

Index 214

Acknowledgements

It is a great pleasure to thank here the many people whose generous assistance has allowed me to complete this book. Kevin Passmore and Garthine Walker first encouraged me to write a book on gender history and have followed the project closely ever since, reading and re-reading more draft chapters than I'm sure either of them cares to remember, and offering intellectual companionship and moral support every step of the way. Karen H Adler, Padma Anagol, Becky Conekin, Sanjay Subramanyan, Emmanuelle Saada, Gregory Mann and Tara Zahra read large sections of the manuscript and offered valuable comments and suggestions. I owe a special debt of gratitude to Lynn Hunt and Nancy Cott, each of whom read the entire manuscript and helped me to sharpen and clarify the arguments. Finally, I am grateful to Christopher Wheeler, formerly of Hodder Arnold Press, for having welcomed this book into the *Writing History* series, and to his successor, Michael Strang, who enthusiastically took on a project that was not originally his own.

Introduction

On 18 March 1920, Virginia Woolf reminded readers of the venerable *Times Literary Supplement* that, despite the existence of isolated works on the history of women (one of which she had reviewed that day), the lives and condition of women in history remained shrouded in profound obscurity: 'It has been common knowledge for ages that women exist, bear children, have no beards, and seldom go bald,' wrote Woolf with acerbic wit, 'but save in these respects, and in others where they are said to be identical with men, we know little of them and have little sound evidence upon which to base our conclusions. Moreover, we are seldom dispassionate.'[1] And indeed, aside from the work of a few maverick pioneers, to whom the history of women offered fresh and challenging terrain, women's history would continue to languish in the shadows of which Woolf had complained until the 1960s, when the first stirrings of renewed political activism (feminism's much-vaunted 'second wave') turned the sustained attention of historians and activists towards the recovery and analysis of those who remained 'hidden from history'.

This volume explores the evolution of historical writing about women and gender since the turn of the twentieth century. It focuses primarily on the literatures generated by European and American historians, and pays special attention to developments since the late 1960s. Throughout the volume, we will consider the epistemological consequences that the birth and development of women's and gender history in tandem with a very present-minded political movement have had for the field as a whole. Yet discussion will focus neither on abstract theory nor on historiography per se, but rather upon the practical application of theory in historical scholarship on women and gender. The chapters are organized more thematically than chronologically, though there is a gradual progression from early to mid- to late twentieth century, as the discussion moves from women's history to gender history and then to poststructuralist challenges to women's and gender history. At the core of each chapter lie detailed analyses of one or two works of feminist scholarship around which I have sought to build a textually grounded discussion of the various debates and developments that have marked the evolution of women's and gender history as sub-disciplines.

Of course, you might ask, why write a book on the development of women's and gender history? The answer to that question is twofold. First, the fields of women's and gender history have expanded dramatically in the 40 years since feminism's second wave first crashed on the shores of Europe and North America, showing great vigour and variety in the breadth of subjects tackled and the range of methodologies explored. The sheer energy with which feminist scholarship has unfolded and the diverse forms it has taken seem justification enough for undertaking such a survey. But there is a second, yet more compelling reason to trace the development of women's and gender history, and that is the central role that feminist scholarship has played in the recent evolution of the historical discipline itself. From the complacent reign of macro-social analysis in the 1960s and 1970s to the 'crisis' of such analysis in the 1980s to the cultural and linguistic (or poststructuralist) turns through which that crisis was expressed at the turn of the 1990s, feminist critics and historians have played a crucial part in the often searing 'theory wars' that have divided the discipline for the last 25 years. Women's and gender history thus provide a privileged vantage point from which to consider the larger epistemological debates that have shaken the discipline since the late 1970s. For, as we will see, those debates were very often driven by the frustration of feminist scholars with the limits of traditional approaches when it came to accounting for the specific experiences of women in history.

Due to constraints of space, and the specifics of my own areas of expertise, I have chosen to analyse at some length a fairly limited series of works drawn essentially from the modern period (1750 to the present), and from France, the UK, Germany and the USA, with brief forays into medieval Europe and colonial Africa and India. While this has required that I leave aside much excellent and important research, I believe the closer focus on a selected number of books and articles will allow certain trends that have shaped the fields of women's and gender history to emerge with greater clarity. As a preliminary to the analysis of major texts and concepts that constitutes the main work of this book, the following brief overview lays out several of these trends in a brief survey of the changing shape of the women's and gender history fields over the period 1970–2000.

From women's history to gender history: an overview

In the early 1970s, feminist scholars and activists founded the first women's studies courses in universities and adult education programmes across the USA and Europe.[2] '1973: the first course on women at Jussieu,' recalls Michelle Perrot. 'On the 7th of November, Andrée Michel opened fire with a lecture on "Women and the family in developed societies." The lecture hall was packed, the atmosphere over-heated by the hostility of leftist [male] students for whom the study of women was but a distraction from the real work of revolution.'[3] But such resistance merely fuelled feminist scholars' determination to recover their own history, a history that had been unjustly banished from view, a history that could serve to reinforce feminist politics by offering a historically grounded account of women's identity as a group distinct from men. As publications accumulated, feminist historians moved from their initial, hesitant question, 'Is it possible to write a history of women?' (and what might it look like?), towards the more confidant formulation that to write a history *without* women was a foolhardy endeavour indeed, for it would be to tell barely half the story.[4]

Fired by an enthusiasm that was at once political and intellectual, feminist scholars, students and activists engaged in individual and collective projects of research and teaching whose accumulated, and sometimes unexpected, results did not always fit smoothly into the existing narratives of history.[5] The problem of integrating the 'women's story' soon prompted feminist scholars to challenge the traditional contours of their discipline by posing a new and difficult question: is women's history merely an 'innocuous supplement' to existing narratives, or does the integration of these new stories and perspectives demand that the analytic structures themselves be reshaped?[6] For if, as the growing body of scholarship on women suggested, gender identity was not a biological given but a social and historical creation, then the task of the historian was no longer merely adding women to an existing narrative whose outlines were familiar. Rather, her task was now to excavate the precise meanings that femininity and masculinity have carried in the past, to demonstrate the evolution of those meanings over time, and so reveal the historically constructed nature of these concepts in our present world.

From early on, then, feminist scholars were committed not merely to adding new material to the historical record, but also to changing the analytic structures of historical practice. Crucial to this ambition was the distinction drawn between biological sex, understood as the material and unchanging ground of one's identity, and the infinitely malleable carapace of gender, a socially constructed series of behaviours that code one as male or female, but that vary across time and space in such a way as to reveal their constructed nature.[7] Women (and men, for that matter) were thus made and not born, and much productive research proceeded on the ground of the sex/gender distinction, as feminist historians smoked out the various ways that gender, understood as a socially constructed system of difference, had operated to shape social relations and understandings of self in societies past.

Women's history was fast transforming itself into a broader history of gender relations, though not without protest from scholars who feared that the turn to gender signalled the abandonment of women's history as a feminist political project.[8] Yet the very move by which women's historians had underscored the constructed nature of male and female roles in society had already destabilized the notion of identity as an essential, natural property. In this sense, gender history was immanent in the very development of women's history, and feminist scholars moved increasingly towards the study of gender as a way to locate the experiences of women in a broader context, while arguing for the gendered nature of all human experience, and not simply that of women.[9]

The shift from women's history to gender history over the course of the 1980s thus had several important consequences, not the least of which was to contribute to the development of an entirely new arena of research: that of masculinity and 'men's studies', a field that was to expand and develop rapidly during the 1990s. But de-essentializing maleness and femaleness by underscoring their historical construction also met a vital intellectual need of the young sub-discipline, by taking these categories out of the timeless realm of eternal verities, where male dominance and women's subordination were written into the very order of things, and returning them to the stream of history. By the same token, de-essentializing the category 'woman' served an equally important political goal, underscoring the historical, and hence changeable, non-necessary content of the category as it is deployed in contemporary politics and social policy.

Finally, it was argued that the turn to gender would give feminist scholarship greater impact on the shape of the historical discipline itself. For by the mid-1980s, it was clear that women's history on its own had failed to transform the epistemological bases of the historical discipline, despite the conviction of many feminist historians that the integration of the women's story rendered such transformation inevitable. Rather, women's history was being researched and taught alongside the standard narratives of 'real' history, without affecting those narratives in any fundamental way. The only way to break out of this intellectual ghetto, it was argued, was to cease focusing exclusively on women and follow instead the mutual construction of masculinities and femininities as they have evolved over time. Drawing heavily from the anthropologist's tool kit, historians of gender sought to render the study of sexual division an instrument of historical analysis by arguing that such divisions are rooted in a more global sexual division of social, symbolic and political space. Any history worth the name would henceforth have to abandon the pretext that the masculine represents a neutral and universal history of the species, while the feminine remains the particular object of a revendicating identity politics. Rather, historians of any subject, whether military, social, political or diplomatic, would henceforth have to identify the gendered constitution of their object of analysis, to demonstrate how it had been coded masculine or feminine and then explain what the consequences of that gendering have been for its evolution in time. For gender (unlike women) was everywhere, or so the theory went.

Feminist scholars' desire to render women visible in history thus resulted ultimately in a broader conceptual vision of the social distinction of the sexes; a less militantly woman-centred concept, perhaps, but one which has nonetheless altered historical practice, not only among feminist scholars but among many of their male colleagues as well. Feminist politics and the demands of scholarship thus remained tightly intertwined in the intellectual history of the discipline, even as its practitioners moved outwards from the particulars of women's history to a more universal history of gender, understood as a fundamental aspect of social being and social order.[10]

Throughout its initial phase of development, women's history had been riding the people's history wave, which, fed by a number of streams (notably the *Annales* school and the 'new social history' movement), peaked in the 1960s and early 1970s. In this, the golden age of social history, where scholars strove to restore the voices of common people to history, women found their place as a prime example of the generally-unheard-from in standard history textbooks.[11] In addition, the link to social history gave women's history a strong orientation towards labour history, which was reinforced by the conviction, common to 1970s feminists in Europe and the USA, that one key to women's liberation from the patriarchal domination of fathers and husbands lay in their finding paid employment outside the home.[12]

Social and labour history would continue to dominate the emerging fields of women's and gender history until the late 1980s, by which point historians in general, and women's and gender historians in particular, began turning away from social history, with its basis in macro-structural forms of analysis (social and economic structures as determinants of individual behaviour), towards more cultural and discursive forms of analysis, often grounded in more micro-historical contexts. Thanks to their long-standing recourse to the notion of social construction in the study of masculinities and femininities past, feminist historians found themselves on the cutting edge of this larger poststructuralist movement in historical analysis. For at the very moment that feminist critiques of an essentializing women's history were driving the growth and elaboration of gender history, the entire discipline of social history was engaged as a whole in the search for more nuanced ways of addressing the relationships among the social, material and cultural aspects of history. Frustrated by the limits of earlier, social-science-driven and/or Marxist perspectives, scholars across the discipline placed increasing stress on the importance of the play between representation and social reality. Here, the use of the notion of social construction (in this case of sex/gender) became a way to navigate between the two.

At a time when the discipline of social history was pushing up against the limits of earlier models and conceptualizations, then, feminist historians carved out an avant-garde role for themselves as theoretical and methodological innovators, developing fruitful new approaches that were grounded in psychoanalytic understandings of gender identity-formation, and in the insights of radical feminist consciousness-raising groups into the inherently political nature of domestic gender relations, which are, after all, relations of power. The feminist challenge to stable social categories like male and female, achieved through the historical study of gender relations as they have shifted in time, thus preceded the arrival of poststructuralist theory in departments of history, which arrived bearing the chic banner of 'French theory'. Although such theory had blossomed in departments of language and literature since the late 1970s, the message came to history rather late in the day, borne notably by Joan Wallach Scott in her famous essay, 'Gender: A Useful Category of Historical Analysis', first published in the *American Historical Review* in 1986.[13]

Feminist historians would thus play a leading role in the theoretical and methodological debates that shook the discipline from the late 1980s into the mid-1990s. As we will see, these debates would upset the epistemological certitudes on which history had confidently rested, notably the idea that textual sources give us a direct window onto the past. At the same time, they challenged the original synthesis of scholarship and politics that had characterized women's and gender history, by casting doubt on the notion that at the core of each individual subject lies a stable and coherent identity. In order to explore more concretely what the turn from women's to gender history – and the subsequent engagement with poststructuralism – have meant for the practice of women's and gender history, the remainder of this book discusses the major theoretical and methodological contributions of feminist scholarship since the turn of the twentieth century through a close analysis of particular texts and arguments and their location within the broader historical discipline.

Endnotes

1 Virginia Woolf, review of Léonie Villard, *La Femme anglaise au XIXe siècle et son évolution d'après le roman anglais contemporain* (Henry Didier, 1920), first published in the *Times Literary Supplement*, 18 March 1920, cited in Rachel Bowlby (ed.), *Virginia Woolf: A Woman's Essays* (London, 1992), 18.

2 While feminism is itself a contested word, and one whose meaning has, moreover, shifted over the course of the women's rights movement, one can nonetheless establish a broad definition of the term, one that embraces all who find women's subordinate status to be unjust, and who, furthermore, believe that there is nothing inevitable about this status: it is

a product of human convention and can therefore be changed through human effort.

3 Michelle Perrot, *Les Femmes ou les silences de l'histoire* (Paris, 1998), xi–xii.

4 I refer here to the famous pair of conferences in women's history organized by the University of Toulouse-Le-Mirail in 1983 and 1997, titled, respectively, 'Une histoire des femmes est-elle possible?' and 'Une histoire sans les femmes, est-elle possible?'.

5 The scope and scale of this rapid 'primitive accumulation' in women's history can be measured by the number of new journals that sprang up overnight, some, like *Pénélope* (France) or *Memoria* (Italy), destined to die after just a few years, others, like *Signs* and *Feminist Studies* (USA), *Women's History Yearbook* (Netherlands), *L'Homme* (Austria) *Arenal* (Spain) and *Women's Studies International Quarterly* (UK), are still going strong some 40 years later. At the end of the 1980s and early 1990s, a new generation of journals appeared, including *Clio* and *Travail, genre et sociétés* (France), *Gender & History* (based in the UK but co-edited in the USA), *Women's History Review* (UK) and *The Journal of Women's History* (USA).

6 On women's history as an 'innocuous supplement', see Joan W. Scott, 'Women's History: The Emergence of a New Field', in Peter Burke (ed.), *New Perspectives in Historical Writing* (University Park, PA, 1989).

7 For more on the sex/gender distinction see Annie Oakley, *Sex, Gender and Society* (London, 1972); Gayle Rubin, 'The Traffic in Women: Notes on the Political Economy of Sex', in Rayna Reiter (ed.), *Towards an Anthropology of Women* (New York, 1975), 157–210; Michèle Barrett, *Women's Oppression Today: Problems in Marxist-Feminist Analysis* (London, 1980); and Joan W. Scott, 'Gender: A Useful Category of Analysis', *American Historical Review*, 91 (1986), 1053–75, reprinted in Joan W. Scott, *Gender and the Politics of History* (New York, 1988). For a critique of the ironclad division between biology and culture on which the sex/gender distinction rests, see Mary Midgley, 'On Not Being Afraid of Natural Sex Difference', in Morwenna Griffiths and Margaret Whitford (eds), *Feminist Perspectives in Philosophy* (London, 1988); and Judith Butler, *Gender Trouble: Feminism and the Subversion of Identity* (New York, 1990).

8 See Judith Bennett, 'Feminism and History', *Gender & History*, 1:3 (Autumn 1989), 251–71; and Joan Hoff, 'Gender as a Postmodern Category of Paralysis', *Women's History Review* 3:2 (1994), 149–68. Of course, plenty of feminist historians see no necessary opposition between women's and gender history, but rather a continuity of aims and practices, notably, the common goal of restructuring the historical record using the analytic tool of sexual difference, understood as a social construct, to recast our understanding of societies past. See Jane Rendall, 'Review Article: Women's History: Beyond the Cage?', *History*, 75 (1990), 63–72.

9 Gianna Pomata has argued that women's history and gender history must be understood as inextricably linked in the dialectic movement from the particular (women's history) to general history and back again, with gender history serving as a conduit between the two: 'With its higher claim to generality, gender history can be the bridge that connects the particulars discovered by women's history with wider social contexts, and therefore with the space occupied by general history.' Gianna Pomata, 'Close-ups and Long Shots: Combining Particular and General in Writing the Histories of Women and Men', in Hans Medick and Anne-Charlotte Trepp, *Geschlectergeschichte und Allgemeine Geschichte* (Goettingen, 1998), 117.

10 'Relations between the sexes are a primary aspect of social organization.' Joan W. Scott, 'Women's History', in Scott, *Gender and the Politics of History*, 25.

11 On this point, see Maxine Berg, *A Woman in History. Eileen Power, 1889–1940* (Cambridge, 1996).

12 The focus on work was especially pronounced in the English literature, but was quite visible in the American, French and German literatures of the 1970s and 1980s as well.

13 The Subaltern school of history, with its concern for understanding the articulation of nation and class, occupied a similarly advanced position theoretically. See below, chapter 8.

1

Prologue: Before the second wave: scholarship on women from the early twentieth century into the 1960s

Clearly the history of women has come a long way since Virginia Woolf first underscored our astonishing ignorance on the subject, for as we have seen, the revival of feminist militancy in the late 1960s inspired a vast outpouring of research on women in both Europe and the USA. Yet well before the upheavals of the 1960s, individual scholars like Ivy Pinchbeck in England, Mary Beard in the USA, and Léon Abensour in France were already beginning to carve out a niche for women's history through the publication of pioneering works whose structure and preoccupations laid out the initial lines along which the field would develop.[1] Inspired by the possibilities that the new practice of social (or 'people's') history opened up for recovering the experiences of ordinary folk in the past, Pinchbeck, Beard and Abensour – along with Alice Clark, Olive Schreiner and Eileen Power, among others – all set out to write books that would restore women of the common people to the historical record.[2] In so doing, they sought to deepen our understanding of the social, political, economic and legal/juridical structures that have shaped women's unequal place in social, economic and political life. But they also sought to demonstrate that women, too, have been agents in history. For despite the resounding silence of history books on the matter, these scholars knew that the world that we have inherited was made not only by men but by women as well.

The period from about 1890 to the mid-1970s constituted a kind of golden age for social and economic history.[3] During these years, scholars across a broad range of fields – historians of industrial labour, to be sure, but also historians of the agrarian world, or of the urban popular classes – strove with militant purpose to bring the voices of common people, women included, into the history books. Later, in the 1970s and 1980s, feminist scholars would define more precisely the specific forms of silence that have haunted women's history, even as they elucidated the gendered structures of society and politics that underpin those forms of silence, and give them such a different meaning from the silences that have dogged people's history in general.[4] But in the first half of the twentieth century, feminist scholars made no such distinction between the invisibility of women in history and that of a broad range of other non-elite people (workers, peasants), all of whom had been unjustly consigned to the margins by historians' exclusive concern with the activities of national elites. The history of the family, and demographic analysis more generally, the history of agricultural and industrial production, and of workers of both sexes, the history of women: all these histories, hitherto dismissed as too small, too quotidian to merit scholarly attention, were now to be rescued from obscurity by the techniques of social and economic history. These were histories that shared a common status by virtue of being defined in opposition to the standard narratives of political, diplomatic and intellectual history, which, taken together, constituted that History-with-a-capital-H that was the glory of each nation. And it was these 'little' histories whose telling, it was hoped, would promote a more democratic and egalitarian understanding of society, with women's vital, yet ever under-sung role at last receiving the attention it deserved.

One important site of production for feminist-inspired social and economic history in the early twentieth century was the London School of Economics (LSE), which first opened its doors in 1895. Here, men and women studied together in a singular experiment in university-level co-education: 'Women were brought into the LSE by its first lecturers, and were given scholarships and academic posts,' writes feminist economic historian Maxine Berg. Moreover, 'intellectual issues were just as important as the institutional framework in attracting women and giving them the opportunity for scholarly achievement. Feminist ideas certainly provided one impetus.' But the perception among activist, reform-minded women of the 'practical and moral role of economic history' also played a vital role in drawing women to study the subject at the LSE.[5] For as Berg reminds us, this was an era in which questions of social policy stood at the heart of British intellectual life. Indeed, concern for contemporary social problems helped to create the disciplines of social and economic history in the first place, by turning the eyes of early twentieth-century scholar-activists to the historical investigation of economy and society. In this fashion, an entire generation of feminist scholars at the LSE took up the complex question of the impact of industrialization on women's work. Inspired by contemporary problems of wages, welfare, consumption and women's employment, Bessie Hutchins, Lilian Knowles, Dorothy George, Alice Clark, Mabel Buer and Ivy Pinchbeck all examined various aspects of the 'women and modern industry' question, in a series of books, articles and social policy tracts published over the period 1910–35.[6]

The range and quality of the work produced by these women seems all the more impressive when one recalls that most of them were working outside or at the very margins of the academy. As American historian of France, Bonnie Smith, has argued, the professionalization of history as a discipline across the late nineteenth and early twentieth centuries was at the same time a process of masculinization. Hence, as history became a recognized discipline with a secure place inside European and American universities, those women who had long been writing history were excluded from or remained on the margins of an increasingly male profession, whose central concerns revolved around the (male) political sphere.[7] The marginal status of this early twentieth-century generation of women scholars would certainly seem to confirm Smith's argument. Indeed, in the case of Great Britain, it would take another 60 years (at least) before feminist scholarship would at last find its way into the centres of academic distinction.

Let us take a closer look at one of the major works produced by this group of scholars, Ivy Pinchbeck's *Women Workers and the Industrial Revolution, 1750–1850.* First published in 1930 (and reprinted three times since), Pinchbeck's study illustrates beautifully the encounter between social history and women's history that was to occupy such an important place in the constitution of women's history as a sub-discipline.[8] As we shall see, her work, along with that of Alice Clark, set in place many of the questions and explanatory frameworks that would guide women's historians in the subsequent revival of feminist scholarship that accompanied feminism's second wave in the 1960s and 1970s: the centrality of work and of women's economic condition more generally in determining their overall social and political status; the importance of the Industrial Revolution in recasting that status over the nineteenth century and into the twentieth; the changing shape of the family and its central role in allocating resources; the issue of patriarchal control of resources and wages; the importance of analysing women's work and wages in relation to those of men, since the two were understood to constitute complementary forms of labour power; the divergent fates of middle- and working-class women across the great divide of the Industrial Revolution – a fact which suggests that the meanings of womanhood were not stable across class lines.[9] All this is woven into a tightly argued and compelling narrative, the story of how the overwhelmingly agrarian economy of mid-eighteenth-century England became the modern industrial one that we recognize today, told from the point of view of the hundreds of thousands of women who, in their incarnation as factory workers, agricultural labourers, shopkeepers and handcraft workers, were central to that transformation. Prefiguring as it does so many of the themes and arguments that would animate women's history after the late 1960s, *Women Workers and the Industrial Revolution* merits our sustained attention.

'But women have always worked': women, work and the Industrial Revolution in Britain, 1750–1850[10]

> It is often assumed that the woman worker was produced by the Industrial Revolution, and that since that time women have taken an increasing share in the world's work. This theory, however, is quite unsupported by facts... for centuries, under the handcraft and domestic systems, the greater part of [women's] work was carried on in the home and there taken for granted. It was only when new developments brought about the separation of home and workshop that a far greater number of women were compelled to follow their work and become wage earners in the outside world...[11]

Thus does Ivy Pinchbeck open her *Women Workers and the Industrial Revolution*, with a ringing declaration of the fact that women have always worked. It is a fact of great consequence for our understanding of the social impact of industrial development in eighteenth- and nineteenth-century England: to what extent and in precisely what ways did such development disrupt and reshape family life after 1750? How were women's activities and opportunities recast by the profound transformations in the economy? Yet it is a fact that has repeatedly been forgotten with disturbing ease; indeed, scholars and social policy-makers alike have proven curiously resistant to hearing it, with the result that the moment at which women first 'really' entered the workplace is forever being rediscovered.[12] The total wars of the twentieth century have long been a perennial favourite for the title. But the Industrial Revolution remains the key moment at which women were thought to have been torn from a life of non-productive wifely and maternal duty and thrown into the insatiable maw of industrial capitalism.[13] As Ivy Pinchbeck demonstrates in telling (and beautifully told) detail, the work that women performed in nineteenth-century factories (particularly textile mills, but also in food production) was often a reconfiguration of the labour they had performed in their own homes for centuries – spinning, weaving, clothing production, cheesemaking, market gardening and the raising of pigs and poultry. The massive entry of women into England's first manufactories is thus more usefully understood as a physical relocation of working women, consequence of the separation of home and work that the development of industrial capitalism entailed.

Pinchbeck opens her story with a fine-grained analysis of women's labour within the traditional agrarian world of estate, village and small town community that was 1750s England. The economy was an overwhelmingly agricultural one, with land forming the basis of wealth, status and power in society. Those small industries that did exist were entirely bound up with the agricultural economy, and the vast majority of working women and men depended on the land, either directly or indirectly, as the prime source of their livelihood. In an economy structured by the harvest, by local markets and fairs, and by various cottage industries whose production could fit into the agrarian rhythms of life (weaving and spinning, lacemaking, glovemaking), women worked in or near their homes, tilling small garden plots, raising chickens, pigs and geese, making cheese and butter, grazing animals, gathering wood for fuel, working at cottage crafts and participating in the harvest, whose heavy labours demanded all available hands, male and female, adult and child. For in a world where women and children were expected to earn their own keep, and men's wages were based on an assumption that they did so, all but the very wealthiest families demanded the active participation of all members, with the exception of the tiniest children, in maintaining the family economy.

From about 1760 on, the basic structures of this agrarian economy were to be shaken, and ultimately overturned, by the activity of large landlords, who began to increase the pace and scope of enclosure, consolidating formerly open fields, pastures and wastes into large fenced-in units that were more economical to farm. This process of consolidation allowed large landowners to adopt more intensive, rationalized agricultural techniques. But the effects on smallholders were often disastrous, as their wealthier neighbours absorbed not only the lands of many a small farm but also great swatches of once commonly used meadows, pastures and woods. Even for those smallholders who managed to retain their plots, loss of access to these collective resources rapidly undermined their already precarious economic base.

Ivy Pinchbeck reveals to her readers the differential impact of this 'capitalist revolution' on the land for women of the wealthy, versus those of the smallholding classes. Thus, the enclosure and more intensive farming of large fields swelled profits and produced rising standards of comfort among the wealthier farmers. And this new prosperity led their wives gradually to withdraw from the everyday management of dairy, brewery, poultry and kitchen garden in favour of more leisured pursuits that would allow them to emulate the gentry: 'a Farmer, now become a Gentleman by swallowing up the farms of his neighbours, would be much affronted to have it even supposed that he would concern himself about such *small matters* [as raising livestock],' wrote one observer of the changing rural scene in 1800, 'and the fine lady, his wife, would faint at the idea of attending at market, like her mother or grandmother, with a basket of butter, pork, roasting pigs, or poultry, on her arm.'[14] Gone were the days when the prosperous farmwife undertook to support the household out of the profits of her own domain (livestock, dairy, poultry, orchard and garden), for as Pinchbeck pithily remarked, 'the Farmer's wife now drove, not indeed to market, but to an Assembly in a post chaise.' Her withdrawal from productive labour cost the wealthy farmer's wife her former economic independence. Yet, as Pinchbeck is careful to remind us, this loss of economic independence did not entail any material hardship and, indeed, was seen to represent a real advance on the social scale.

Once again, and not for the last time, a newly leisured wife became a marker of recently acquired social status. It was quite the opposite for the wives of those small farmers who had lost access to open pastures and woods, or, worse yet, any hold on the land at all. Indeed, the impact of agriculture's 'capitalist revolution' was no less than catastrophic for those hundreds of thousands of smallholding families, reduced to abject poverty by the loss of their lands. Women who had once earned their keep by raising animals, making cheese and cultivating kitchen gardens were now forced into long hours of domestic industrial production, at wages so low they generally had to be supplemented by parish assistance, or into the great gangs of women and children agricultural labourers who were hired out by the day or the week to work on the newly consolidated fields of large landowners. As the supply of day labourers generally exceeded the demand, wages were minimal and employers did not hesitate to use the cheaper labour of women and children to drive down the rates paid to male day labourers. Indeed, sometimes, they replaced those men altogether on tasks such as hoeing turnips and other root crops, which women and children performed just as well, if not better than men, and at half the wages.[15]

Work in the gangs was not only poorly paid, but the conditions of work were also deeply fatiguing, even physically injurious, especially to the bodies of child gang labourers: long hikes of as much as seven or eight miles each way to reach the fields, followed by nine hours' heavy labouring (seven during the shorter days of winter) in all seasons and all weathers. 'I'm forced to let my daughter go, else I'm very much against it,' testified the mother of an 11-year-old girl before the 1843 Parliamentary Commission on Women and Children in Agriculture. Her daughter had been working as a gang labourer since the age of nine:

> She has complained of a pain in her side very often; they [gang foremen] drive them along – force them along – they make them work very hard. Gathering stones has hurt my girl's back at times. Pulling turnips is the hardest work; they get such a hold of the ground with their roots; when the land's strong it's as much as we can do sometimes to get 'em out, pull as hard as we can pull. It blisters their hands so that they can hardly touch anything... My girl went 5 miles yesterday to her work, turniping. She set off between seven and eight; she walked; had a piece of bread before she went; she did not stop work in the middle of the day; ate nothing till she left off; she came home between 3 and 4 o'clock. Their walks are worse than their work; she is sometimes so tired, she can't eat no victuals when she comes home.[16]

Agricultural revolution on the land, followed by the gradual transfer of industrial production from home to factory, thus entailed deep misery for those generations who lived through this profound transformation of the English economy. For women, in particular, and especially married ones, the initial stages of this transformation destroyed most opportunities for employment at home. Only later, with the development of large-scale manufacturing in the last quarter of the eighteenth century would new opportunities arise, as their daughters and granddaughters eventually found new employment outside their homes, in the first 'manufactories' of the dawning industrial economy.

Yet the passage of women and children from their hidden labours at home into new and more public spaces of production was met with great ambivalence. Perhaps this should not surprise us; after all, the 'dark, satanic mills' were England's most visible symbol of a dawning industrial economy whose apparent impact on social life (notably the alleged dismemberment of working-class families) gave rise to great public anxiety. Inevitably, then, the transfer of women and children workers from domestic industry into the new mills nourished the popular Victorian myth that women and children were industry's first and most vulnerable victims, sacrificed to the new industrial regime's boundless appetite for labour. One of the most original aspects of *Women and the Industrial Revolution* lies in the author's capacity to look past the alarmist discourse on industry's dissolution of working-class family life in order to evaluate more coolly the actual impact of industrial labour on the lives and fortunes of working women, in relation to those of their mothers and grandmothers. After a thorough survey of the full range of women's occupations within the domestic and industrial systems, Ivy Pinchbeck finds that, contrary to Victorian stereotypes, the Industrial Revolution was, on the whole, beneficial to women. For those women who remained in the home, it relieved them of the 'drudgery and monotony that characterised much of the hand labour previously performed in connection with industrial work under the domestic system.'[17] And for those women who worked outside the home, the Industrial Revolution ultimately delivered better conditions, a greater variety of openings and, most importantly, an improved status as independent wage earners.

Ivy Pinchbeck thus wrote against the popular vision of the pre-industrial world as a kind of golden age, where families had laboured together, in harmony and close to nature, before the arrival of industry tore them apart and condemned them to labour in isolation from one another, bound no longer to nature but to the pitiless rhythms of the machine. Without downplaying the real hardships that the industrial economy imposed on workers of both sexes – the long hours, low wages and poor working conditions that gnawed away at the health and well-being of England's early industrial proletariat – Pinchbeck nonetheless refuses the catastrophic narrative of industrial labour as a descent into hell and instead resolutely compares industrial conditions for women with those that had previously prevailed in smallholding agriculture and domestic industry. Here, she never allows her reader to forget how monotonous and laborious were the basic tasks of assuring a family's subsistence with only the hand technologies of the pre-industrial world. Nor was she inclined to minimize the highly problematic position of economic dependence that women's implication in the pre-modern family economy entailed. For if the gendered and asymmetrical complementarities of the domestic system (in which women were crucial, but nonetheless second-class workers) assured married women fairly stable employment in their homes, it often spelled extreme poverty for single women and those widows or abandoned wives who were thrown upon their own resources.

Women Workers and the Industrial Revolution thus offers a nuanced portrait of the occupational changes that, in Pinchbeck's estimation, played a central role in improving women's social position over the period 1850–1950. For if 'political enfranchisement has been represented as the crowning achievement of the emancipation of women, [t]he occupational changes which played so large a part in their emancipation ... have been curiously neglected ...'.[18] In redressing the historiographical imbalance between the political and social histories of English women, Pinchbeck established many of the concepts and categories that would, 40 years hence, shape women's history as it established itself in the great feminist revival of the 1960s and 1970s: the notion that productive labour outside the home is the key to women's autonomy; the idea that women's political emancipation in the twentieth century was grounded in far more fundamental social and economic developments that, over the long term, lifted women's socio-economic status relative to men's; the separation of home and work as a consequence of industrial capitalism (with all that that implies regarding women workers' 'double burden' of labour in both home and factory); the careful distinctions of class made between bourgeois and working-class women in the analysis of industrialism's impact on women (with each woman's class determined by that of her husband).

Each of these insights, concepts and distinctions contributed to the construction of women as objects of social analysis. And this, in turn, allowed Pinchbeck to explore not only the various ways that different groups of women (married and single, bourgeois and working class) were affected by the upheavals of industrial development, but also the crucial role that women played in shaping the nature of that development. In addition, her thoughtful exploration of the shifting sexual divisions of labour across the agrarian and industrial revolutions reveals the relational nature of gender as a category of social being. Although Pinchbeck herself never uses the term 'gender', her analysis of the shift from male to female (and child) labour in the hoeing of root crops, or of the gendered switchovers that attended the mechanization of spinning and weaving (the traditionally female task of spinning in the home became a skilled male job in the textile mills, whereas the mixed, but predominantly male task of handloom weaving was instantly feminized with its mechanization and transfer to the factory), show an acute sensitivity to the construction and reconstruction of gender roles in relation to particular forms of work. In a period when the forms of work were undergoing radical transformation, who got hired for specific work roles depended largely on how individual employers perceived the particular qualities of men and women, girls and boys. For strength and stamina, resistance to monotony and docility were qualities that, in the eyes of most employers, were possessed in unequal measure by the two sexes, with men winning on the former count and women on the latter. Forty years before the women's movement was to put the sexual division of labour on the table as one of *the* major feminist issues, Ivy Pinchbeck had already begun shaping the analytic tools that would allow scholarship on this topic to move forward.

Women and the Industrial Revolution thus places women squarely with the stream of events and structures that were to shape the modern industrial economy. As a consequence, women are revealed as both actors in history and as acted upon by history; no more and no less subject to the great social and economic forces of the era than were the men alongside whom they lived and laboured. As Kerry Hamilton wrote in her introduction to the 1981 edition of this great classic, 'women's history owes Ivy Pinchbeck a great debt.'[19] It was a debt that would only come due some 35 to 40 years hence, when, in a period of renewed feminist militancy, women's history ceased to be the preoccupation of a small band of dedicated pioneers and become instead the collective mission of an entire generation.[20]

Endnotes

1 Ivy Pinchbeck, *Women Workers and the Industrial Revolution, 1750–1850* (London, 1930, reprinted by Virago, 1981); Mary Beard, *Woman as a Force in History: A Study in Tradition and Realities* (New York, 1946); Léon Abensour, *Histoire générale du féminisme des origines à nos jours* (Paris, 1921). For an illuminating discussion of writing about women before the turn of the twentieth century, see Gianna Pomata, 'History, Particular and Universal: On Reading Some Recent Women's History Textbooks', *Feminist Studies*, 19:1 (Spring 1993), 7–50.

2 Alice Clark, *The Working Life of Women in the Seventeenth Century* (London, 1919); Eileen Power, *Medieval English Nunneries* (Cambridge, 1922); Olive Schreiner, *Women and Labour* (London, 1911).

3 As Natalie Zemon Davis points out in her illuminating article, '"Women's History" in Transition: The European Case', *Feminist Studies*, 3:3/4 (Spring/Summer 1976), 83–103 (reprinted in Joan W. Scott (ed.),

Feminism and History (Oxford, 1996), 79–104), social history as a form goes back to the eighteenth century. Moreover, social historians of both sexes, from William Alexander to Friedrich Engels to Georgina Hill, were concerned to expand the boundaries of their discipline so as to include the activities of women, questions of family life, etc. Indeed, a number of (generally male) scholars, notably Engels and J.J. Bachofen, used the relations between the sexes as a way to characterize different stages of human society. (Using male–female relations as a benchmark for 'civilization' was, of course, a popular way to talk about the unevolved state of colonized peoples, and so justify European rule or 'tutelage').

4 On this point, see Carolyn Steedman, *Childhood, Culture and Class in Britain. Margaret McMillan, 1860–1931* (New Brunswick, NJ, 1990), especially her concluding chapter.

5 Maxine Berg, *A Woman in History. Eileen Power, 1889–1940* (Cambridge, 1996), 9.

6 A number of the women who studied at the LSE also belonged to the Fabian Socialist's Women's Group. See Bessie L. Hutchins, 'The Working Life of Women', Fabian Women's Group Series, *Fabian Tracts*, 157 (London, 1911); and Hutchins, *Women in Modern Industry* (London, 1915); Lilian Knowles, *The Industrial and Commercial Revolutions in Great Britain During the Nineteenth Century* (London, 1921); Dorothy George, *London Life in the Eighteenth Century* (London, 1925); and George, *England in Transition* (London, 1931); Mabel Buer, *Health, Wealth and Population in the Early Days of the Industrial Revolution* (London, 1926).

7 Bonnie Smith, *The Gender of History: Men, Women and Historical Practice* (Cambridge, MA, 1998).

8 Pinchbeck herself studied with two pioneers in the fledgling field of economic history: Lilian Knowles (1849–1929: the first woman to hold a chair in economic history in Britain) and Eileen Power (1889–1940: renowned medievalist, co-founder of the British Economic History Society, founder of the *Economic History Review*, and appointed to the LSE's Chair in Economic History in 1934). A fellowship from Mrs Bernard Shaw allowed Pinchbeck to complete her manuscript. The LSE was a kind of social-science think-tank, where history was understood to be a science that one pursued with larger goals of social reform in mind. (This at a time when the social sciences were just finding their feet as disciplines.) Founded by a group of Fabian socialists in 1895, the LSE was conceived as a laboratory of social reform and was particularly invested in the higher education of women, as well as the scholarly investigation of women's social, political and economic condition. It also drew students from a broader range of social and cultural backgrounds, and from a wider age range, than one normally found in the university milieu of *fin-de-siècle* Britain. See Maxine Berg, 'The First Women Economic Historians', *Economic History Review*, 45:2 (1992), 308–29; and Berg, 'Eileen Power

and Women's History', *Gender & History*, 2 (1994), 265–74. On the LSE's links to adult education and the Workers' Education Association, see Berg, *A Woman in History*.

9 On the contribution that Alice Clark's *Working Life of Women in the Seventeenth Century* made to subsequent historiography on women and work, see Natalie Zemon Davis, '"Women's History" in Transition', and Olwen Hufton, 'Femmes/hommes: une question subversive', *Passés recomposés. Champs et chantiers d'histoire* (Paris, 1995), 235–42. See also Maxine Berg, *A Woman in History*, esp. 9.

10 Drawn from the title of Sylvie Schweitzer's comprehensive survey, *Les Femmes ont toujours travaillé. Une histoire du travail des femmes au XIXe et XXe siècles* (Paris, 2002).

11 Pinchbeck, *Women Workers*, 1.

12 See Schweitzer, *Les Femmes ont toujours travaillé*, for an eloquent exposition of this persistent amnesia regarding the pervasiveness of women's labour in nineteenth- and twentieth-century France.

13 The term 'Industrial Revolution' refers to the vast social, demographic and economic changes that were bound up with the acceleration in economic and technological development from about 1750 on. The term was first coined by Toynbee, and while the 'revolutionary' status of these changes has more recently been contested by economic and labour historians, the notion that this period saw an industrial 'revolution' still held sway in 1930 (and, indeed, would continue to do so into the 1970s).

14 J. S. Girdler, *Observations of the Pernicious Consequences of Forestalling, Regrating, and Engrossing* (1800), 9, cited in Pinchbeck, *Women Workers*, 34.

15 Pinchbeck, *Women Workers*, 59.

16 *Report on Women and Children in Agriculture* (1843), vol. XII, 224, cited in Pinchbeck, *Women Workers*, 89.

17 Pinchbeck, *Women Workers*, 4.

18 Pinchbeck, *Women Workers*, Preface to the 2nd edn, October 1968.

19 Kerry Hamilton, 'Introduction to the Third Edition', in Pinchbeck, *Women Workers*, 1981.

20 Maxine Berg notes that post-World War II Britain saw a sharp drop in the number of women historians holding academic posts, and comments wryly on the post-war 'loss' of the intellectual legacy of Pinchbeck's generation. Berg, *A Woman in History*, 12.

2

Second-wave feminism and the rediscovery of women's history, 1968–1975

In the late 1960s, Europe and the USA saw a powerful revival of feminist activism that began at the heart of that vast congeries of social, cultural and political movements that constituted ''68' – the black freedom movement and the anti-war protests in the USA, the strikes and student movements that erupted in the spring of 1968 all across Europe and North America, the emergence of a more self-consciously political 'new' left. In the USA, small groups of radical women began meeting as early as autumn 1967 to discuss the problem of male supremacy (within the movement, but also in society at large), while in England and France, women who had been involved in the '68 protests and the social movements that grew out of them were, by 1970, organizing all-female consciousness-raising groups.[1] 'The first Women's Liberation Group met in Birmingham in February 1970,' recalls British historian Catherine Hall:

> Many of us were young mothers with children who had started talking informally about the things that felt wrong with our lives, especially our isolation... Most of us had some kind of history in left politics, and a university education. Some of us attended the first women's movement conference at the end of 1970... Feminism placed the issue of power on the political agenda, just as the black power movement did in the United States... The recognition of the multiplicity of sites of power between men and women was linked to the concept that 'the personal is political'... the understanding that *sexual politics*, the politics of power relations between men and women, is part of everyday personal life.[2]

If the heart of male–female power relations was indeed to be found in the private realm of the home, then the purely political rights gained during feminism's first wave (which stretched from the early nineteenth century until the attainment of the vote, in the first half of the twentieth) would no longer serve by themselves to redress the problem of male domination. Politically active women, newly awakened to the domestic bases of their own second-class status, threw themselves heart and soul into a struggle whose goal was to reveal the hidden sources of male domination and to extirpate them at their root.

It was in this atmosphere of heightened political awareness that women's history was transformed from a minority strand in historical practice to a widespread intellectual movement. Indeed, for many scholars working in the heat of feminism's second wave, the determination to recover the still-hidden history of women was an integral part of a life of militant commitment in which political and intellectual work were inextricably linked: 'If the personal was political, so too was the historical,' writes Carroll Smith-Rosenberg of that heady mix of political fervour and intellectual discovery that characterized the re-founding of women's history in the late 1960s:

> Self-conscious feminism strengthened the resolve of those who insisted upon restructuring the scholarly canon to make the study of women's roles and visions, power and oppression central to historical analysis... Perhaps the most revolutionary aspect of contemporary women's history was our refusal to accept gender-role divisions as natural. Gender, we insisted, was man-made, the product of cultural definitions. No universal femaleness or maleness existed. Rather, economic, demographic, and ideational factors came together within specific societies to determine which rights, privileges, and personalities women and men would possess. For us, the search to determine what concatenation of factors had decreed the particular gender assumptions the Western world imposed upon its women and its men was far from academic. These assumptions had shaped our own lives.[3]

For activist scholars of the second wave, then, the pursuit of women's history was inseparably bound to a larger feminist political project. Indeed, one might say that politics was the motor that drove the rapid expansion of women's history after 1968. The link to contemporary politics carried several important consequences for scholarly practice in the nascent sub-field. For one thing, women's historians (like other feminist scholars), strove to build a new style of scholarly interaction, one that stressed cooperation and dialogue, as opposed to the competitive, aggressive and individualistic styles associated with a male-dominated academy.[4] More profoundly, the desire to promote social change through one's scholarship often determined the initial choice of research subject, as well as the kinds of questions that were posed. Moved by and often engaged in contemporary struggles around equal pay or abortion, feminist historians searched the past in precisely those fields that seemed most immediately relevant: the struggle for the vote and for access to higher education, the history of women's industrial and agricultural labour, women's struggle to attain control over their own bodies and sexuality, the history of prostitution. 'No other field of history seemed so directly linked to a social movement,' recalled French historian Françoise Thébaud, as she looked back some 25 years later on a body of scholarship whose very present-minded and political goal was to 'constitute a collective memory [for women]' that might reinforce (or create anew) a shared sense of female identity.[5] A kind of synergy thus grew up between academic labour and the demands of present-day feminism – for full equality with men in the public realms of politics, work and education, for abortion rights and improved access to cheap and safe contraception, for a more equitable division of labour between men and women in the home, in sum, for recognition of women's full personhood and the establishment of grounds on which that personhood might be realized at an individual level.

The tight links binding women's history to feminist politics clearly lent a sense of immediacy and urgency to the early narratives of women's history, rendering them less abstract and distant than is, alas, too often the case in historical writing. But the close tie to politics also raised the danger that the past would be understood and interrogated in terms of present-day needs and values, rather than on its own terms, thus preventing what Italian historian Gianna Pomata has called 'a true dialogue with women of the past.'[6] Women's historians have had to tread this narrow path, drawing inspiration from the present-day urgency of their subject without obscuring the deep gulf of difference that separates the present from worlds past.

One of the most striking consequences of the new sub-discipline's political origins was to be found in the widespread, almost millenarian hope that the very practice of women's history – the new kinds of questions being posed, the new sources being consulted, and the very different kinds of experiences being uncovered – might recast some of the basic categories and concepts on which the historical discipline rested.[7] This transformative potential was most immediately apparent in the matter of rethinking the chronologies that shape larger historical narratives, for as Joan Kelly argued in her famous article, 'Did Women Have a Renaissance?' (1977), an era of progressive change for men might well have quite different, even opposite, effects on women.[8] Beyond the matter of periodization, however, women's history seemed clearly poised to reconfigure some of the fundamental categories of analysis that shape historical inquiry. Our understanding of the nature and deployment of power, for example, looks very different when the optic is shifted away from the public settings of government and party politics toward its private exercise – over women but also *by* women – in domestic and local settings.[9] Even such basic categories as class take on a different configuration and dynamic when the question of women's activities and class position are put into the picture. As we will see, women's historians of the 1960s and 1970s would open a lively debate with traditional (male-focused) labour history around precisely these questions, arguing that the integration of women's labours into the story requires that historians rewrite the history of production itself. For, as British historian Sally Alexander put it, class divisions are shaped not only by the struggle between labour and capital, but through 'the development of a particular form of the sexual division of labour in relation to that struggle.'[10]

One final consequence of the close link between feminist politics and scholarly endeavour can be read in the tendency of feminist scholarship to reflect quite directly conflicts in the political arena. Nowhere is this more evident than in the matter of differences among women. The 'problem' of difference, whether of race, ethnicity, class, religion or sexual orientation, erupted very early in the women's movement, troubling the would-be smooth surface of feminist identity politics with the complicating factor of women's highly varied social situations.[11] That the differences among women should have posed such a problem for 1970s feminism is perhaps not all that surprising. After all, women's identity, newly found (or newly forged) through the all-important consciousness-raising groups, played a fundamental role in structuring a feminist politics that drew its strength from the notion that 'we are one, we are woman.'[12] It was a powerful vision; one that inspired many a middle-class woman to step outside the bounds of convention and join her newly discovered 'sisters' in the systematic denunciation of male domination. The problem was that for poor women and women of colour, the forms of masculine domination that they encountered at home were not always the most problematic forms of discrimination and inequality that marked their lives. Indeed, on issues of racial and economic inequality, women of colour often felt they had more in common with their brothers, sons, husbands and fathers than with the white, middle-class 'sisters' who dominated the movement in the late 1960s and 1970s.

While this may seem incredibly obvious, viewed from the vantage point of the early twenty-first century, one must recall how powerful, and ultimately blinding, was feminists' need for complete unity among women. Indeed, the desire for an uncomplicated sisterhood of women was so strong that it made it quite difficult for mainstream (i.e. white, middle class) feminists to really hear the voices of feminists of colour in the 1970s and early 1980s, as the latter sought to broaden the movement's definition of 'woman' from its implicit basis in the experiences of white, middle-class women. 'There can be no discussion of feminist theory... without examining our many differences, and without significant input from poor women, black and third-world women, and lesbians,' urged poet and feminist theorist Audre Lorde at New York University's 'Second Sex' conference in

October 1979. Lorde made no bones about the political limitations of a mainstream feminism that refused the very deep differences among women, frantically papering over those differences in the name of a universal and singular model of women's oppression. For behind the naïve and simplistic rallying cry, 'we are one, we are woman', crouched the 'pretence to a homogeneity of experience... that does not in fact exist.'[13] Until feminists could acknowledge and work with the differences among women, sisterhood would remain a fantasy, an appeal to a fictive identity among women that had no basis in social and political reality.

But this shift in consciousness was not to be achieved overnight, entailing as it did the abandonment of the comfortable notion that women automatically fall into a single sociological category, a single political collectivity. Indeed, as Catherine Hall recalls,

> it took the angry black voice demanding 'What exactly do you mean when you say WE?' – which must have been heard at countless tense meetings and encounters, insisting that white women must recognize the specificities and limitations of their own experience and the existence of difference – to disrupt that collectivity.[14]

Over the course of the 1980s, feminist scholars would gradually hear the message, thanks in part to the arrival of more and more women of colour in positions of intellectual authority in British and North American universities. By the end of the decade, broad acknowledgement of the socio-political force of difference, whether of race, religion, ethnicity, sexuality or class, would lead to the eventual disaggregation of second-wave feminism's uninterrogated 'we', as feminists of all colours and conditions worked to rethink the category 'woman' and the feminist project in such a way that the recognition of difference lay at its core.[15]

But what about those first 15 or so years after 1968? What did women's history look like in this initial phase of second-wave enthusiasm, before the question of differences among women had assumed such a vital place in the conceptualization of 'women' and 'gender' as categories of historical analysis? In the following two chapters, I will offer brief sketches of two distinct approaches that were widely adopted, and equally widely debated by feminist historians in the 1970s: first, the socialist-feminist approach, which placed at the forefront of women's history the problem of understanding the articulation between class and gender, between capitalist and patriarchal modes of domination; and, second, the study of women's 'culture', pursued from within the optic of separate spheres – that is, the notion that, in one way or another, all human societies divide social space into dichotomous and gendered realms of public and private. Now socialist-feminist and separate spheres approaches both foregrounded patriarchy – defined as the domination of women by men, to the political, economic and psychological benefit of the latter – as an important source of women's oppression. But socialist feminists tended to view patriarchy as distinct from and often secondary to the more fundamental and far-reaching forms of domination on which capitalism is founded.[16] Some even went so far as to argue that working-class men were equally the victims of class-based domination, and so lacked altogether the power to oppress women; a position that harmonized nicely with the socialist-feminist politics of building a common, class-conscious politics with working-class men. Separate spheres feminists, by contrast, tended to see patriarchy as the oldest and most universal form of domination, the one that is most deeply embedded in human psychology, the one that has provided the model for other, more recent forms of race and class-based domination. From this perspective, patriarchy has constituted *the* constant force in human history, and the task of the historian is not to demonstrate women's agency but to recount the many and varied forms that the patriarchal oppression of women has taken. Separate spheres analysis constituted the scholarly face of so-called 'radical feminism', which turned away from traditional feminist efforts to break into a man's world on equal terms, and instead stressed the construction of separate female spaces, based on a distinctively female culture, as an alternative to (or refuge from) patriarchy.[17]

For purposes of clarity, I discuss each of these approaches in the context of a nationally situated case study, beginning with the development of the socialist-feminist paradigm in Britain and then passing to the elaboration of the separate spheres model in the USA. I adopt this nationally focused approach in order to place the particular works that I discuss – by Jill Liddington and Jill Norris, Barbara Taylor, Laura Lee Downs and Caroline Bynum – in their most proximate historiographical contexts. For the socialist-feminist analysis of patriarchy saw its most thorough elaboration in the UK, where at the end of the 1960s Marxist understandings of class dominated the left-wing political and scholarly circles from which the British feminist movement first emerged. In the USA, by contrast, leftist politics were more eclectic and less exclusively focused on issues of class. It was in this more heterogeneous soil that radical feminist analyses of patriarchy first took root, traversing the Atlantic to England and France only at the end of the 1970s.[18] It is important to recall, however, that the socialist-feminist analysis of patriarchy and capitalism did not halt at Britain's shores, nor did efforts to identify specifically female forms of cultural expression confine themselves to the North American continent. Women's history was, after all, an international movement, shaped not only by debates within a single national historiographical tradition, but also by international encounters and exchanges among feminist scholars. Methods and approaches being developed in one place thus circulated rapidly through the increasingly dense network of national and international conferences that have brought women's historians together since the early 1970s.[19]

As you read about British feminists and the debate over socialist-feminism, or US discussions of the distinct worlds that women created for themselves, it is important to bear in mind that these debates and discussions were also being pursued elsewhere. For much important work was done by French and US historians under the sign of the capitalism-versus-patriarchy debate, while British and French feminist historians strove with equal vigour to describe the multiple forms that women's culture and women's sociability have taken in factories and in rural villages, in convents and in schools, whether in the fifth-century BCE Greek polis or in the colonies of eighteenth-century New England.

The international nature of the exchange among feminist scholars regarding models and methods in women's and gender history is perhaps best exemplified by Catherine Hall and Leonore Davidoff's *Family Fortunes*, which is discussed briefly at the end of chapter 5. This important book strove to integrate the two analytic frameworks, bringing the separate spheres model together with a socialist-feminist account of middle-class class formation in nineteenth-century Britain in order to demonstrate the profoundly gendered nature of class as a social category.

Endnotes

1 On radical feminism in the USA, see Alice Echols' superb study, *Daring To Be Bad: Radical Feminism in America, 1967–1975* (Minneapolis, MN, 1989).

2 Catherine Hall, *White, Male and Middle-Class: Explorations in Feminism and History* (Oxford, 1992), 15.

3 Carroll Smith-Rosenberg, 'Hearing Women's Words: A Feminist Reconstruction of History', in Smith-Rosenberg, *Disorderly Conduct: Visions of Gender in American History* (Oxford, 1985), 11–12. Smith-Rosenberg further notes that women's history 'revolutionized historians' understanding of the family, of the process of economic change, and of the distribution of power within both traditional and industrial societies ...', Smith-Rosenberg, *Disorderly Conduct*, 11.

4 The search for more horizontal, dialogically based relations spilled over into the classroom, as feminist teachers strove to impart new and empowering knowledge of forgotten and repressed forms of female identity to a younger generation of 'sisters'.

5 Françoise Thébaud, *Ecrire l'histoire des femmes* (Fontenay-St-Cloud, 1998), 44.

6 Gianna Pomata, in Maria Cristina Marcuzzo and Anna Rossi-Doria (eds), *La ricerca della donne* (Torino, 1987), 199–200.

7 'Especially important, the study of the sexes should help to promote a rethinking of some of the central issues faced by historians – power, social structure, property, symbols, and periodization.' Natalie Zemon Davis,

'"Women's History" in Transition: The European Case', *Feminist Studies*, 3:3/4 (Spring/Summer 1976), reprinted in Joan W. Scott (ed.), *Feminism and History* (Oxford, 1996), 89. Near the end of her article, Davis identified two new goals for women's history as it strove to develop on the basis of cutting-edge social-science techniques in 1970s Europe and the USA: first, scholars had to engage more seriously with the history of sexuality, and second, rather than focusing exclusively on women, feminist historians needed to ground their work in an analysis of the social relations of the sexes. With the wisdom of hindsight, Natalie Davis's article shows remarkable prescience, for the areas she staked out for future research – the history of sexuality and the broadening of women's history to encompass the social relations of the sexes – have seen considerable development across Europe and North America over the past 25 years or so. Yet the central concerns of her article, stressing the importance for women's history of historical demography, statistical modelling and the history of the family, remind us of the extent to which the birth of women's history as such in 1960s and 1970s Europe and the USA took shape in relation to the various forms of social history then being practised across Europe and North America.

8 Joan Kelly, 'Did Women Have a Renaissance?', in Catherine Stimpson (ed.), *Women, History and Theory. The Essays of Joan Kelly* (Chicago, IL, 1984), 19–50, first published in Renate Bridenthal and Claudia Koonz (eds), *Becoming Visible. Women in European History* (Boston, MA, 1977). On the centrality of periodization to the constitution of the historical discipline, see Ludmilla Jordanova, *History in Practice* (London, 2000), 114–40, esp. 135: 'The manner of naming periods contains assumptions about where historical agency lies and about what the most formative aspects of a given society are.'

9 French philosopher, Michel Foucault also looked at these questions but is curiously silent on the gendered aspect of power relations.

10 This insight had already been foreshadowed in the work of Ivy Pinchbeck and Alice Clark. Sally Alexander, 'Women's Work in Nineteenth Century London: A Study of the Years 1820–50', in Anne Oakley and Juliet Mitchell (eds), *The Rights and Wrongs of Women* (London, 1976). Alexander drove home her argument by pointing out that in mid-nineteenth-century London, the often casual and sweated occupations of labouring women – charring, prostitution, needlework and other forms of subcontracted industrial labour at home – fit poorly with the conventional definitions of 'the working class', which was generally defined with reference to factory labour.

11 For an excellent discussion of early manifestations of difference among women, see Echols, *Daring To Be Bad*.

12 Ann Snitow, cited in Echols, *Daring To Be Bad*, 208.

13 Audre Lorde, 'The Master's Tools Will Never Dismantle the Master's

House', in Cherrie Moraga and Gloria Anzaldua (eds), *This Bridge Called My Back: Writings by Radical Women of Color* (New York, 1981), 98–9. 'In other words, the womanness underneath the black woman's skin is white woman's, and deep down inside the Latina woman is an Anglo woman waiting to burst through.' Elizabeth Spelman, *Inessential Woman. Problems of Exclusion in Feminist Thought* (Boston, MA, 1988), 13, 80–113.

14 Hall, *White, Male and Middle-Class*, 21–2. See also Hazel Carby, 'White Women Listen. Black Feminism and the Boundaries of Sisterhood', in Centre for Contemporary Cultural Studies (ed.), *The Empire Strikes Back* (London, 1982); Evelyn Brooks Higginbotham, 'Beyond the Sound of Silence: Afro-American Women in History', *Gender & History* 1:1 (Spring 1989), 50–67. bell hooks, *Feminist Theory: From Margin to Center* (Boston, MA, 1984); and Elizabeth Spelman, *Inessential Woman.* Note the centrality of experience to feminist understandings of differences among women in the 1970s and 1980s. By the 1990s, poststructuralist feminists would introduce an entirely different way of conceptualizing difference into the theoretical pot: difference as positional meaning within language. (This concept depends on the Saussurean insight that meaning is constructed via linguistic opposition, rather than by a relationship of correspondence between signs and the things they signify ('signifiers'), via the relationships of binary opposition among signs, which oppositional relations endow those signs with meaning. See below, chapter 7, and postscript to chapter 8).

15 Denise Riley, *'Am I that Name?' Feminism and the Category of 'Women' in History* (Minneapolis, MN, 1988).

16 As Joan Kelly (among others) has pointed out, the term 'patriarchy' actually refers to a form of the family in which political, social and economic authority over all other family members, male and female alike is vested in the father. Nonetheless, feminists of the second wave used the term 'patriarchy' as shorthand for 'male supremacy'. Among other things, the term patriarchy carried the additional benefit of conveying the eminently political significance of male (patriarchal) power. See Joan Kelly, 'Family and Society', in Stimpson (ed.), *Women, History and Theory,* 110–55, esp. 120. See also Zillah Eisenstein (ed.), *Capitalist Patriarchy and the Case for Socialist Feminism* (New York, 1978).

17 Kevin Passmore, 'Introduction' to Passmore (ed.), *Women, Gender and Fascism in Europe, 1919–45* (Manchester, 2003), 2. For an astute historical analysis of the 'radical' feminism of women's culture and its renunciation of the politics of direct confrontation with male power, see Echols, *Daring To Be Bad*.

18 See Sally Alexander 'Women, Class and Sexual Differences in the 1830s and 1840s: Some Reflections on the Writing of Feminist History', *History Workshop Journal*, 1984, 128: 'Radical feminism offered a breath-takingly

audacious understanding of the relations between the sexes in history. Sexual divisions prefigure those of class, was the message that Shulamith Firestone and Kate Millett flung at a male-dominated intellectual world; patriarchy the concept which they restored to the centre of debates around social formations and the social relations between the sexes.'

19 To list just three of the more vital international fora: the Berkshire conference (which first met in 1973), the 1982 congress at Toulouse, 'L'Histoire des femmes, est-elle possible?', and the International Federation for Research in Women's History (IFRWH, which is attached to the International Historical Congress). Although the IFRWH has hosted a series of major, tri-annual conferences in such cities as Montreal, Melbourne and Oslo, the Federation carries out the majority of its work through the various national organizations that are federated to it (which numbered some 26 in 2001).

3

Feminist historians and the 'new' social history, 1968–1995

If feminist political conviction constituted one vital source of inspiration for women's historians of the second wave, contemporary forms of social history constituted the mould that structured feminist historical inquiry throughout the 1970s and well into the 1980s. Indeed, women's historians built their own practice in contest and dialogue with social historians, notably of the *Annales* school but also with historians from the 'new social history' movement of the 1960s and 1970s. Nowhere was this dialogue with social history more evident than in Britain, where, as we have seen, the field of women's history first took shape within the great tradition of social, and socialist, history of working-class life and labour. It was an intellectually and politically vibrant tradition, one that would, by the mid-1960s, give rise to a 'new social history' that stressed the agency of working-class people in making their own history.

The epistemological base of the 'new social history' rested on Edward Palmer Thompson's famous articulation between agency and structure, between experiences (of exploitation), social identity (class consciousness) and politics. 'Class is defined by men as they live their own history,' declared Thompson in an oft-quoted passage from the introduction to his path-breaking study, *The Making of the English Working Class*, first published in 1963. Far from constituting a mere 'structure' or static descriptive category, class is something that in fact 'happens when some men, as a result of common experiences (inherited or shared), feel and articulate the identity of their interests as between themselves and against other men whose interests are different from (and usually opposed to) theirs'.[1] Thompson thus recast class as a dynamic process that is set in motion by individual agents as much as by material conditions. In this process, individual experience plays a vital role in forming collective identities. But it does so thanks to the key, mediating force of inherited cultural tradition. Hence, in the case of

Thompson's study, pre-existing notions of the 'rights of free-born Englishmen' enabled individual (male) artisans to transform their experiences of exploitation into a collective identity, based on a shared consciousness of their exploitation as a class.[2] For practitioners of the new social history, individual experiences, interpreted in light of inherited cultural tradition, formed the indispensable ground of political and revolutionary action.

But if it was the chain binding experience, social identity and politics that constituted the epistemological ground of early feminist scholarship, it was the vast, if poorly paid, domain of popular and adult education that gave Britain's first generation of feminist historians a precarious institutional anchor. Working outside the four walls of traditional universities, in programmes that were often located in working-class neighbourhoods, socialist historians of both sexes offered courses on the lives and labour of British workers. In so doing, they sought to bind socialist intellectuals more closely to the working-class movement by returning to the people the history of their own class.[3] It was here, in this politically alive – if institutionally somewhat marginalized – atmosphere that feminist scholars of the 1960s and 1970s first began to research and teach the history of women and work as an integral aspect of people's history.

British women's history thus put down its first institutional and epistemological roots in the socialist movement for a people's history, organized around a new social history that, while methodologically innovative on a number of fronts, remained largely a history of men. Dominated by images of barrel-chested miners shouldering their axes, or sooty metalworkers hammering away like devils before the roaring flames of the forge, the initial narratives produced by the new social historians seem to have forgotten that the nation's first industrial proletariat, called to work in the weaving sheds of early nineteenth-century Lancashire, was predominantly female. Only with the flourishing of feminist-socialist scholarship after 1968 would this picture slowly begin to change, as the figures of women, bent over in the fields, or standing at the loom, were gradually restored to view.

Over the next ten years or so, the majority of feminist scholars in Britain would continue to work on the margins of the university, teaching history in adult education or neighbourhood women's centres while participating in a flourishing array of autonomous associations that sprang up around the history of women: The Women's Research and Resources Centre in London (which later became the Feminist Library), The Feminist Archive (Bath), The Lesbian Archive (Manchester), the numerous informal feminist history groups that met in London, Bristol, Brighton and Manchester (to name but a few), and the Virago Press, dedicated to publishing new work in women's history while reissuing handsome editions of out-of-print works as well.[4] 'The margins can be a very productive terrain', wrote Catherine Hall in 1992, 'a space from which both to challenge establishments and develop our own perspectives, build our own organizations, confirm our own collectivities.'[5] For feminist scholars of the 1970s, this marginality also served to remind them of the overarching political purpose of women's history: to restore women's voices to history while using these discoveries to transform present-day gender relations.

During the 1980s, feminist scholars moved gradually from adult education into the universities. In part, this movement was an involuntary one, for the severe budget cuts of the Thatcher years forced many programmes in adult education to sharply reduce staff, if not to close their doors entirely. At the same time, the first interdisciplinary programmes in women's studies began putting down roots in certain of the 'new universities', including Bradford, Essex, Kent, Warwick and York.[6] The need to create interdisciplinary programmes gave rise to fruitful exchanges among feminist scholars across the disciplines, breaking their isolation from one another inside separate departments (where they were often the lone exponents of women's studies) while reinforcing the cross-disciplinary nature of women's and gender history. And yet very few of the participants in these first women's studies programmes were historians, for until the end of the 1980s, the British historical discipline as a whole proved reluctant to concede that women's and gender history might be legitimate fields of research.[7] Numerous key works were thus produced by scholars in sociology (Leonore Davidoff), social policy (Pat Thane), education (Penny Summerfield, Carol Dyhouse) or social science administration (Jane Lewis) – scholars in the social sciences who found that adopting a historical approach was crucial to the success of their enterprise.[8]

A look at two classic works from this period illustrates the shape that feminist historians' overarching preoccupation with the world of labour, and with the often tense relation between socialist feminists and their male comrades, assumed in the guise of history. Thus, Jill Liddington and Jill Norris's *'One Hand Tied Behind Us': The Rise of the Women's Suffrage Movement* recounts the hitherto untold story of the radical suffrage movement among women textile workers in turn-of-the-century Lancashire.[9] Both authors were teaching in adult education in Manchester at the time (1978), and their book is the fruit of an enormous labour of research conducted in local archives and through interviews with the surviving daughters and granddaughters of such local activists as Selina Cooper and Doris Chew. Burdened by a double load of domestic and factory labour, these women sought the vote not merely as an end in itself, but as a means to the larger end of improving the conditions of life and labour for working-class men, women and children. Lancashire's radical suffragists thus fought equally hard to gain those social and economic rights which they judged every bit as important as the simple right to vote: equal pay, better educational opportunities, birth control, child allowances and the right to work on an equal footing with men. In order to piece together the tale of this all-but-forgotten movement, Liddington and Norris had to write against the conventional tale of exclusively middle-class heroics first propagated by middle-class and London-based activists, such as Sylvia Pankhurst and Rachel Strachey, militant suffragists for whom the social and political activism of women workers was but a distant echo of their own, more narrowly vote-based struggle.[10] Inspired by the convictions of 1970s socialist-feminism and sustained by the structures of popular education in a region that was heavily populated by retired textile workers, Liddington and Norris used their contacts in the milieu to recover the unwritten tale of a political movement, led by the women workers themselves, in which feminist politics and class struggle were inextricably linked.

Barbara Taylor's *Eve and the New Jerusalem: Socialism and Feminism in the Nineteenth Century* explores the encounter between feminism and Owenite socialism in early nineteenth-century England in what is, ultimately, a sustained meditation on the often fraught relationship of feminism to socialism.[11] Taylor's richly documented study shows how Owen's moral critique of gender inequality within the family constituted an essential pillar of so-called 'utopian' socialism in the 1820s through to the 1840s. Unlike the 'scientific' socialists of the later nineteenth century, for whom the struggle for gender equality was always subsumed under the banner of class struggle, Owenite socialists placed women's liberation at the heart of their political project to liberate all of humanity from all forms of oppression and inequality, be they class- or gender-based. Once again, one can read the preoccupations and discontents of 1970s socialist-feminists in the study of a long-since marginalized movement in which the liberation of women formed an integral part of the larger struggle, and not just a coda, left to the tender (and studiously vague) mercies of 'after the revolution'.

Socialist-feminist historians of the 1970s and early 1980s thus privileged working-class history and the study of women's work, sometimes adapting terms and categories of Marxist analysis – 'sex-class', 'sex struggle' and 'patriarchal mode of production' – in order to extend a materialist analysis of women's exploitation from the factory to the family, and so unmask the material basis of male domination. In some instances, patriarchy (understood as a system of relations that is generated entirely outside the workplace) travelled alone in its relentless exploitation of women's domestic and reproductive labour.[12] More often, however, socialist-feminists analysed patriarchy in its unholy alliance with capitalism, a 'dual system' whose elements had to be analysed simultaneously in order to explain women's double burden of labour (and exploitation) – in the factory, to be sure, but also in the home. 'The present status of women in the labor market and the current arrangement of sex-segregated jobs is the result of a long process of interaction between patriarchy and capitalism,' concluded American economist Heidi Hartmann in her influential article, 'Capitalism, Patriarchy and Job Segregation by Sex'.

> Capitalism grew on top of patriarchy: patriarchal capitalism is stratified society par excellence. If nonruling-class men are to be free they will have to recognize their cooptation by patriarchal capitalism and relinquish their patriarchal benefits. If women are to be free they must fight against both patriarchal power and capitalist organization of society.

Men will therefore have to be 'forced to relinquish their favoured positions in the division of labour – in the labour market and at home – both if women's subordination is to end and if men are to begin to escape class oppression and exploitation.'[13] The tension that this first generation felt between feminism and socialism, between gender versus class as the privileged category of analysis, thus expressed itself in the long debate over whether patriarchy or capitalism should be regarded as the prime source of working women's oppression.[14] While much important work was produced under the sign of this 'dual systems theory', its underlying hermeneutic, in which patriarchy and capitalism are treated as autonomously functioning structures of oppression, would remain unchallenged until the early 1990s, when the history of women's experiences of work was broadened to embrace the study of gender divisions inside the workplace itself. The workplace then revealed itself to be a world in which notions of masculinity and femininity have always played a central role in shaping divisions of labour and hierarchies of authority, a world in which the two structures (patriarchy and capitalism) are in fact inextricably bound together in a single, gendered order of production.[15]

Hence, feminist historians would never really resolve the long and ultimately sterile debate over the relative weight of capitalism versus patriarchy in the oppression of working women. Rather, they set the debate aside altogether in favour of more fruitful and far-reaching analytic approaches based on the adoption of gender as a central axis of investigation. Let me illustrate the point by offering an example from my own research, on the gendered reconfiguration of production in the French and British metalworking industries after 1914. While this entails making a brief fast-forward in time, from the socialist-feminist work of the late 1970s to the gendered labour history of the mid-1990s, such a leap recommends itself on the grounds of analytic coherence, for it allows us to bring the socialist-feminist story to its gendered conclusion within the confines of a single chapter. We will then return in the next chapter to the late 1970s, in order to pick up the tale of evolving analytic frameworks in women's and gender history, with a discussion of women's culture and the notion of separate spheres.

'Boys will be men, and girls will be boys': gender and the reshaping of industrial production in France and Great Britain, 1914–1939[16]

In the summer of 1917, a Scottish lady who was 'prominently' engaged in welfare work among women munitions workers acidly remarked that with this war, 'the Kaiser handed British women an opportunity which their own fathers and brothers and mothers and husbands had ever denied them.'[17] *Manufacturing Inequality* is an exploration of that opportunity, of the shape and extent of the new fields that, after 1914, opened to women in the metalworking industries of France and Great Britain – iron and steel, machine-building, automobiles, airplanes and electronics, all of which were centrally implicated in the production of arms and munitions. The story really begins in the spring of 1915, when the crisis of protracted industrial war drew thousands of women into the previously male world of metalworking. Pressed by the sharply spiralling demand for weapons at the very moment when much of their traditional workforce had left for the front, employers found themselves experimenting with new, mass-production technologies of work, grounded in the subdivision, routinization and mechanization of formerly skilled jobs, even as they introduced female workers *en masse*. From the outset, then, women workers were associated with the new, more productive technologies introduced by the crisis of war. Over the next four years French and British employers would reclassify types of work and types of workers in relation to the newly fragmented labour process. In so doing, they gave precise definition to a category of worker hitherto unknown in the metals and engineering trades: the woman metalworker.

What is perhaps most significant in all this is how similarly French and British employers responded to this challenge. Despite differences in political culture, industrial organization and even level of industrial development, employers in both nations strove to assimilate the simultaneous transformations in technology and personnel by integrating a new distinction, that of gender, into an existing system of skill differences. These men reorganized productive hierarchies and allocated tasks between the sexes in accordance with their understanding of the ways in which male–female difference manifested itself on the assembly line or at the machine. The result was a structure of inequality that was taken to be both inevitable and economically rational, anchored in the solid bedrock of 'natural' difference and articulated through a newly gendered language of job skill.

Manufacturing Inequality thus recounts the entry of women into the war factories, and the adaptation of women to the work and of work to the women. Along the way, it tells the tale of strikes and labour protests among women for whom the prolonged hours of heavy labour, justified by the war emergency, proved a crushing burden in the long run. Hence, if many women looked back on their wartime employment with a certain degree of pleasure, recalling with pride their success in the arduous but highly valued (and well-paid) labours of weapons and munitions-building, others remember only the drudgery and exhaustion of those years: 'Some of us fell asleep in the WC [during the night shift]', one woman bullet-maker recounted. 'If it hadn't been for Sundays [off], three-quarters of us would have died. Some did die.'[18] Despite these manifold hardships, the domestic truce of sacred union held good throughout the first two years of war. Ultimately, however, the pressures of life on the home front – long shifts at work followed by hours spent hunting down increasingly scarce foodstuffs at ever-spiralling prices, not to mention the endlessly bad news from the front, where the butchery continued unabated – finally took their toll, and from the end of 1916, women in both nations began taking their grievances to the streets. They protested against poor working conditions, lack of rest and unequal wages for a job equal to if not better than that performed by the man being replaced. At times, they even protested the conduct of the war and demanded that 'their' soldiers be returned from the front and various 'draft dodgers' be sent in their place. And when the economy of war at last gave way to peacetime production, women workers were first fired in the extreme dislocation of post-war demobilization, only to be hired again soon after, and in ever-greater numbers, to labour in expanding and newly feminized sectors of this formerly male industry, whose technology, organization and labour demands had been permanently altered by the experience of war production.

The central chapters of the book are devoted to a detailed analysis of the process by which important sectors of the metalworking trade were feminized after 1914, a process that rested on employers' efforts to identify women's skills and capacities and arrange them in complementary relation to those of men. They did this through observation, interpreting women's performance at work in light of the socio-biological 'facts' of women's essential nature. These facts were constructed at the mental confluence of observation and prior conviction about the nature of gender difference. In other words, employers' observations of women at work were shaped by what they already 'knew' to be true of women in general and of working-class women in particular. Thus French and British employers alike observed that women maintained a swifter, more regular rhythm than did their male counterparts, for their nimble little fingers allowed them to excel at jobs requiring 'quick and delicate manipulation'. Indeed, on such jobs, women routinely out-produced men.[19] These men soon came to believe that there was something inherently feminine about repetitive motion itself; indeed, employers regarded speed, dexterity and regular, precise motions as specific to women, qualities whose origin, shape and meaning were to be found in the household division of labour. Hence, when they looked at women before their lathes, employers did not see individuals, held to a new level of precision and regularity in motion by the unprecedented automatism of the newly installed machine tools. Rather, they believed they were looking at something they had seen before: women engaged in the timeless rhythms of domestic labour: 'The machines that the women operate function similarly to the men's but seem to run more continuously, at a more regular rhythm, because of the gentleness of women's movements, and because of their vigilance,' reported journalist Gaston Rageot from inside one of France's great national arms factories. 'There remains a housewife in every woman turning shells at the lathe, and women produce metal parts as they do sweaters.'[20]

Women's excellence in repetition work was balanced by a presumed timidity and lack of initiative: 'one must never demand an impromptu or unexpected vigilance from them,' asserted one French employer near the end of the war. 'Women draw parallels, they compare, but they are incapable of inventive thought.'[21] Employers thus concluded that women's patient execution of rapid, detailed work sprang from some set of qualities intrinsic in women, and not from the structures of mass production into which the new workers had been slotted.[22] Further, the naturalization of women as repetition workers *par excellence* travelled hand in glove with employers' insistence that men were particularly *un*suited to these new forms of work, for the male's restless drive and imagination – the very qualities that made good skilled mechanics of some men – interfered with the ability of his less-skilled brother to execute repetition work satisfactorily. Thus, while inexperienced workers of both sexes were initially placed on simple repetition jobs, employers declared a distinct preference for women, who were regarded as a more 'delicate class of unskilled labour', endowed with agile fingers that could, without prior training, manipulate small metal parts far more easily than men, whose hands, untrained, remained stiff and clumsy.

Over the course of the war, then, employers distinguished light repetition work from physical labouring, reserving the former to unskilled women and the latter to unskilled men. But the common appellation 'unskilled' shrouded a visible difference in the technical ability required for women's versus men's unskilled work, for if an unskilled male labourer were to be promoted, his first step up the ladder entailed training for the very machine work that allegedly 'unskilled' women routinely performed. 'Unskilled' women thus possessed technical capacities that, in the employers' eyes, came from their natural endowment as women, including the ability to accomplish, without training, tasks that lay beyond the reach of unskilled men. But since the capacity came from 'nature', and not from any programme of apprenticeship, it received no official recognition, nor was it rewarded on the same basis as the hard-won skills of the male. At the level of more highly skilled work, for which but a handful of women were trained during the war, employers ended by making a similar distinction between the 'imitative' skills of women and the 'initiative' skills of men. While this gendered classification granted grudging recognition of the 'remarkable' work done by skilled women during the war, it nonetheless maintained a sharp hierarchical distinction between women's lower, 'imitative' forms of skill and the higher, executive brand possessed by skilled men.[23]

At all levels, then, employers naturalized women's skills as qualities that women, as women, carried with them into the factory, rather than seeing such dexterity as the product of a broader social division of labour in early twentieth-century Europe in which girls, far more than boys, were trained from an early age to use their hands for household crafts (knitting, embroidery, lacemaking, sewing.) In this fashion, gender difference, conceived as a system of fixed and natural antinomies, was gradually woven through the system of division and hierarchy that ruled the metalworking factory floor.

Employers' conviction that gender forms a salient, stable and meaningful distinction in human character and capacity thus played a key role in the restructuring of industrial labour during and after World War I. Indeed, the very move by which employers sought to comprehend and contain the new female workforce – defining women as a particular kind of labour within an existing system of skill divisions – had the unintended effect of ensuring that wartime changes in the sexual division of labour would endure well past the Armistice. For if the wartime experience had linked women contingently with the new technologies, employers then cemented this connection by enshrining it in the language of job skill. In concrete terms, this meant that for many employers, efficient production had become unthinkable in the absence of a significant contingent of women employed on appropriately female tasks. At the war's end, then, employers were less interested in a wholesale return to pre-war practices (which would have entailed abandoning the more productive methods introduced since 1914 and eliminating women workers entirely) than in achieving what they now perceived as a more 'rational' distribution of employment between the two sexes. And this entailed turning over to women entire classes of work that, for years, had been performed men, a practice whose unproductive consequences were roundly condemned in 1919 by the head of Britain's Engineering Employers' Federation: 'Most firms have been doing women's work by men and calling it men's work and that is a thing which has got to be gone into very carefully... and a line of demarcation laid down.'[24] Of course, the very notion that a firm and unchanging boundary could ever be laid down once and for all was pure illusion, for with ongoing technological change and repeated restructuring of the labour process, management and workers of both sexes pressed constantly on that gendered frontier, renegotiating the contours that distinguished men's work from women's. But if that gendered boundary proved to be a mobile one, the underlying conviction on which it rested – that some kind of gender division was both natural and necessary – remained stable and unshaken, enshrined as it was in the newly gendered language of job skill elaborated during the war. Indeed, it was the very stability of gender division as a fundamental principle of social and technical division that lent an illusion of permanence and inevitability to particular, local distributions of work between women and men.

After 1914, then, the principle of sexual division became yet another party to broader struggles over wages, shop-floor authority and the redivision of labour in the metalworking factories of Great Britain and France. In the course of these struggles, gender acquired new, technical meanings that, despite employers' oft-invoked domestic analogies in describing the labours of women, bore little direct relation to any broader discourses on women's and men's social roles. Rather, ideas about gender difference travelled in a technical idiom within the factory, a realm where femaleness meant dexterity and speed within the new, 'scientifically' ordered work process, while maleness signified a clumsier brute strength, but also the exclusively male capacity to gain the highest forms of skill and so rise to positions of technical and moral authority on the factory floor.

By analysing the restructuring of production in metalworking through the lens of gender, understood as a social distinction between the sexes, *Manufacturing Inequality* demonstrates that, far from working separately, capitalism and patriarchy were fully imbricated in the structures that governed the industrial order in early twentieth-century Europe. Indeed, the two forces were perfectly intertwined in the gendered language of job skill that was the instrument of classification and command on the factory floor. Far from constituting a set of ideas and practices outside the rational economic practice of capitalist employers, 'patriarchy' was partially constitutive of that practice – an integral element in the system of technical and social relations that governed metals production after 1914.

The adoption of gender as a central category of analysis by labour historians in the late 1980s and early 1990s would thus resolve certain of the epistemological difficulties that had dogged women's history from its origins, moving the field beyond the simple (and misleading) opposition of patriarchy versus capitalism to a more global analysis of the gender divisions that underwrite all forms of work. Moreover, the shift in object – from women's experiences of work to the gendered analysis of production – broadened considerably the reach of feminist scholarship in the field of labour history. Indeed, the shift to gender analysis suggested that any work of labour history that failed to address the gendered nature of work was at best partial, and at worst, missed entirely one of the central aspects in the organization of labour.

Endnotes

1 Edward Palmer Thompson, *The Making of the English Working Class* (London, 1963), 11, 9. The new social history was defined largely by the

work of Thompson, Eric Hobsbawm and the young Gareth Stedman Jones. (I refer here to Stedman Jones's early work, notably his *Outcast London: A Study in the Relationship Between Classes in Victorian Society* (Oxford, 1971). Over the next 13 years, Stedman Jones would gradually turn away from the Thompsonian preoccupation with the relationship between structure and agency in favour of exploring the links between culture and politics. See G. Stedman Jones, *Languages of Class: Studies in English Working-Class History, 1832–1982* (Cambridge, 1983).

2 As feminist historian Joan Wallach Scott would later point out, Thompson's artisans relied not only on the freeborn Englishman but on pre-existing ideas about gender as well. See Joan W. Scott, 'Women in *The Making of the English Working Class*', in Joan W. Scott (ed.), *Gender and the Politics of History* (New York, 1988), 68–90.

3 Adult education in the UK goes back to the University Extension movement, at the end of the nineteenth century, followed by the Workers' Education Association, which was organized at the turn of the century. See Raphaël Samuel, *People's History and Socialist Theory* (London, 1981), especially the articles by Ken Worpole, 'A Ghostly Pavement: The Political Implications of Local Working-Class History', Jerry White, 'Beyond Autobiography', and Stephen Yeo, 'The Politics of Community Publications'.

4 Virago thus reprinted numerous out-of-print classics, like Ivy Pinchbeck's *Women Workers and the Industrial Revolution, 1750–1850* (London, 1930, reprinted by Virago, 1981), alongside an entire series of socio-economic studies published in the early twentieth century by socialist researchers from the Fabian Women's Group, such as Barbara Drake, *Women in Engineering* (1917) and Drake, *Women in Trade Unions* (1920), not to mention a host of less well-known works of women's fiction.

5 Catherine Hall, *White, Male and Middle-Class: Explorations in Feminism and History* (Oxford, 1992), 34.

6 The 'new' universities were founded in the aftermath of World War II in order to assure higher education to the masses. Elite universities like Oxford and Cambridge would continue to hold themselves aloof from such Johnny-come-lately disciplines as women's studies until the mid- to late 1990s.

7 Hence, a partial survey of history departments in Britain in 1991 revealed that despite the fact that nearly half the students were women, only 17 per cent of lecturing jobs in a sample 53 universities were held by women, while only 12.7 per cent of senior lecturers, 6.6 per cent of readers and 3 out of 134 professors were women. *Times Literary Supplement*, 7 June 1991, cited in Hall, *White, Male and Middle-Class*, 34.

8 To list but a few key works by these scholars from this period: Leonore Davidoff, 'Mastered for Life: Servant and Wife in Victorian and Edwardian England', in A. Sutcliffe and P. Thane (eds), *Essays in Social History*

(Oxford, 1986); Davidoff, 'Class and Gender in Victorian Society: The Diaries of Arthur Munby and Hannah Cullwick,' in J.L. Newton, M. Ryan and J. Walkowitz (eds), *Sex and Class in Women's History* (London, 1983); Pat Thane and Gisela Bock (eds), *Maternity and Gender Politics: Women and the Rise of the European Welfare States, 1880s–1950s* (London, 1991); Penny Summerfield, *Women Workers in the Second World War: Production and Patriarchy in Conflict* (London, 1984); Carol Dyhouse, *Girls Growing Up in Late Victorian and Edwardian England* (London, 1981); Dyhouse, *Feminism and the Family in England, 1880–1939* (Oxford, 1989); Jane Lewis, *Women in England, 1870–1950: Sexual Divisions and Social Change* (Brighton, 1984); Lewis, 'Women Lost and Found: The Impact of Feminism on History', in Dale Spender (ed.), *Men's Studies Modified: The Impact of Feminism on the Academic Disciplines* (Oxford, 1981).

9 Jill Liddington and Jill Norris, '*One Hand Tied Behind Us*': *The Rise of the Women's Suffrage Movement* (London, 1978).

10 Sylvia Pankhurst, *The Suffragette* (New York, 1911); Rachel Strachey, *The Cause* (London, 1978, first published 1928).

11 Barbara Taylor, *Eve and the New Jerusalem: Socialism and Feminism in the Nineteenth Century* (New York, 1983).

12 Christine Delphy, *L'Ennemi principale: l Economie politique du patriarcat* (Paris, 1998). It is worth noting that those who approached women's history under the sign of the capitalism-versus-patriarchy debate were from the outset struggling with the theoretical difficulties that one particular form of difference among women – that of class – posed for the creation of a unitary feminist approach to historical analysis.

13 Heidi Hartmann, 'Capitalism, Patriarchy and Job Segregation by Sex', in Zillah Eisentstein (ed.), *Capitalist Patriarchy and the Case for Socialist Feminism* (New York, 1979), 230.

14 See Sylvia Walby's *Patriarchy at Work* (Minneapolis, MN, 1986) for a thorough introduction to the scholarship on theories of patriarchy and women's work. See also Heidi Hartmann, 'The Unhappy Marriage of Marxism and Feminism: Towards a More Progressive Union', in Lydia Sargent (ed.), *Women and Revolution* (Boston, MA, 1981). For an important critique of Hartmann, see Veronica Beechey, *Unequal Work* (London, 1987).

15 See, for example, Sonya Rose, *Limited Livelihoods: Gender and Class in Nineteenth-Century England* (Berkeley, CA, 1992); Miriam Glucksmann, *Women Assemble: Women Workers and the New Industries in Interwar Britain* (London, 1990); and Laura Lee Downs, *Manufacturing Inequality: Gender Division in the French and British Metalworking Industries, 1914–1939* (Ithaca, NY, 1995).

16 The phrase 'boys will be men, and girls will be boys' is taken from a British munitions employer's summary of the wartime redivision of labour in his

own factory. Parliamentary Papers 1918, Cd. 9073, Board of Trade, *Report of the Departmental Committee*, 16, quoted in Downs, *Manufacturing Inequality*, 223.

17 'Fair Play for Women', *People's Journal*, 27 January 1917, found at the Imperial War Museum (London), Press Cuttings, Box on Trades Unions, 1917.

18 Intereview with 'Mme X', who worked in the Cartoucherie d'Issy throughout the war and again in the interwar period, after her husband's death (he had been gassed in the trenches and died in 1928). Mathilde Dubesset, Françoise Thébaud and Catherine Vincent, 'Quand les femmes entrent à l'usine. Les ouvrières des usines de guerre de la Seine, 1914–1918', mémoire de maîtrise (Université de Paris VII, 1974), 441, cited in Downs, *Manufacturing Inequality,* 52. For more positive accounts of munitions work, see Downs, *Manufacturing Inequality*, chapters 2 and 3.

19 Downs, *Manufacturing Inequality*, 212–25.

20 Downs, *Manufacturing Inequality*, 213.

21 Downs, *Manufacturing Inequality*, 215.

22 The fact that the small handful of women who were trained to perform fully skilled work in French and British war factories vigorously repudiated the mind-numbing labour of their less-skilled sisters reminds us that, given the choice (as few women and many men were), women were no more 'naturally' drawn to repetition work than were men.

23 Downs, *Manufacturing Inequality*, 222, 221.

24 Downs, *Manufacturing Inequality*, 223.

4

Is female to male as nature is to culture? Feminist anthropology and the search for a key to all misogynist mythologies

While socialist-feminist historians were busily thrashing out the problem of patriarchy's relationship to capitalism, their radical feminist counterparts, who, initially, were working mostly in America, were developing tools for the analysis of patriarchy as a sociocultural phenomenon, universal in scope and organized around a series of gendered dichotomies on which human societies build their social, political and economic orders: nature versus culture, private versus public, female versus male.[1] Cultural anthropology, as deployed by feminist scholars, would play a key role in this development. Hence, in the 1950s, anthropologists had already begun experimenting with the idea of interpreting cultures as if they functioned like language; closed systems that are based on an underlying structure of binary oppositions (private versus public, female versus male) that give meaning to social organization and to the ordinary acts of everyday life. This methodological insight into the deep structures of human culture inspired a 'semiotic revolution' in cultural anthropology, as scholars, feminist and non-feminist alike, turned away from the study of social structures and towards the semiotic analysis of the symbols, rituals, discourses and cultural practices that weld a given society together. By the mid-1970s, feminist anthropologists would build a coherent, gendered analysis of human culture and society from the observation that the gendered division of symbolic space is fundamental to social organization across a wide range of cultures, both 'primitive' and 'advanced'. Indeed, when examined through the lens of cultural anthropology, the gendered distinction between public and private stood forth as a universal feature of human society, past and present: 'An opposition between "domestic" and "public" provides the basis of a structural framework necessary to identify and explore the place of male and female in psychological, cultural, social, and economic aspects of human life,' wrote Michelle Rosaldo in 1974.

> Though this opposition will be more or less salient in different social and ideological systems, it does provide a universal framework for conceptualising the activities of the sexes. The opposition does not determine cultural stereotypes or asymmetries in the evaluations of the sexes, but rather underlies them, to support a very general (and, for women, often demeaning) identification of women with domestic life and of men with public life.[2]

In identifying the domestic–public divide as a universal social structure, Rosaldo and her colleagues gave voice to feminists' powerful felt sense that the source of women's oppression lay in their confinement to domestic activities, 'cut off from other women and from the social world of men'.[3] But they also sketched a compelling vision in which the gendered separation of space constituted no less than the 'deep structure' of human culture and society, subject to variation in form and intensity, but invariably present wherever human beings have come together to create society. This vision of a divided social whole in which all human activity unfolds within the distinct, yet interdependent spheres of private and public rendered the domestic sphere no less than the public one a site of social historical analysis. Those who sought to grasp a society in its entirety could no longer content themselves with the view from the public end. Henceforth, women's domestic activities would have to be subjected to the same kinds of social and economic analysis as the public activities of men.

The separate spheres model thus enabled historians to grasp the function and significance of gender division and sex segregation across society as a whole. As such, it accomplished what no individual work of women's history had yet been able to achieve: it moved women's history 'out of the realm of the trivial and anecdotal into the analytic of social history.'[4] Indeed, by the late 1970s, the separate spheres/women's culture model had become 'the most widely used framework for interpreting women's past in the United States', according to US women's historian Nancy Hewitt, whose important review essay, 'Beyond the Search for Sisterhood', published in 1985, traces the mechanisms whereby the separate spheres model gained such rapid authority in the US academy at the end of the 1970s and early 1980s: 'The articles and arguments presented by the architects of the paradigm are widely quoted, reprinted frequently, summarized in textbooks and popular histories, reproduced in curriculum packets, and elaborated upon in an array of scholarly studies.' Feminist historians thus imported into their own research the fundamental political premise of second-wave feminism, namely, that 'gender is the primary source of oppression in society and [gender oppression] is the model for all other forms of oppression', inspiring those secondary forms of oppression (race and class) that are, in this vision, less profoundly anchored in the human soul.[5]

By underscoring the culturally constructed nature of the symbolic linkage of women and domesticity, feminist anthropologists made a vital contribution to the work of denaturalizing the gendered division of labour and social space, revealing the gendered order of society to be mere human artefact (and hence subject to change), rather than the inevitable outcome of men's and women's 'natural' and divergent destinies.[6] Hence, one very important outcome of anthropologists' intense reflection on the gendered division of society was the clear articulation of the distinction between one's biologically given sex and her culturally constructed gender identity. The sex/gender distinction gave feminist historians a new tool for writing against the age-old proposition that where women are concerned, biology is destiny, and that women, caught up in the timeless, cyclic rhythms of nature (childbirth, nurturance and death), have no history. 'When I speak of cultural construction of gender, I mean simply the ideas that give social meaning to physical differences between the sexes,' wrote anthropologist Harriet Whitehead in 1981, 'rendering two biological classes two social classes, men and women, and making the social relationships in which men and women stand toward each other appear reasonable and appropriate.'[7] Not only are women and men made rather than born as such, but the entire edifice of gender identity is burdened with the ideological weight of naturalizing, and thus sustaining, the prevailing relationships between the sexes.

But the 'universal' theory of gendered spheres also gave rise to a decade or more of intensive scholarly investigation into the distinct worlds that women have made for themselves from within the confines of domesticity. Here, historians like Bonnie Smith and Carroll Smith-Rosenberg deployed the interpretive tools of cultural anthropology, notably the semiotic analysis of ritual, symbol and cultural practice, in order to reconstruct female worlds of love and ritual, maternity and sorrow, in nineteenth-century France and the USA. Uncovering a rich array of work cultures, reform activities and friendship networks among white middle- and working-class women, Smith, Smith-Rosenberg and a host of other women's historians subtly shifted the focus of attention away from the political question of male domination and towards the exploration of women's separate 'cultures', which were generally conceived of as havens of female solidarity created by and among women.[8]

The public/domestic model was clearly a powerful one, inspiring at least a decade of research into the hidden realms of female culture. And yet the notion that public/private constitutes the single, universal key to understanding the forms and dynamics of male domination came under critical scrutiny almost as soon as the concept was born. Feminist scholars were soon asking themselves, just how 'universal' is the public–private distinction anyway? After all, anthropologists have identified societies in which such distinctions play a scant role in organizing the culture.[9] Closer to home, scholars like Bonnie Thornton Dill and Jacqueline Jones were quick to underscore the extremely limited applicability of this notion to poor women and women of colour, who have always been obliged to go out to work, and whose domestic space is hardly private, subject as it is to the interventions of private and state-based philanthropy.[10] Among other things, the very lack of a clear public–private divide in the lives of poor women and women of colour suggests that, rather than describing actual lived realities, public–private constituted an ideal (and an ideology) that was premised on a false separation of politics from the private, social worlds that politics was meant to regulate from afar.

As feminist scholars confronted the diverse and, at times, conflicting sources of oppression that have weighed upon the category 'woman', doubts about the universal reach of separate spheres (or any other universal analytic) multiplied rapidly. These doubts were reinforced by scholars' growing recognition that work within the separate spheres optic tended to depoliticize male–female relations, retreating to a world of feminine sociability where the controlling hand of male domination was hardly visible. As Michelle Perrot put it, research within the separate spheres model belonged to a phase of 'euphoric re-evaluation of women's history', a rejection of the woman as subjugated victim in favour of women as active agents in their own history, rebellious, self-asserting, drawing strength from the various female communities to which they belonged. But in stressing female agency in all-female contexts, separate spheres tended to drain the picture of all gender conflict: 'it is too systematic, too dichotomous,' wrote Perrot in 1984. For in the end, research on women's culture too often bracketed the larger structures of male domination within which those gendered spheres arose, celebrating women's 'social power' without sufficient attention to the broader relations of domination that shaped and constrained that power.[11]

The harder they looked, the more feminist historians began to suspect that the gendered separation of public and private, far from being a universal description of lived experience, was in fact a historically created ideology, the product of a particular, nineteenth-century and bourgeois way of thinking about the relationship of home and world, family and public, female and male.[12] Disturbed by the idea that their newly honed analytic tool of gendered spheres might in fact be a mere artefact of male domination – 'the reflection of longstanding categories within the minds of our intellectual oppressors', as one feminist scholar nervously suggested – feminist historians began to take critical distance from the concept, moving away from the notion that 'separate spheres' describes the actual lived reality of women and men past towards analysis of the concept as an ideological construct.[13] In making this critical move, feminist historians drew inspiration from the work of political theorists like Carole Pateman, Jean Bethke Elshtain, Joan Landes and Susan Moeller Okin who, by the very late 1970s, were already inquiring into the creation of the categories 'public' and 'private', seeking to describe the ways such distinctions have arisen in particular historical contexts and how they have been deployed in both political theory and social practice. As we will see in chapter 9, pursuit of the public/private distinction as an ideological creation, one that justified both male domination in the home and the exclusion of women from public life, would prove a very fruitful avenue for analysing the 'gendering' of citizenship in Europe and North America at the very moment (seventeenth to nineteenth centuries) that the concept of citizenship was first taking shape.

Separate spheres, or arguments against it, thus constituted a vital organizing concept for women's and gender history in the 1970s and early 1980s, informing a rich vein of research on both sides of the Atlantic. In order to evaluate the long-term impact of this research on the shape of the field, I would like to look more closely at a work that deploys to great effect the notion of a separate women's culture, Caroline Bynum's *Holy Feast and Holy Fast: The Religious Significance of Food to Medieval Women.* Though first published in 1987, this erudite and ambitious book clearly took shape over the late 1970s and early 1980s. Hence, its underlying structures (questions asked, approaches adopted) bear the stamp of the author's sustained reflection on the various debates that were animating the rapidly growing field of women's and gender history across this period: Should feminist scholarship directly reflect present-day issues in feminist politics, in this case the problem of anorexia? How best can the tools of cultural anthropology, and the insights of feminist anthropologists into the gendering of social space, be deployed in the historical analysis of religious expression? Over the course of her magisterial analysis of food symbolism among religious (Catholic) women in fourteenth- and fifteenth-century Europe, Caroline Bynum produces some thoughtful and unexpected responses to these questions. *Holy Feast and Holy Fast* thus engages not only with the bizarre and even disturbing symbolic practices of religious women, it also addresses some of the most burning methodological issues that continue to plague women's and gender history today. As such, it has much to say to gender historians of the early twenty-first century.

Holy anorexia? Women, food and spiritual practice in fourteenth- and fifteenth-century Europe

Holy Feast and Holy Fast is organized around a very complex and difficult question: How can a historian, working in the late twentieth century, make sense of the centrality of food to the religious practices and world-view of late medieval women and to what extent can we discern the impact of trans-historical mechanisms, whether biological or psychological, in the constitution of these practices? Put differently, to what extent do the fasting girls of the late middle ages stand in continuity with today's anorexics? Caroline Bynum's answer is very clear.

While in both the fourteenth and the twentieth centuries, we find excessive fasting to be far more widespread among women than men, girls than boys, the significance that such fasting holds in each cultural context is so different as to render any trans-historical comparison utterly misleading. Bynum then situates medieval women's 'excessive' fasting in its proper setting, a layered series of socio-historical and religious contexts that lent a very specific meaning to forms of self-denial that, to the secularized eyes of the twentieth-century west, seem pathologically self-destructive.

She begins with the late medieval context, a world in which food was scarce and where feasting and fasting took on heightened significance in the eyes of both women and men. She then turns to a more specific analysis of the diverse meanings and symbolism of food within Catholic Christianity of the fourteenth and fifteenth centuries: Christ on the cross as sacrifice and redemption, but also as food for his people, an article of faith that is ritually re-enacted in the eucharist through the miracle of transubstantiation, in which the host becomes actual body and blood; miracles of food multiplication recounted in Scripture (the miracle of the loaves and the fishes) and in everyday life (in the tales of similar miracles performed by saints of both sexes). Food was thus a crucial and polyvalent symbol, available for manipulation by fervent believers of both sexes. Why, then, were the practices Bynum describes – heroic, even miraculous fasts, devotion to the care and feeding of the poor and sick, the transformation of one's own body into food via miraculous exuding – so much more the province of women and girls than of men? The answer, she tells us, is to be found in the actual separation of male and female space, male and female activity, and male and female forms of devotion and sanctity within Catholic Europe of the late middle ages. For if men and women religious shared a common desire to imitate Christ's sacrifice through heroic sacrifice in their own lives, the choice of what they would in fact sacrifice was largely determined by the gendered structures of their society, in which ownership of worldly possessions was controlled by men, while the preparation and distribution of food was handled by women. Small wonder, then, that the former should have chosen to give away money, household goods, even their clothing and sandals, while the latter renounced the one material good over which they exercised some control: food.

Bynum makes clear that the extreme behaviours of the handful of men and women whom she describes were not the stuff of which everyday religious observance was made but rather constituted the outward manifestation of these particular individuals' very powerful yearning for God's presence. Through their fervent and absolute self-denial they strove for no less than the imitation of perfection in this world, that is, of Christ's suffering on the cross. In so doing, they enacted key elements of Catholic theology in their search for a more profound connection with the divine: 'The notion of substituting one's own suffering through illness and starvation for the guilt and destitution of others is not "symptom" [of anorexic pathology] – it is theology,' writes Bynum in an effort to distinguish modern-day pathology from medieval sanctity. 'Fasting was not merely a substitution of pathological and self-defeating control of self for unattainable control of circumstance. It was a part of suffering; and suffering was considered an effective activity, which redeemed both individual and cosmos.'[14] She then takes the argument one step further: In the case of women, who were consigned to second-class citizenship within both Church and the larger society, and excluded from the priesthood altogether, such extreme practices gave these women a certain measure of control in defining the circumstances that would govern their lives:

> to reject unwanted marriages, to substitute religious activities for more menial duties within the family, to redirect the use of a father's or husband's resources, to change or convert family members, to criticize powerful secular and religious authorities, and to claim for themselves teaching, counselling, and reforming roles for which the religious tradition provided, at best, ambivalent support.[15]

To invoke a term that was very popular in feminist circles of the 1970s and 1980s, fervently religious women used their often extreme practices around food and eating to create a space for themselves from which they could exercise limited forms of agency. Bynum gives this point a human face through a series of poignant and beautifully told tales of women like Catherine of Siena, who read in the tragically abbreviated life of her older sister the unmistakeable message that the wages of marriage could well be an early death in childbirth. Her choice of a different, celibate path, over and against the will of her father – a choice whose contours were marked out by increasingly rigorous fasting – gave her a certain measure of power in determining the circumstances and scope of her own life and activity. But religious women's agency did not stop at the boundaries of their own lives, argues Bynum. Rather, through charity, miracle and fasting, women forged for themselves an 'alternative role' to that of the priest, 'an essentially lay and charismatic role – authorized not by ordination but by inspiration, not by identification with Christ the high priest but by imitation of Christ the suffering man... Women saw themselves as authorized to teach, counsel, serve, and heal by mystical experience rather than by office.'[16] Far from the self-defeating and self-destructive starvation that today's anorexics impose on themselves, the holy fasting of late medieval women enabled these women to construct for themselves 'complex, spiritually effective, and distinctive roles within the medieval church.'[17] For if today's anorexic finds herself an isolated casualty, wrapped inside her own pathology in a society where self-starvation holds no transcendent meaning, it was quite the opposite for women mystics of late medieval Europe, whose behaviours unfolded in a context where such suffering and sacrifice were imbued with social and spiritual significance.

Caroline Bynum thus tacks back and forth between the present and the past; between a present concern with the epidemic of eating disorders among well-to-do young women and a past that is replete with evidence that young women of similar social circumstance (who are the ones of whom we have written traces) engaged in self-denying behaviours that, on the surface, bear a striking resemblance to those of their late twentieth-century 'sisters'. Through her thoughtful and far-reaching analysis of the social and symbolic/religious structures of the period, informed as it is by the interpretive methods of cultural anthropologists such as Victor and Edith Turner, Bynum resolutely separates past from present, Catholic from secular, the un-individualist society of late medieval Europe from the deeply individualist one that we inhabit.[18] The reader is thus left in no doubt as to the folly of facile, trans-historical comparisons. At the same time, however, the author makes clear that her own reflections on the subject were nourished precisely by the play between present-day feminist concerns and that unbridgeable gulf of difference that separates Bynum from her late medieval object of study. Of course, all history gets written from within the creative tension that arises between the world of the historian and the very differently structured world of the past of which he or she writes. And yet this tension takes on a very specific shape when the concerns of feminism are also present.

This emerges most clearly at the beginning of her book, where Bynum explains how the idea of studying women's food practices first took shape in the dialectical tension between the author's feminist consciousness, informed by present-day concerns, and her scholarly awareness of the gaps and deficiencies that marred both the existing feminist literature on late medieval women and more 'traditional' (read male) scholarship. Feminist research on the medieval world in the 1970s and 1980s had thus tended to seize on negative stereotypes of women's sexuality and on women's lack of worldly power and sacerdotal authority, largely 'because these issues are of such pressing modern concern'.[19] But the vision of traditional medievalists was no less partial, for if such historians had striven self-consciously to recreate the vantage point of medieval people themselves, they had in fact tended to assimilate all religious views and practices to a single model, that of male religiosity: 'When studying women, they have tended to look simply for women's answers to questions that have always been asked about men,' observes Bynum, 'questions generated in the first place by observing male religiosity... which was concerned with the renunciation of wealth, privilege and sexuality'.[20] The question of food had thus fallen between the cracks, 'chiefly because it is not, in modern eyes, a primary concern, but also because, to medieval men, it was one among many religious symbols and pious renunciations'.[21] Bynum's self-appointed task, then, was to recreate the vantage point of medieval women, a vantage point that she is able to distinguish from that of medieval men thanks to her feminist awareness that the views, opinions and practices of women past have too often been assimilated to those of the men around them. Once Bynum had restored to view women's distinctive spirituality, renunciation of food took its place alongside the foreswearing of other worldly goods – wealth, privilege and sexuality – as a key signifier of piety. Indeed, among women, who had precious little else that they might renounce, food became the primary means by which they sought greater spiritual effectivity in this world, and greater proximity to the Divine.

Caroline Bynum thus treads the narrow path between present-day feminist concern and respect for the absolute 'otherness' of the past. In so doing, she establishes a 'true dialogue' with women of the past.[22] What is more, she persuades her reader that late medieval women did indeed create distinct forms of spiritual expression and even leadership, building a distinctly female religious 'culture' within the male-dominated Catholic Church. One of the great advantages of her approach is that she is able to demonstrate with precision the points at which women's religiosity was continuous with male Christianity, as well as underscoring those points at which the two diverged. Bynum's study of a particular 'women's culture' thus pushed the envelope of women's history as it was then constituted, pressing beyond the narrowly circumscribed study of women's culture toward an understanding of the social and spiritual relations of the sexes on which any specifically feminine subculture rested. *Holy Feast and Holy Fast* is thus not only a work of women's history; it is equally work of gender history. Writing at a moment when feminist scholars were avidly debating the advantages and dangers of broadening the analytic focus outwards from women's history towards a more universal, if less militantly woman-centred history of gender, Bynum combined the two genres quite naturally, without fanfare or comment. Her book, which was widely read at the time (and continues to draw a broad readership), thus contributed to demonstrating that there is no necessary opposition between women's and gender history, but rather a continuity of aims and practices. For as *Holy Feast and Holy Fast* makes clear, the two genres share the common goal of restructuring the historical record using the analytic tool of sexual difference, understood as a social construct, to recast our understanding of societies past.[23]

With its central analysis organized around the reconstruction and interpretation of women's culture and women's experience, *Holy Feast and Holy Fast* bears the traces of its grounding in a particular moment in women's history. Yet it also transcends that moment through the sheer profundity of the author's reflections on both her subject and on questions of historical method. It is a work that was pioneering on a number of levels – in its use of cultural anthropological modes of interpretation and its quiet adoption of gender as a central category of analysis, but also in its carefully framed effort to locate women's subjectivity (sense of self/identity) at the intersection of religious expression, experiences of and ideas about the body, and constructions of masculine and feminine in fourteenth- and fifteenth-century Europe. In this latter sense, *Holy Feast and Holy Fast* was to provide a model in yet one more domain, the as-yet unwritten history of the body, a history of which scholars merely dreamt in the late 1980s. For the body lies at the heart of Caroline Bynum's analysis: the suffering bodies of male and female saints, the manipulation of the body's hidden capacities in search of a spiritual aim, sudden transgressions of gender identity at moments of liminality (for example, when Jesus appeared in the visions of both men and women as a nurturing mother). *Holy Feast and Holy Fast* is thus, above all, a tale of women and men religious whose bodies constituted the locus of their gendered subjectivity. And this is perhaps the main reason that Bynum's book remains so widely read today. For in her reflections on the multiple ways that human beings relate to and manipulate their bodies, going so far as to deploy them as central symbols in religious experience, Caroline Bynum prefigured some of the central concerns that the gendered history of the body would take up in the 1990s.[24]

Endnotes

1 See the introduction to Judith Newton, Mary Ryan and Judith Walkowitz, *Sex and Class in Women's History* (London, 1983), in which the authors state quite bluntly that the great difference between the British and the American practices of women's history was to be found in the fact that the British emphasized class, whereas the Americans had developed 'a theory of gender and of women's culture'.

2 Michelle Rosaldo, 'A Theoretical Overview', in Michelle Rosaldo and Louise Lamphere (eds), *Women, Culture and Society* (Stanford, CA, 1974), 23–4.

3 Rosaldo, 'A Theoretical Overview', 41.

4 Linda Kerber, 'Separate Spheres, Female Worlds, Woman's Place: The Rhetoric of Women's History', *Journal of American History*, 75 (June 1988), 37.

5 Nancy Hewitt, 'Beyond the Search for Sisterhood: American Women's History in the 1980s', *Social History* 10:3 (1985), 301, 299.

6 Sherry Ortner, 'Is Female to Male as Nature is to Culture?', in Rosaldo and Lamphere (eds), *Women, Culture and Society*, 67–87. See also Gayle Rubin, 'The Traffic in Women: Notes on the "Political Economy" of Sex', in Raynia Reiter, *Toward an Anthropology of Women* (New York, 1975).

7 Harriet Whitehead, 'The Bow and the Burden Strap: A New Look at Institutionalized Homosexuality in Native North America', in Sherry Ortner and Harriet Whitehead (eds), *Sexual Meanings, The Cultural Construction of Gender and Sexuality* (Cambridge, 1981), 83.

8 Bonnie Smith, *Ladies of the Leisure Class: The Bourgeoises of Northern France in the Nineteenth Century* (Princeton, NJ, 1981); Carroll Smith-Rosenberg, 'The Female World of Love and Ritual', *Signs*, *1* (Autumn 1975), 1–30. For a useful evaluation of the vast literature on women's culture in the US history field, see Kerber, 'Separate Spheres'. The turn to studying women's culture, while clearly animated by anthropologists' development of public–private as a tool of analysis, was also influenced by political trends, as feminists retreated in the mid-1970s from the confrontational politics of battling male domination head-on towards the elaboration of a feminist identity politics, structured around the idea of a distinct and superior female nature and of separatist women's culture. See Echols, *Daring To Be Bad*, for a fine analysis of the cultural turn in feminist politics as a retreat from politics into the affirming comforts of female identity.

9 Michelle Rosaldo, 'The Use and Abuse of Anthropology', *Signs*, 5:3 (1980). By 1980, Michelle Rosaldo herself was backing off from the claim that public–private constitutes a universal analytic grid: 'Male dominance, though apparently universal, does not in actual behavioural terms assume a universal content or a universal shape... It now appears to me that woman's place in human social life is not in any direct sense a product of the things she does (or even less a function of what, biologically, she is) but of the meaning her activities acquire through concrete social interactions.' Rosaldo, 'Use and Abuse', 394, 400.

10 Bonnie Thornton Dill, 'Race, Class, and Gender: Prospects for an All-Inclusive Sisterhood', *Feminist Studies*, 9 (Spring 1983), 131–50; Jacqueline Jones, *Labor of Love, Labor of Sorrow. Black Women, Work and the Family from Slavery to the Present* (New York, 1985); Cherrie Moraga and Gloria Anzaldua (eds), *This Bridge Called My Back: Writings by Radical Women of Color* (New York, 1981); Barbara Smith (ed.), *Home Girls: A Black Feminist Anthology* (New York, 1983); Gloria T. Hull, Patricia Bell Scott and Barbara Smith (eds), *All the Women Are White, All the Blacks Are Men, But some of Us Are Brave: Black Women's Studies* (Old Westbury, CT, 1982 271–93).

11 Michelle Perrot, 'Les femmes, le pouvoir, l'histoire', in Perrot (dir.), *Une histoire des femmes, est-elle possible?* (Marseille, 1984), 206–22, 210. For a useful critique of the depoliticizing tendencies inherent in the 'women's culture' approach, see Cécile Dauphin *et al.*, 'Women's Culture and Women's Power: Issues in French Women's History', *Journal of Women's History*, 1:1 (Spring 1989), 63–88 (originally published in *Les Annales, E.S.C.*, mars–avril 1986, 271–93).

12 Eleanor Leacock was among the first to suggest this possibility in her introduction to the 1972 re-edition of Friedrich Engels, *On the Origins of the Family, Private Property and the State*, ed. Eleanor Leacock (New York, 1972).

13 Dorothy Helly and Susan Reverby, 'Introduction' in Helly and Reverby (eds), *Gendered Domains. Rethinking Public and Private in Women's History. Essays from the Seventh Berkshire Conference on the History of Women* (Ithaca, NY, 1992), 8.

14 Caroline Bynum, *Holy Feast and Holy Fast: The Religious Significance of Food to Medieval Women* (Berkeley, CA, 1987), 206, 207.

15 Bynum, *Holy Feast*, 220.

16 Bynum, *Holy Feast*, 233, 235.

17 Bynum, *Holy Feast*, 237.

18 Victor and Edith Turner, *Image and Pilgrimage in Christian Culture: Anthropological Perspectives* (Oxford, 1978).

19 Bynum, *Holy Feast*, 29.

20 Bynum, *Holy Feast*, 29.

21 Bynum, *Holy Feast*, 30.

22 Gianna Pomata, in Maria Cristina Marcuzzo and Anna Rossi-Doria (eds), *La ricerca della donne* (Torino, 1987), 199–20.

23 For an eloquent statement of the continuities between women's and gender history, see Jane Rendall, 'Review Article: Women's History: Beyond the Cage?', *History*, 75 (1990), 63–72. For contemporary critiques of the turn to gender, see Judith Bennett, 'Feminism and History', *Gender & History*, 1:3 (Autumn 1989), 251–71; and Joan Hoff, 'Gender as a Postmodern Category of Paralysis', *Women's History Review*, 3:2 (1994), 149–68.

24 Bynum herself has written most persuasively on the ways that historians of gender and sexuality seized upon the body in the early 1990s as the key to unravelling a host of knotty problems surrounding identity, politics and individual agency. See Caroline Bynum, 'Why All the Fuss About the Body? A Medievalist's Perspective', *Critical Inquiry*, 22 (1995), 1–33.

5

Beyond separate spheres: from women's history to gender history

By the mid-1980s, the prolonged interdisciplinary conversation among anthropologists, political theorists, psychologists and historians over the merits and dangers of the separate spheres model had given rise to more subtle approaches that set aside the search for a single universal account of women's oppression and focused instead on analysing the many and diverse shapes that separate spheres ideologies have assumed in particular historical contexts. One can already see the movement in this direction in *Holy Feast and Holy Fast*, where the analysis of women's distinct religious subcultures is also an analysis of the gendered forms of religious expression in late medieval Europe. Feminist historians' growing concern with the interaction of gender with other forms of social hierarchy, notably those of race and class, would press separate spheres models further in this direction, stressing the range of gendered identities that different conceptions of public and private have produced across both space and time. As we shall see, the notion of 'separate spheres' starts to fade into the background in this literature, while the notion of gender, understood as a central axis of social organization, comes increasingly to the fore.

Let us begin our exploration of the evolution of separate spheres models away from the focus on the universal force of patriarchy and towards a more flexible, historically situated concept of gender, with a close reading of Jacqueline Jones's remarkable study *Labor of Love, Labor of Sorrow*, which follows the history of black women in the USA from slavery to emancipation and beyond. Jones's research took shape at a moment when feminist historians who were concerned with the distinct experiences and identities of women of colour were demonstrating across a broad range of contexts that the shape of the public/private divide, and hence the meanings of gender, were by no means stable across regional, ethnic, racial and religious lines. Indeed, particular constructions of womanhood – the languidly dependent, white southern planter's wife versus the ever-toiling black bondswoman, for example – played a key role in distinguishing dominant groups from subordinate ones, in this case free planters and their families from the men and women they enslaved. Moreover, the role of gender relations in upholding the hierarchical distinction between free and slave (or colonizer and colonized, for that matter) was never innocent, for the gender relations of the dominant group stood as the principle outward sign of their more 'civilized' way of being. This 'civilized' status was then invoked to justify their rule over conquered or enslaved populations.

The chapter concludes with a brief analysis of Leonore Davidoff and Catherine Hall's *Family Fortunes: Men and Women of the English Middle Class, 1780–1850*, which explores the interactions of class and gender in early industrial England through a detailed study of the ways that separate spheres ideologies recast gender identities at the turn of the nineteenth century, even as such ideologies shaped the formation of the industrial middle class. One of the great strengths of Davidoff and Hall's research, as we shall see, is its tight focus on the political work that the naturalization of a gendered public–private divide performed in the establishment of the industrial middle classes as a new kind of elite in nineteenth-century England.

'All the women are white, all the blacks are men': African-American women's history and the debate over differences among women, 1975–1985[1]

When she first began teaching a course in women's history at Wellesley College in 1977, Jacqueline Jones discovered the extent to which the convictions of second-wave feminism (a political practice built around the felt oppressions of white, middle-class women) could obscure even the most basic facts that have shaped black women's history in the USA: 'Widely held among my (mostly white, middle-class) students was the conviction that work outside the home always amounted to a "liberating" experience for women, regardless of their race, age, or marital status'.[2] But as Jones's widely influential book, *Labor of Love, Labor of Sorrow*, demonstrates, work outside the home had never, in and of itself, constituted any kind of liberation for those women 'whose foremothers [had been] brought to this country in chains as slaves'.[3] Jones elaborates this point across 150 years of African-American history in a gripping narrative that moves effortlessly from the individual (micro-historical) to the collective (macro-structural) level and back again. This rich tapestry of individual stories is undergirded by a strong socio-economic structuralism that carries the salutary reminder that these women's hard lives were not the mere product of happenstance or bad luck. Rather, they were shaped by the interaction of three powerful and pitiless hierarchies – race, class and gender – that continue to structure economic and social life in the USA to this day. In each of the binary and vertically ordered oppositions that make up these three hierarchies – white over black, rich over poor, male over female – black women constitute the losing term, the bottom rung of each ladder, the triply damned in a society that has long accorded power and value to white, wealthy males. But as we shall see, Jones's ability to tack back and forth between her tripartite analytic structure and the dense and varied mass of evidence on which her narrative rests enabled her to push past the additive vision of race-plus-class-plus-gender that underlay much of the scholarship on women of colour in 1980s North America. Indeed, one of the author's most remarkable achievements is her demonstration, in eloquent and living detail, that the social category 'black woman', as it is constructed and reconstructed at the confluence of race, class and gender, is something other than the simple sum of its parts.

But *Labor of Love* is not a story of women thrice victimized by slavery (then poverty), racism and sexism. It is a tale of resistance, survival and creativity in the face of overwhelming odds. And it is also the story of a particular black women's culture (or series of cultures) that was anchored in the daily realities of work and organized primarily around community and family, with this latter seen not as source of patriarchal oppression (or not solely so, in any event) but rather as a haven for members of all ages and sexes from the harsh, at times murderous force of racism.[4] Jacqueline Jones thus drew from both the women's culture literature and from radical economic theory (including, but not limited to the capitalism-plus-patriarchy school) in order to avail herself of analytic tools that might comprehend the full range of experience among women who, 'while not removed from the larger history of the American working class, shouldered unique burdens at home and endured unique forms of discrimination in the workplace.'[5] In so doing, she transformed those tools so that they might adequately explicate the specific structures that have shaped the lives of black working women.

Jones opens her analysis in the mid-nineteenth-century South, where the institution of slavery gave distinctive meanings to childhood, manhood and womanhood, and to black family life in general – meanings that would prove decisive in shaping the dreams of both women and men as they exited from slavery in the mid-1860s. In a world where families could be broken up by the decision of the owner to sell off one or more members to another planter, and where women were constantly vulnerable to sexual abuse at the hands of their masters, the ties of kin and family took on heightened significance, a fragile haven in a truly heartless world. At the same time, those ties were differently constituted from the family ties of free whites, for the laws upholding and defining slavery, which barred slaves of both sexes from owning property or acquiring literacy skills, established a kind of negatively defined gender equality among slaves. This 'equality', grounded in the fact that 'neither sex wielded economic power over the other', found further reinforcement in the refusal of plantation owners to sharply differentiate the work of male and female slaves.[6] Jones thus describes the endless and back-breaking labours of women and men who toiled out of doors together for up to 14 hours a day, 'often under a blazing sun'.

> In the Cotton Belt they plowed fields; dropped seed; and hoed, picked, ginned, sorted and moted cotton. On farms in Virginia, North Carolina, Kentucky and Tennessee, women hoed tobacco, laid worm fences; and threshed, raked and bound wheat. For those on the Sea Islands and in coastal areas, rice culture included raking and burning the stubble from the previous year's crop; ditching; sowing seed; plowing, listing and hoeing fields; and harvesting, stacking, and threshing the rice. In the bayou region of Louisiana, women planted sugar cane cuttings, plowed, and helped to harvest and gin the cane. During the winter, they performed a myriad of tasks necessary on 19th century farms: repairing roads, pitching hay, burning brush, and setting up post and rail fences... Slaves of both sexes watered the horses, fed the chickens, and slopped the hogs. Together they ginned cotton, ground hominy, shelled corn and peas, and milled flour.[7]

In their relentless search for efficiency, slaveowners tended to downplay gender differences among slaves, especially when it came to assigning adults to field labour: 'The things that my sister May and I suffered were so terrible... It is better not to have such things in our memory,' recalled Hannah Davidson, some 70 years later, remembering her childhood as a slave in Kentucky. 'Work, work, work... I been so exhausted working, I was like an inchworm crawling along a roof. I worked till I thought another lick would kill me.'[8] The testimony of women like Hannah Davidson reminds us how little the gender 'equality' among slaves meant, circumscribed as it was inside the larger structures of bondage. For if their lack of private property or access to wages of any kind deprived bondsmen of 'the means to achieve economic superiority over their wives, one of the major sources of inequality in the ("free") sexual order', their common status as slaves nonetheless reduced black women and men alike to a state of powerlessness that rendered 'virtually meaningless the concept of equality as it applies to marital relations, especially since black women were so vulnerable to attacks by white men'.[9]

The institution of bondage thus denied black men access to patriarchal privilege/power in the larger economic and political sense.[10] Nonetheless, Jones finds that in the extremely restricted scope of cabin life, which unfolded only at the end of the long working day, a clear sexual division of labour prevailed, and that, moreover, bondsmen 'actively scorned' women's work, which included cooking, sewing, cleaning, washing clothes and intimate forms of childcare.[11] While she can only speculate about the origins of the sexual divisions that marked the private lives of bondsmen and women – did they trace back in some way to 'West African cultural preferences'? – Jones has other reasons for pursuing the related questions of gender 'equality' under slavery and the fluidity, even absence, of gendered divisions of labour in field work. For in her discussion of these points in her opening chapter on slavery, Jones lays the groundwork for two larger arguments that she will pursue throughout the 150 years that her book covers: First, she wishes to underscore that family life marked by a domestic sexual division of labour might mean something very different to people to whom domestic life has been denied. Second, Jones uses her evidence to demonstrate that two socio-economic orders – owners and slaves – were defined and upheld on southern plantations, in part through two distinct understandings of gender relations and, by extension, two distinct understandings of the meanings of masculinity and femininity. The planter class was thus defined by a set of gender relations in which wives and daughters were economically dependent on fathers and husbands, their bodies and minds too frail to survive outside the protective circle of masculine tutelage/domination. The slave class, by contrast, was defined through a set of gender relations in which sexual divisions of labour were fluid at best, if not absent altogether. Bondswomen's 'femininity' thus resided in their bodily strength, their capacity to serve as both 'work-oxen and brood-sows', lining the masters' pockets through the alienation of both their productive and reproductive labours.[12] Bondsmen's masculinity also resided in bodily strength, minus, of course, the ability to produce a new slave generation, even as they bent their backs over the cotton crop. It would seem that bondswomen and the white wives of slave owners, though equally female, were quite differently gendered beings, possessed of distinct and opposing kinds of femininity that took shape inside the distinct gender orders that defined their respective classes (black, poor and enslaved versus white, wealthy and free). In later chapters, Jones will demonstrate that poor and working-class white women lived inside yet a third set of gender relations which was neither that of the slave and then post-emancipation black family, nor that of the wealthy whites who dominated them.

Hence the differences between white and black, between free and slave, were articulated through distinct sets of gender relations, through distinct and opposing visions of what constitutes masculine and feminine. *Labor of Love* thus mounts a compelling argument for the proposition that gender is not an axis that operates independently of race and class, creating from a single mould women who will then be subjected to various class- and race-based experiences. Gender relations and notions of ideal masculinity and femininity are, rather, partly constitutive of both racial and class hierarchies, and therefore take on specific forms and meanings within those hierarchies. In this way, *Labor of Love* provides a convincing rebuttal to those who would argue that women's oppression takes a singular form, and that feminist identity (and politics) is therefore reducible to a single, shared experience. For in tracing the historical construction and reconstruction of black women's work and of black family life, understood simultaneously as social constructions and lived experiences, Jacqueline Jones leaves little doubt in the reader's mind that crucial feminist issues, such as work and family, have occupied a very different place in the lives of black women. These are insights of tremendous importance for the history of women and gender; they are insights that emerge with stark clarity in the history of black women in America, first under slavery, then under various states of freedom.

Subsequent chapters on the immediate post-emancipation era underscore the glacial pace of social, political and economic change in the Old South, where the vast majority of African-Americans continued to reside. In this rural economy of dispersed habitat, it was not unknown for slavery to continue in isolated regions, unaffected by the Civil War or by the post-war efforts of the federal government (personified by the Freedmen's Bureaus) to break the grip of the old ways and introduce into the South an economic order based on free, waged labour. Jones thus tells of entire plantations of slaves in remote areas of Kentucky or Tennessee who lived 'in such rural isolation – and under such tyranny – that they remained in servitude until the mid-1880s: "We didn't even know we were free",' recalled one old woman from Kentucky.[13]

During these post-emancipation years, the material condition of ex-slave families often deteriorated, as southern employers systematically underpaid the black men and women who worked for them, sometimes refusing to pay them altogether. While some freed men and women migrated to small southern cities, hoping to escape the known tyrannies of rural life and labour, most families remained on the land, working as sharecroppers on large cotton and tobacco plantations under highly disadvantageous 50-50 contracts (half the crop went to the landlord, the other half to the sharecropping family) that kept them bound to the land and to their landlords in a vicious cycle of poverty and debt.

Freed men and women thus continued to labour long hours in the fields for a very meagre return (the life expectancy of black children at birth was only 33 years in the early twentieth century, due to poverty, disease and poor nutrition).[14] Yet the post-emancipation period did see one striking and much-commented-on change: the partial withdrawal of married freed women from waged labour on the land. Jacqueline Jones explains this phenomenon in terms of that which had been denied to black families under slavery, namely stable family life with a wife and mother whose caretaking labours belonged solely to husbands, children and kin. 'The female field hand who plowed, hoed, and picked cotton under the ever-watchful eye of an overseer came to symbolize the old order,' writes Jones.[15] Withholding their labour from former owners was thus one way for women to mark their passage to freedom, to assert the domestic and family life that had for so long been denied them. Equally important, such withdrawal enabled black women to protect themselves from the sexual assaults of male overseers, and those women whose circumstances permitted (i.e. those who had access to the wages of an able-bodied man) abandoned waged work in favour of toiling on behalf of their families. Of course, under the sharecropping system, this does not mean that these women left the agricultural labour force; far from it. Such women continued to plow, hoe and pick cotton alongside their husbands and children, producing a crop that would be split 50-50 between sharecroppers and landlord. They simply refused (when they could) to work in the gangs of agricultural labourers overseen by white men.

Alongside married women's partial withdrawal from paid agricultural labour, Jones notes a sharpening of gendered divisions of labour within rural black families after emancipation: 'Wives and mothers and husbands and fathers perceived domestic duties to be a woman's major obligation, in contrast to the slavemaster's view that a female was first and foremost a field or house worker and only incidentally a member of a family'.[16] In this context, the patriarchal family constituted a site of collective resistance to the powerful forces of racism, in particular to employers' undying conviction that black men and women were there to be exploited in the fields, that black women had no right to 'put on airs' and confine their labours to the domestic sphere, in imitation of their white 'sisters'. One might legitimately wonder how women who had lived under slavery's regime of negatively defined equality came to accept their husbands' abrupt, post-emancipation assertion of the right to rule 'self-consciously' over their wives and children, directing their labour and dispensing discipline as they saw fit.[17] The implication of Jones's argument, however, is that patriarchal authority lay at the heart of the very thing freed people had been denied under slavery, namely a stable family life, as that was understood in late nineteenth-century North America. Hence, 'freedwomen perceived freedom to mean not a release from back-breaking labor, but rather the opportunity to labor on behalf of their own families and kin from within the protected spheres of household and community'.[18] There was to be no reinventing of the family here along more egalitarian lines; freed men and women alike grasped at domestic and family life as it was organized in the world around them. In so doing, they rejected the regime of gender-indifferent toil with which the gender 'equality' of bondsmen and women had been associated.

Having established the importance of family life to freed men and women in the post-emancipation South, Jacqueline Jones goes on to make a bold claim:

> In rejecting the forced pace of the slave regimen and embracing a family-based system of labor organization, freed people exhibited a preference for

> work patterns typical of a 'tradition' rural society in which religious, regional and kinship loyalties are the dominant values, as opposed to personal ambition or the nationalistic goal of social and economic 'progress.'[19]

In other words, black families and communities in the Old South were bound by ties of cooperation and mutual assistance that were not only necessary to their very survival but that ran counter to the dominant values of competitive individualism that prevailed elsewhere in the industrializing nation. The cooperative ties of this 'traditional' family-kin-community structure (which Jones also characterizes as typical of 'pre-modern' society) provided a context in which women's domestic and economic functions overlapped. Black women were thus far less 'dramatically dependent' on their husbands than were middle-class white wives, while public–private and male–female distinctions were less tightly drawn within black families and communities than among middle-class whites.[20] Once again, the reader is reminded of the very different meanings that family has held for black Americans. For if reconstructing the patriarchal family was one of the first gestures by which former slaves marked their passage to freedom, the grinding poverty within which freed people laboured ensured that upholding distinctions of gender along white, middle-class lines (in particular, the non-labouring wife) would remain a luxury well beyond their grasp.

It was this family, characterized by productive labour on the part of all its adult members, and enmeshed in the values of cooperation among kin, that would gradually move off the land and into more urban contexts; first to the towns and small cities of the South (after 1860), then migrating north after 1915 to take advantage of widening economic opportunities in the industrial cities of Chicago, Detroit and New York. Already in 1870, freed women outnumbered freed men in the cities of the Old South, for single mothers had a hard time making it on the land, and so tended to migrate to towns or cities in search of paid labour. By the last quarter of the nineteenth century, as many as 30 per cent of urban black households in the South were headed by women, twice the figure for rural households.[21] The demographic imbalance prevailing among freed people in southern towns and cities was only reinforced by the distinctly urban structures of opportunity. Hence, the city provided plenty of steady employment to black women, so long as they were willing to work as domestic servants or laundresses. Black men, however, found only sporadic and temporary work in southern cities (which Jones contrasts with the 'labor-voraciousness' of the cotton plantation), jobs that lasted only the length of a particular construction project or contract.

The spectacle of young men, hanging idly about the streets while their wives toiled long hours in white households would help feed the dawning image of black families 'deformed' by the fecklessness of fathers and the 'excessive' power and authority of their labouring mothers. For already, at the end of the nineteenth century, the black family was starting to draw the attention of concerned social workers, who saw this family as dangerously deviant from the white, middle-class norm. This 'deviance' was most visible in two arenas: first, the widespread and highly visible paid labour of wives and mothers, most of whom toiled as domestics in white households; and, second, the notorious 'lack of ambition' shown by fathers who, in the face of an implacable racism whose most basic form was economic, lacked any incentive to strive for extra money, so that they might improve the family's status. Jacqueline Jones is quick to point out that women's 'relative equality of economic function' within this doubly deviant family did not imply any equality of domestic authority, 'hence the use of the term patriarchy to describe [black] family relationships'.[22] Nonetheless, contemporary teacher-social workers like Georgia Washington, concerned with the impact of poverty and racism on black family life, showed a curious inability to uncouple paid labour from domestic authority when they turned their eyes upon the labour of women in poor black families. This is doubly striking because where it was a question of white, working-class wives' employment, no one seems to have expected that such work would grant them additional authority within their families. But contemporary observers were convinced that black families were doomed by what all agreed were 'unnatural', gender-reversed structures. Within these structures women enjoyed 'excessive' authority, thanks to their near-universal wage-earning function, while men, caught as they were inside the dead-end categories of a racially stratified labour market, suffered from a pathological lack of such authority, rooted in what was construed as their utter lack of drive and ambition.[23]

The image of the 'strong, overburdened black mother' that first took shape in the observations of late nineteenth-century teacher-social workers would ultimately give rise to the famous 'black matriarchy thesis' that was destined to have such long life in the sociological analysis of black families. 'It is a cruel historical irony that scholars and policymakers alike have taken the manifestations of black women's oppression and twisted them into the argument that a powerful black matriarchy exists.'[24] But as the author well knows, this ideologically charged vision of gender disorder as the root of family dysfunction is not the outcome of mere 'historical irony'; indeed, this stubbornly long-lived vision is of necessity one of Jacqueline Jones's prime targets. She could hardly proceed otherwise, for any analysis of black women's work and family life worthy of the name must address not only the raced, classed and gendered structures of black women's work, but also the full panoply of gendered stereotypes that have constructed a fictive, but nonetheless highly effective image of a dysfunctional black family populated by powerful, 'castrating' matriarchs and weak-kneed fathers with one foot halfway out the door. The author places her faith in the power of history to destroy the disabling myth, declaring that 'the persistent belief that any woman who fulfills a traditional male role, either as breadwinner or as household head, wields some sort of all-encompassing power over her spouse and children is belied by the experiences of black working women'.[25]

The final chapters of *Labor of Love* follow black women's gradual move out of domestic service and into new forms of employment, notably in industry, but also in the professions and, after 1945, the tertiary sector (clerical and sales) as well. These chapters also recount the necessary backdrop to black women's hard-won escape from domestic service, namely the growing political activism of black communities in both North and South, an activism that was intimately entwined with the dense network of churches that had long bound these communities together. Along the way, Jones stops to cast a critical eye on the race-and-gender-inflected terms of US welfare policy that, far from representing a break with past structures of inequality, merely confirmed those structures in a new context.

Tracing the contested history of black women workers' shift into industrial labour reveals most starkly how the triple forces of capitalism, patriarchy and racism converged to define a narrow, ill-paid niche of labour at the very bottom of the industrial hierarchy, a niche of employments that were distinct from those performed by black men, and very often distinct from those performed by white women as well. The enormous disparity in earnings between black women and their white counterparts, which had long hidden itself behind the occupational ghettoization of black women workers within domestic service, was harder to mask, let alone justify, when black and white women worked together on the same factory floor. Yet employers did nothing to hide the sharp wage differentials that cut across their factory floors where, as a general rule, blacks received about half the wages paid to whites, and women earned about two-thirds of the male wage within their respective race categories. (In other words, black women earned two-thirds of the black male wage; white women, two-thirds of the white male wage). Black women were nonetheless drawn to industrial labour by the higher level of wages overall, for even their low rates of pay far exceeded that which they could earn as domestics. Moreover, industrial employment held out the promise of greater personal freedom to women who were all too accustomed to toiling at the beck and call of white mistresses: 'All the colored women like this work and want to keep it,' explained one railroad yard worker in 1918. 'We are making more money at this than any work we can get, and we do not have to work as hard as at housework which requires us to be on duty from six o'clock in the morning until nine or ten at night, with light [*sic*] little time off and at very poor wages...'.[26]

But black women's niche in industry was not only narrow and ill-paid, it was quite precarious as well, as they found themselves eternally in the position of 'last hired, first fired'. Until the end of the 1950s, black women would periodically abandon domestic service for more lucrative industrial employment, notably during the tight labour markets of the two world wars, only to find themselves returning to service as soon as post-war industrial labour markets slackened in the least. Black women thus constituted a mere 5.4 per cent of the industrial labour force in 1930. Outside the exceptional demand of wartime, they were concentrated in several highly feminized (hence poorly paid) industries: clothing and food processing in the North and tobacco and cigar factories in the South. Black women who sought to escape domestic service via clerical or sales work, both of which absorbed increasing numbers of white working women over the first half of the twentieth century, found the doors shut firmly against them until after World War II.[27] Indeed, the major form of non-manual employment open to black women was the job of schoolteacher. Teaching constituted 'a special category of black women's work', Jones tells us, 'for it implicitly involved a commitment to social and political activism'. But if teaching carried certain undeniable advantages – a vital role in the community, the opportunity to put one's education to good use – it brought black women no material advantage whatsoever. In fact, black women teachers were paid so little that they often had to supplement their earnings with work as laundresses or seamstresses, particularly during the long school vacations, just in order to make ends meet.[28]

Jones's final chapters also trace the racist foundations of US welfare policy, which were first laid down during the economic crisis of the 1930s. The federal government's insistence that relief be handled by local federal authorities produced an uneven patchwork of work provision – under the Works Progress Administration (WPA) – and welfare relief – under the Aid to Dependent Children (ADC) programme. Needless to say, the level and quality of assistance offered under these locally managed programmes varied considerably from state to state and from region to region. While a fair share of WPA jobs went to black men and women in the North, providing some kind of safety net, however threadbare, the actions of federal administrators in the South showed how little these white men's attitudes had changed since the days of slavery. 'Whether they were plantation owners or government officials, they saw black wives and mothers chiefly as domestic servants or manual laborers, outside the pale of the (white) sexual division of labor.' This meant that during the Depression, federal funds would be used for the first time, and on a large scale, 'to preserve the fundamental racial and sexual inequalities in the former Confederate states'.[29]

ADC exerted its negative effects on black families with a far more uniform force, regionally speaking. Hence, in the North as much as in the South, the programme's targeting of single mothers with dependent children had the perverse effect of encouraging fathers to desert their families, especially in times of economic hardship, so that their wives might then qualify for assistance. Of course, levels of assistance were so minimal that black mothers often had to keep working even if they did qualify for ADC. Thanks to the perverse set of incentives established to guarantee that aid went only to the neediest, then, the poor black family began to look ever more 'deformed' by paternal fecklessness and undue maternal 'power' (read: economic activity). By the mid-1960s, this vision of a fearsome black matriarchy, ruling the roost and thereby robbing black men of all self-respect, would receive new legitimacy in sociologist Daniel Moynihan's famous report, 'The Negro Family: The Case for National Action'. In language which should by now be all too drearily familiar, Moynihan fingered single black mothers for the crime of disseminating a 'female culture' to their children, and so undermining their sons' chances to enjoy a healthy sex-role development. The inevitable result of such maternal overbearance could, of course, be read in the statistics on juvenile crime in the ghetto, as boys, in frantic flight from this terrifying female influence, constructed for themselves 'an utterly masculine world... a world away from women, a world run by strong men of unquestioned authority...'.[30]

I have dwelt at some length on certain elements of Jacqueline Jones's argument (at the expense of other, equally vital aspects, notably her discussion of political activism) in order to demonstrate precisely how the author realized her larger historiographical ambition, stated in the opening pages of her book: to 'open a wider discussion on the interrelationships among work, sex, race and class.'[31] As I hope is clear from the preceding discussion, Jones succeeds admirably in her endeavour. Indeed, through her work of historically grounded analysis, Jones helped press the discipline beyond a simplistic 'add-and-stir' vision of difference, in which differences of race and class are added on to the presumably unchanging and universal ground of gender, towards a confrontation with the far more complex social realities and social identities that are produced by the mutual interactions among multiple forms of oppression. We thus see black working women struggling against fates that are peculiarly their own. At many points, the force of racism operates so powerfully that the fate that bound black men and women together seems far more powerful than the gender differences that divided them. This is especially striking under conditions of slavery, where black men and women were reduced to a common state of powerlessness in the face of their owners. In an interesting and subtle way, Jones's discussion of the negative gender 'equality' that reigned among slaves helps to put into perspective two pillars of second-wave feminism, namely the call to abolish male privilege within the family, and sexual divisions of labour in the workplace. Far from constituting a universally applicable solution to all misogynies, these demands stand revealed in Jones's text for what they really are: feminist rallying cries that were linked to the specific political and economic condition of free, white, middle-class women in the mid-twentieth-century west.[32]

But tracing the shifting paths of gender difference and sexual division across 150 years of black history in North America allows Jones to make an even deeper point, one that is perhaps immanent in the notion of the social construction of gender difference, but that nonetheless had to wait for a sustained analysis of black women's history before it was actually made: that people who are born female do not all have the same gender (nor do those who are born male, for that matter). Hence, the construction of whiteness in North America rested on a particular set of relations between men and women within that group, a particular conception of what constitutes masculine and feminine that was not only not shared by blacks, but was in fact used by whites as a way to differentiate more sharply between the two groups. The very lack of a strict sexual division of labour, with both parents going out to work, was thus seen to characterize the black family and black culture as a distinct and inferior form. Of course, white working-class families were also somewhat tainted by this form of inferiority – to the extent that working-class wives and daughters were seen to be labouring and economically productive, they, too, were perceived to be somehow less than women. And this, in turn, was a mark of their families' social inferiority and lack of 'civilization'. The white upper class was thus defined by an extreme differentiation in the status and activities of men and women, a differentiation that was organized to underscore the economic dependency of wives and daughters. Moreover, this extreme form of gender division had become the dominant ideal over the course of the late nineteenth century, constituting the benchmark by which all other kinds of gender relations and family structures were to be judged. *Labor of Love* thus demonstrates, in eloquent and telling detail, that gender does not operate independently of race and class, creating women out of a single mould. Rather, gender relations and notions of ideal masculinity and femininity are partly constitutive of both racial and class hierarchies. As we will see, this is a point that would often be made again in the literature on colonial society, where gender relations became a marker of difference that distinguished, hierarchically, the dominant class from the 'barbarian' cultures being brought under colonial 'tutelage'.

Of course, Jacqueline Jones does not say in so many words that the different race-class orders were grounded in different gender orders. But that is the inescapable conclusion of the story she tells and the evidence she gives. Moreover, there is much evidence that whites, too, understood the differences of race at least partially in terms of the distinctive gender relations and different notions of masculinity and femininity that marked different races, and perhaps different social classes as well. After all, poor and labouring women were often seen as more animal-like than human. None of this was welcome news to those who wished to uphold the comfortingly universal 'we' of white, middle-class feminism. Yet it was precisely the work of black feminist scholars, applying the tools of feminist analysis – gender, women's culture, patriarchy-plus-capitalism – that would help lift feminist scholarship out of the narrow parochialism of women's history and move it towards a more universal history of gender.

Family Fortunes: engendering class in early Victorian England

The publication, in 1987, of Leonore Davidoff and Catherine Hall's highly influential book, *Family Fortunes: Men and Women of the English Middle Class, 1780–1850*, marked a decisive moment in the turn to gender history in Britain, and in gender's diffusion outward into historical practice more broadly.[33] The product of nearly ten years' collaboration between the historian (Hall) and the sociologist (Davidoff), *Family Fortunes* recounts in detail the formation of the provincial middle classes in turn-of-the-nineteenth-century England, a process whose roots lie, the authors argue, in the progressive separation of public (male) space from the private and female-dominated realm of the middle-class home. At the heart of the book lies the ambition to analyse the construction of gendered identities within a particular society, with identity conceived as the link between individual psychology and the larger collectivity. In this sense, *Family Fortunes* contributed mightily not only to the broader diffusion of gender as a tool of historical analysis, but also to the turn in the late 1980s towards subjectivity as an object of historical study.

Of course, the idea of separate male and female spheres was far from new in 1987, for feminist scholars across Europe and the USA had long deployed the model as a description of middle-class social organization – or at least of an *ideal* of middle-class social organization – in modern western societies. What was new was Hall and Davidoff's ambition to lay bare and analyse the gendered foundations of large social processes like class formation. Some five years after the publication of *Family Fortunes*, Catherine Hall wrote:

> We wanted not just to put the women back into a history from which they had been left out, but to rewrite that history so that proper recognition would be given to the ways in which gender, as a key axis of power in society, provides a crucial understanding of how any society is structured and organized... What was the specific relation of women to class structures and how should women's class position be defined? How was class *gendered...?* Do men and women have different class identities? Are their forms of class consciousness and class solidarity the same?... D[o] women have an identity as women which cut across forms of class belonging?[34]

The result is a book that speaks of both men and women and of the formation of the middle classes during the Industrial Revolution on the basis of a gendered distinction in social space and social function.

This gendered distinction between the moral world of the home, where acts are reciprocal and performed for love, not money, and the competitive, amoral world of business and politics, is one that the authors trace back to the texts and practices of Protestant evangelical religion. To my mind, the exploration of the religious sources of gender distinction constitutes one of the most original aspects of Hall and Davidoff's argument. Among other things, it allows the authors to document in some detail the very particular visions of masculinity and femininity that emerged in this world of middle-class evangelicals; visions that were hardly congruent with those of the landed aristocracy, on the one hand, nor with those of the labouring poor on the other. Evangelical religion thus gave a specific moral meaning to the strict and gendered segregation of space and activity, to the productive activity of men in the world, and to the economic dependence of women, who remained close to the hearth and held aloft the pure flame of domesticity. Here, the pious husband would always find a morally uplifting retreat from the unavoidable sullying of hands and spirit that his implication in the competitive and treacherous worlds of business and politics entailed. Across the decades that *Family Fortunes* covers, gender and class are perpetually constructed and reconstructed in relation to one another and in the context of the gendered separation of public and private. And this, in turn, implies that the class consciousness of both men and women must, of necessity, take gendered forms.

With its uncanny capacity to reveal and analyse the gendered underpinnings of such fundamental social processes as class formation, Hall and Davidoff's book became something of a classic almost overnight. It was widely taught in university courses from the late 1980s, and not only in women's studies but in general history classes as well. Yet *Family Fortunes* also drew substantial criticism, often from feminist historians who criticized the separate spheres model for its functionalist logic, as well as for its proximity to the world-view of the very bourgeois whom it purports to analyse. And indeed, there is something deeply disturbing in the peaceful harmony with which the tale of the complementary division of public and private unfolds. It is a tale in which all hint of male domination as a political problem fades behind the comfortable harmonies of gender complementarity. It is a tale that, as Carolyn Steedman astutely observed, 'repeats the imperative of the *Bildungsroman*, which, in its many forms, typically symbolizes the process of socialization, and makes its characters and its readers really want to do what it is that they have to do anyway (be married, have children, clean the stairs...)'.[35] Yet the separate spheres model was seductive – a structure of binary classification that allowed feminist researchers to move beyond social history and to integrate women and gender into more political histories as well, notably into studies of the gendered contours of social and political citizenship. Studies of male–female relations and the construction of gendered identities in a wide range of social contexts began to multiply rapidly, and the history of women and work inexorably lost its privileged position in feminist research.

Feminist scholars' exploration of the various constructions of separate spheres ideology, and the multiple constructions of gender thereby produced, thus honed the category of gender as a tool of social-historical analysis. Across the 1980s and into the 1990s, gender would continue to evolve as scholars deployed it in conjunction with other categories of social analysis (notably those of race and class) to produce histories in which gendered identities, far from holding any stable or universal status, were understood as constantly shifting elements in larger strategies of social organization, and in the notionally stable social and racial hierarchies on which such strategies rested.

Endnotes

1 Taken from the title of Gloria T. Hull, Patricia Bell Scott and Barbara Smith (eds), *All the Women Are White, All the Blacks Are Men, But some of Us Are Brave: Black Women's Studies* (Old Westbury, CT, 1982).

2 Jacqueline Jones, *Labor of Love, Labor of Sorrow. Black Women, Work and the Family from Slavery to the Present* (New York, 1985), xi.

3 Jones, *Labor of Love*, 3.

4 Her analysis owes much to the work of previous scholars like Angela Davis, in particular, her path-breaking article, 'Reflections on the Black Woman's Role in the Community of Slaves', *Black Scholar*, 3 (December 1971), 2–15, and her widely read book, *Women, Race and Class* (New York, 1981). Jones thus builds on Davis's observation that, in the context of slavery, black women's 'ministering to the needs of the men and children around her' (who were not necessarily members of her immediate family) constituted 'the only labor of the slave community which could not be directly and immediately claimed by the oppressor' (Davis, 'Reflections', 7). But she goes further, taking this insight into the profoundly different meanings that domestic labour might have for black and white women and pursuing it across time, and across different political and economic contexts: post-emancipation, northern industrial versus southern agrarian contexts, etc.

5 Jones, *Labor of Love*, 9.

6 Jones, *Labor of Love*, 13–14. The extent to which sexual divisions of labour were observed or not by those who organized the work of slaves is a point of debate among scholars of black women's history. Deborah G. White's research thus stresses the importance of sexual divisions of labour in structuring the work performed by slaves, particularly in the master's house, where work was highly sex-segregated, and black men were never assigned women's work, even under dire circumstances. In field work, however, the 'customary' sexual division of labour ('women hoed while men ploughed') was often ignored when the need arose, and White

proffers a list of heavy outdoor labours that were routinely performed by bondswomen – clearing land, cutting trees, hauling lumber, digging, driving teams of draft animals – a list whose contours recall Jones's enumeration of women's labours in the field, and, further, suggests that out of doors, sexual divisions of labour in field work were far less rigid. Deborah G. White, 'Female Slaves: Sex Roles and Status in the Antebellum Plantation South', *Journal of Family History* (Fall 1983), 248–61.

7 Jones, *Labor of Love*, 15–16.

8 Jones, *Labor of Love*, 15, 13.

9 Jones, *Labor of Love*, 41–2.

10 Jones, *Labor of Love*, 36.

11 Jones, *Labor of Love*, 38.

12 Jones, *Labor of Love*, 42.

13 Jones, *Labor of Love*, 47.

14 The data on infant mortality are from Jones, *Labor of Love*, 91–2.

15 Jones, *Labor of Love*, 58–9.

16 Jones, *Labor of Love*, 63.

17 Jones, *Labor of Love*, 104.

18 Jones, *Labor of Love*, 78.

19 Jones, *Labor of Love*, 68.

20 Jones, *Labor of Love*, 99.

21 Jones, *Labor of Love*, 74.

22 Jones, *Labor of Love*, 104–5.

23 Indeed, the thesis of the excessively powerful black mother doubtless stemmed in large part from her husband's weak position in the labour market, which made for a far lesser gap between her earning power and his than prevailed in most white working-class families, where all-white and all-male labour organizations fought with some success to impose something approaching the male breadwinner wage. The far greater gender gap in white working-class salaries doubtless underscored paternal authority in homes where the woman's wage, however necessary to the family income, nearly always made up the smaller part, and could therefore be cast in the role of mere 'supplement'. No such mythologies could circulate in homes where the mothers' and fathers' wages were more nearly equal, and equally essential to family survival.

24 Jones, *Labor of Love*, 7.

25 Jones, *Labor of Love*, 7.

26 Jones, *Labor of Love*, 166–7.

27 Jones, *Labor of Love*, 166.

28 Jones, *Labor of Love*, 143, 146.

29 Jones, *Labor of Love*, 220.

30 Moynihan Report, quoted in Jones, *Labor of Love*, 312.

31 Jones, *Labor of Love*, 8.

32 This is not to say that patriarchal privilege at home and sexual divisions at

work have posed problems for women only in the mid-twentieth-century west, which is clearly not the case, but rather to relativize the place of these tools in feminist analysis. As Jones's own text makes clear, the analysis of patriarchy at home and of arbitrary sexual and racial divisions at work, remain powerful tools of feminist analysis. Indeed, both are central to *Labor of Love*.

33 Leonore Davidoff and Catherine Hall, *Family Fortunes: Men and Women of the English Middle Class, 1780–1850* (London, 1987).

34 Catherine Hall, *White, Male and Middle-Class: Explorations in Feminism and History* (Oxford, 1992), 12–13.

35 Carolyn Steedman, 'Bimbos from Hell', *Social History*, 19:1 (January 1994), 65. Also Steedman, '"Public" and "Private" in Women's Lives', *Journal of Historical Sociology*, 3:3 (1990). For an elegant critique of the entire separate spheres concept, see Amanda Vickery, 'Golden Age to Separate Spheres? A Review of the Categories and Chronology of English Women's History', *Historical Journal*, 36:2 (1993), 383–414. For an intelligent and extremely useful exploration of the ways that the widely variable range of individual character and experience constantly threatens to destabilize the binary constructs (such as public and private) that underpin ideologies of gender difference, see Mary Poovey, *Uneven Developments: The Ideological Work of Gender in Mid-Victorian England* (Chicago, IL, 1988).

6

Gender history, cultural history and the history of masculinity

In 1994, Joan Hoff published an article ('Gender as a Postmodern Category of Paralysis') whose arguments were symptomatic of a widespread concern among second-wave women's historians that the feminist revolution in the academy was being stolen by various opportunists who were ruthlessly profiteering from the turn to gender analysis. In this defensive vision, gender's capacious skirts were sheltering an unholy alliance of male infiltrators, working under the sign of 'Men's Studies', and a new generation of relentlessly careerist young women. This new generation had forgotten (or worse, carelessly cast aside) the harsh struggles of their foremothers in the race to embrace gender as a more all-inclusive category of analysis than mere 'women'; a category that was, in Hoff's bitter analysis, more favourable to individual career advancement. Lurching back and forth between anger at gender historians' hijacking of 1970s-style women's history and nostalgia for the time when 'women's experiences [could] be used to create feminist theory', Hoff's article thoroughly captures the grave suspicion with which the category of gender was greeted by many a fervent women's historian in the late 1980s and early 1990s.[1] Of course, much of the sound and fury directed against gender had to do with the 'theory wars' that erupted at the end of the 1980s in both British and US universities – a struggle over historians' deployment of postmodern epistemologies and over the use of 'theory' in general, which we will examine more closely in the following chapter. For if gender took shape gradually over the course of the late 1970s and early 1980s as a 'useful' category of analysis in history, its efflorescence within the discipline clearly coincided with the rise of poststructuralism after 1985.

Yet feminist scholars' suspicion of gender also reflected a genuine conflict, already present in the mid-1970s, between those for whom doing women's history was an act of militant (and separatist) scholarship, and those like Natalie Davis, or Michelle Perrot, for whom the study of women always implied the study of men as well: 'It seems to me that we should be interested in the history of both women and men, that we should not be working only on the subjected sex any more than a historian of class can focus entirely on peasants,' wrote Davis in her highly influential article, '"Women's History" in Transition: The European Case', first published in 1975. 'Our goal is to understand the significance of the *sexes*, of gender groups in the historical past.'[2] But if the argument for gender history is immanent in the practice of women's history itself – that is to say, if gender analysis is immanent in the insight that discourses about women are always also discourses about men, and vice versa – the deeply political significance that the practice of *women's* history bore for many second-wave feminists nonetheless ensured that the prospect of 'moving on from recovery of women's history to the history of gender [would] seem a dangerous one, giving hostages to an already hostile establishment'.[3] Nowhere was this more visible than in the ambivalent reaction to the arrival of 'Men's Studies' and the history of masculinity, via the Trojan Horse of gender. For if scholars like Natalie Davis understood from the outset that the study of men as a gendered group was indispensable to any serious feminist history, the links that still bound women's history to a feminist political project that was at times conceived in separatist terms has made the arrival of gender, and its *enfant terrible* Men's Studies, seem like a frontal assault on the still fragile achievements of second-wave activists.

The split between women's history and gender history was doubtless widened during the 1990s by the rising interest that a new generation of scholars of both sexes showed in the history of masculinity. While programmes in women's studies sought to heal the split by re-baptizing themselves programmes in women's and gender studies, the basic divide remains. And as gender historians have in large majority moved to embrace some or all of the poststructuralist and linguistic 'turns', women's historians, with their emphasis on 'lived experience' and 'common gender identities' as the indispensable basis for feminist scholarship and activism, have continued to lose ground.[4]

Let us take a closer look at the precise shape that histories of masculinity have taken within the larger embrace of gender history over the 1980s and early 1990s. For by exploring the various ways that maleness has been constructed, historians of masculinity have put flesh and substance onto the term 'mutual construction' of femininity and masculinity, a concept that had remained a bit abstract and theoretical so long as the focus was turned exclusively on the feminine side of the equation. In so doing, they have underscored the labile nature of masculinity, an entity that, even in feminist history, often functioned as a kind of still point around which notions of femininity shifted. The history of masculinity thus promised to bring back within the circle of social construction those beings who, in Gisela Bock's telling formulation, 'could appear to exist beyond gender relations'.[5]

The 'sex in mourning': putting men as *men* into gender history

In 1984, Alain Corbin published a brief article, 'Le "sexe en deuil" et l'histoire des femmes au XIXe siècle', in which he proposed that women's historians cease their one-sided preoccupation with the sorrows and suffering of women and investigate seriously the suffering of men, 'which suffering produced, in large measure, the marginalization and silencing of women' throughout the nineteenth century.[6] Taking women's historians to task for their 'ostentatious *mise en scène* of female suffering', Corbin suggested that such historians would do well to analyse the less visible forms of masculine suffering that stood half-shrouded behind nineteenth-century Frenchmen's impossible ideals of masculinity: 'Nineteenth-century man... was expected to conduct himself according to a model of warrior-like virility, even, perhaps especially, among the popular classes,' writes Corbin.

> To this end, boys' education was harsh indeed, punctuated by various kinds of physical discipline; the brutal brawling in the *compagnonnages*, the prestige of sheer muscle in rural settings, the dark and omnipresent violence among workers in the Paris building trades all testify to the power of this model.

Lest one imagine that bourgeois youth had an easier time of it, Corbin is quick to note that 'up until the Second Empire [1851–70], the bourgeoisie preferred to keep its girls close to home while consigning its boys to the filthy, stinking cold atmosphere of the boarding school, where they suffered a bodily discipline whose severity contributed immensely to shaping masculine *mentalités*'.[7]

Taking as his point of departure the notion that historians of women and gender must also (and perhaps above all) concern themselves with the history of sexuality, Corbin was among the first to suggest that we cannot really understand the suffering of women without investigating the oppressive social and familial structures within which both male and female identities and sexualities were constructed. Hence, in his 1978 classic *Les Filles de noce. Misère sexuelle et prostitution au XIXe et XXe siècles*, Corbin had already argued that in nineteenth-century France, the demands of social order and, particularly, of orderly property transmission among both urban and rural families weighed especially heavy on the young of both sexes.[8] For the larger inheritance and marriage strategies that animated bourgeois and peasant/artisan families alike required that youth of both sexes delay marriage in the name of those strategies. This entailed a certain degree of frustration for all younger family members, and even condemned certain of them to lifelong celibacy: 'In those milieux where late marriage was particularly widespread, frequent trips to the local bordellos, along with masturbation, constituted a form of sexuality-in-waiting for those obliged to accept a prolonged period of celibacy'.[9] If migration to the city enabled some men to escape the very narrow economic prospects offered by family farm and home village, such migration did little to resolve the problem of sexual misery among these 'sexual proletarians'. Indeed, the pronounced gender imbalance of early nineteenth-century cities (where young men far outnumbered young women) combined with the straitened circumstances of many a young migrant – whose urban employment left him 'too poor to support a girl, or even to dream of marriage' – to ensure that houses of prostitution would play an ongoing and vital role in the lives of a male proletariat condemned to sexual marginality.[10]

In this narrative of repression and frustration, then, prostitution constituted one outlet for such frustrations: 'Women's misery arises directly here from men's... [for] the feelings of the partner, wife or concubine cannot be understood in isolation from the forms of expression or inhibition, of satisfaction or of frustration of masculine desire'.[11] Well before the concept of social construction had passed into common currency, Alain Corbin was already taking seriously the notion that gendered identities are mutually constructed, that 'one's representation of the other and one's image of self are never fashioned independently each of the other', but are, in fact, interdependent.[12] Driving this process of mutual construction is the imperative force of human sexuality, the powers of both male and female desire (though with male 'needs' clearly taking the commanding role), pushing at the boundaries of those social conventions (marriage, property law) erected precisely in order to protect social order from the blind force of human passion.

Corbin's critique of women's history, cast as a contest over which sex could legitimately claim the most victimized status, might well bring a smile to your face, recalling as it does the peculiar orientation of 1970s identity politics, in which the moral stature of one's group identity was directly linked to that group's status as victim of unjust suffering. Nonetheless, his larger point – that gender identities are mutually constructed, and that to understand that construction, historians must delve into the history of sexuality – proved remarkably prescient. Over the next two decades, sexuality would move swiftly to the centre of gender historians' concerns, displacing earlier problematics, such as the sexual division of labour, which had driven so much of the initial research in the field. While the turn to the history of sexuality had much to do with the influence of French philosopher Michel Foucault, not to mention the growing influence of gay and lesbian scholarship in the human sciences more generally, it is nonetheless clear that for at least some historians of masculinity, Corbin's rather different approach to these questions, which might be characterized as a kind of social history of the emotions (one that falls under the broad aegis of the history of *mentalités*), was also decisive.[13] Hence Robert Nye's pioneering work on *Masculinity and Male Codes of Honor in Modern France*, published in 1992, acknowledges the great intellectual debt that the then fledgling sub-discipline (history of masculinity) owed to Corbin.[14] For by placing at the heart of his research an inquiry into the history of male sexuality and masculine suffering, Corbin flew in the face of a long tradition of scientific and psychoanalytic analysis that has treated male sexuality (and hence men themselves) as somehow more straightforward, less 'problematic' than the sexuality of women.[15] In so doing, he provided a salutary reminder that to insist on the 'simplicity' of men's sexuality, relative to the 'complexity' of women's, simply reproduces a particular, nineteenth-century way of thinking about the sexual 'natures' of men and women, one that was burdened with the tremendously important ideological work of underpinning a specific, bourgeois form of the family. Rather than helping us to understand how men and women past might have experienced their sexual identities, such an ideologically charged vision of male and female sexuality merely sets up a barrier to such understanding, denying all experience that falls outside its very narrow purview.

I think it is perhaps no accident that a major work on sexuality, prostitution and the mutual constitution of masculine and feminine identities appeared so early in France, and that it appeared not in the guise of women's history but rather under the sign of the history of *mentalités*. For the history of sexuality constitutes a part of what historians call cultural history, the history of those cultural and symbolic practices that define and shape human communities, including those practices involving people's own bodies.[16] And social and cultural history have enjoyed a long and fairly harmonious cohabitation in France. Hence, soon after its foundation, in 1929, the most famous school of French social history, *Les Annales*, integrated a special kind of cultural history, the history of *mentalités*, into the practice of social history.[17] The term '*mentalités*' refers to the attitudes, customs and world-views that constitute the almost unconscious bedrock of mental and cultural life. Because they are intimately bound up with highly durable social structures, *mentalités* are quite slow to change; indeed, they form yet another layer in the *ossature* that structures human societies, though one that is more cultural and perceptual than social or economic.

By analysing *mentalités* in relation to social structures, French social historians achieved a kind of synthesis between social and cultural forms of analysis, and cultural history, pursued as the history of *mentalités*, has flourished in post-World War II France.[18] In the Anglophone world, on the other hand, the relationship between social and cultural history has been far more contentious; indeed, British and US scholars have tended to see social and cultural analysis as distinct approaches that are grounded in opposing epistemologies. The former thus aspires to a realistic reconstruction of the material and social foundations on which past worlds have rested, understanding those foundations to be prior to, and determinitive of ideas, images and other modes of cultural expression.[19] Cultural historians, by contrast, are interested precisely in exploring those forms of expression which social historians have been only too happy to dismiss as mere superstructure, those baffling layers of cultural mystification that cover over and distort the crystalline certitudes of economic and social relations. In both the UK and the USA, then, the increasing interest in writing histories of sexuality was inscribed in the larger 'cultural turn' that many social historians took some time near the end of the 1980s.[20] Frustrated with the limited capacity of social history to engage with the more cultural and expressive dimensions of human existence, these newly converted cultural historians viewed their cultural turn as an epistemic rupture with social history's more narrowly materialist analysis: 'Social history has brought us to the brink of a new history of culture, where society may not be primary after all and culture may not be derivative,' wrote US historian of France Patricia O'Brien in 1989. 'The result is a period of confusion and perhaps crisis in the rise and fall of paradigms'.[21] It is a rupture whose consequences British and US historians continue to struggle with today, as we will see in the next chapter, on the impact of poststructuralism in the 1990s.

But let us return to the case of France, where cultural history, far from implying any kind of break with social history, has constituted instead a compatible and complementary element of social analysis. Having never drawn so sharp a distinction between material and cultural forms of analysis as their Anglophone neighbours, historians in France disposed from early on of an analytic framework (the history of *mentalités*) that allowed them to approach the history of sexuality from a more integrated sociocultural perspective. Already in the 1970s, then, Alain Corbin could analyse the shifting structures and social locations of prostitution in order to grasp the precise forms of 'sexual misery' endured by men and women of both the popular and upper classes in nineteenth- and twentieth-century France. Indeed, by taking seriously the complementary construction of gender identities, Alain Corbin's work on the sorrows of masculinity provided one suggestive point of departure for what was to become a veritable growth industry in the 1990s, namely a history of masculinity that could reinstate the particularity of men as a 'social group and gender category'.[22]

Constructing bourgeois masculinity: valour, male honour and duelling in nineteenth-century France

One of the most thoughtful and suggestive contributions to this project came from a US historian of nineteenth-century France, Robert Nye, whose *Masculinity and Male Codes of Honor in Modern France* stands at the crossroads of the history of *mentalités* and a more Foucaldian approach to the history of sexuality. Drawing on Pierre Bourdieu's extremely fruitful notion of sexual identity as a 'practical sense' that is embodied in both gesture and bearing, Nye brings together the analysis of bodies and sexuality, forms of male sociability and the shifting medico-political constraints that sought to define and channel male sexuality toward eugenic and reproductive ends in a rich and revealing study of upper-class masculinity across a very long nineteenth century, from the end of the *ancien régime* to the early 1920s.

Nye's interest in Bourdieu's concept of sexual identity as a 'practical sense' stems in part from the author's concern with a problem that should by now be familiar to you, namely that of anachronism. For like Caroline Bynum before him, Nye was concerned that through the very analytic devices that they use to interpret the past, historians can all too easily impose anachronistic perspectives on their objects of study. In Bynum's case, the potential culprit was the late twentieth-century concern with women's eating disorders. In Nye's case, the problem lay in the very tool that allowed him to unlock the question of masculinities past, that is, the sex/gender distinction. Now, we early twenty-first-century beings are quite familiar with this distinction, on which the notion of socially constructed gender identities rests. 'Our post-modern consciousness encourages a distrust of all determinisms and stimulates in us the conceit that we may reconfigure ourselves infinitely, select new identities, slip in and out of roles in protean fashion,' writes Nye in his eloquent introduction.

> Our ability to think of sex as a constructed *identity* therefore provides us with a valuable analytic tool for understanding sex as a historical artefact furnishing individuals with particular kinds of self-awareness and modes of self-presentation... By historicizing sex we can escape the bind of thinking about it as an adamantine and transhistorical category of being.[23]

But what of our ancestors who had no such sophisticated tools for destabilizing (and thereby putting at a safe distance) their own sexed identities? How can the historian usefully profit from the insights to be gained via the sex/gender distinction without wrongfully imposing a postmodern sense of the self as a voluntarily chosen subjectivity on men and women for whom sex really *was* destiny, 'an *amor fati* that swept them along in its powerful currents'?[24] How can he or she convey the powerful influence that the all-encompassing sense of sex as destiny exercised in shaping male and female subjectivities, while at the same time retain sufficient critical distance in order to analyse those subjectivities? It is here that Nye seizes upon Bourdieu's concept of 'practical sense', hoping thereby to capture the double-edged quality of sexual identity as at once culturally constructed *and* lived, embodied reality.[25]

The author does this by posing a novel problem. In societies that do not distinguish sex from gender (a category that includes most European societies, including that of nineteenth-century France), patrolling the boundaries of gender-appropriate behaviour entails recalling deviant members to their 'true' sex. But how in the world did people actually recognize 'true' sex? For if 'traditional societies' possess some 'collective understanding' against which individual sexual identities are evaluated ('invariably some form of the binary opposition "male–female"'), how is this identity actually constituted? In other words, what is the relationship between individual gendered identities and the larger collectivities within which those identities are inscribed? Drawing on Pierre Bourdieu's notion that sexual identity is not a 'state of mind' based on formal rationality but is, rather, a 'state of the body', a 'practical belief' that is inscribed directly on the body, Nye argues that sexual identity was 'experienced and regarded in the past as a *natural* quality, expressed in and through the body and its gestures'.[26] Individuals acquire and reproduce this 'practical sense', not by conscious imitation but rather through a process of embodiment that occurs 'below the level of consciousness':

> The body believes in what it plays at; it weeps if it mimes grief. It does not represent what it performs, it does not memorise the past, it *enacts* the past, bringing it back to life. What is learned by the body is not something that one has, like knowledge that can be brandished, but something that one is.[27]

Bourdieu's 'practical sense' thus helps us to understand how easy it is for sex and gender to be experienced as a single, seamless quality of the self, for 'the gestures and practices of sexual identity are… as corporeal in their lived reality as the sexual anatomy and secondary sex characteristics with which they are correlated'.[28]

Armed with this sophisticated approach, Nye set out to study men's 'lived relation to their world', not in present-day society, where the evanescent gestures that express this relation are constantly and everywhere visible, readily presenting themselves for analysis, but in the now-vanished world of France's nineteenth-century elites. The site on which Nye reconstructs those long-gone expressions of manliness is that of the male honour code, whose ideals and values, though originally shaped by France's military and landowning nobility, were eagerly seized upon by the French bourgeoisie as an instrument for anchoring, affirming and valorizing bourgeois masculine identity and ideals of masculine behaviour. Such codes were effective in shaping masculinity largely because they regulated the social relations among groups of men. But they also provided a basis for settling private disputes between individuals, the duel being 'only the most spectacular representation of this function of the honor code; on a more prosaic level, honor codes informed the day to day relations of men in professional life, sports, the political arena, and other areas of public life'.[29] Behind the voice of Pierre Bourdieu, then, echoes that of sociologist Norbert Elias, whose magisterial *Civilising Process* analyses bourgeois norms of conduct in modern France as the outcome of a trickle-down of aristocratic manners, values and caste-consciousness across the seventeenth and eighteenth centuries, and on into the nineteenth century as well: 'By provoking... constantly renewed efforts at emulation by the vulgar, the cream of society served as the engine that drove the whole social organism toward a horizon of greater cultivation,' writes Nye in a neat summary of Elias's argument.[30]

Yet the voice that resonates most powerfully in Nye's text is that of Michel Foucault, whose *History of Sexuality* influenced an entire generation of US historians: 'The bourgeoisie's "blood" was its sex,' writes Foucault in a meditation – fully cited by Nye – on the transmission of aristocratic concepts of caste downwards to the early nineteenth-century bourgeoisie. Upon arrival, such concepts underwent a significant transformation, appearing 'in the guise of biological, medical or eugenic precepts. The [aristocratic] concern with genealogy became a preoccupation with heredity...'.[31] And, as Nye amply demonstrates, the bourgeois notion of male honour was saturated with medico-sexual preoccupations, notably around male sexuality, which, it was believed, exercised determinitive force in shaping the health and gender of the offspring. He who properly managed and disciplined his finite sexual energy would thus be rewarded with vigorous offspring and numerous sons, while he who carelessly spent his vital sexual force through masturbation, excessive coitus or frequent recourse to prostitutes squandered and endangered his limited sexual capital. The results of such debauched behaviour were all too painfully visible in his sickly and effeminate offspring, if indeed he produced any offspring at all. Because the continuity of bourgeois fortunes depended not only on inheritance but also on the production of 'viable and talented *inheritors*', the paterfamilias was saddled with the dual obligation to manage simultaneously the family's financial and genetic capital, a job that began with the careful conservation of his own sexual vitality and hygiene.

Honour thus had both a private and a public face, 'the honor embedded in the sex of the male body and its sexual hygiene, and the public rites of honor expressed in male sociability and the duel'.[32] Creatively deploying the feminist insight that public and private are in fact fatally connected, Robert Nye demonstrates with great precision how the concept of honour entered into and organized masculine behaviour and ideals in both their private and their public lives. The male honour code thus enjoined self-discipline and self-control in the home (a.k.a. the sexual sphere) and the courage, group loyalty and refusal to accept insult that, in the public realm, were the outward signs of one's free and honourable status: 'My study reveals in particular how the bodies and sexuality of upper-class males and their modes of sociability and conflict were related to their elite social and political status,' writes Nye, for 'honor was *embodied* in bourgeois men as a set of normative sexual characteristics and desires that reflected the strategies of bourgeois social reproduction'.[33] An appropriately masculine domination of one's dependants in the home (wife, children, servants) was thus one indispensable ground on which bourgeois men's public honour rested; a combination of prideful, dignified bearing and unbreakable loyalty toward one's peers constituted the other.

Among other things, this approach allows the author to specify the relation between the 'individual' and the 'social' in the construction and maintenance of masculine identities. For if the ideals of masculinity were anchored in a public code of honour, a 'collective representation', then masculine identity cannot be analysed solely in terms of individual psychology; the role of public culture in shaping such identities was simply too important, at least in the case of nineteenth-century France.[34] Across the entire space of his book, then, Nye moves back and forth between the public and the private, using the honour code to explore the relation between bourgeois men's social and sexual identities. Such identities were, of course, never secure, being grounded in a concept (honour) that required constant affirmation and was perpetually open to challenge.[35] Nonetheless, honour provides the point of anchorage, the institutionalized location at which a host of cultural codes around masculine ideals came together across the long nineteenth century in France.

Beginning with the era of the French Revolution, 'when men and women were first identified in law and medicine as opposite but complementary beings whose unequal social status was expressed in their bodies and sexuality', Nye shows us the masculine face of 'separate spheres' in nineteenth-century France; an ideology and a social practice that produced bourgeois males whose conduct and identity were no less rigidly controlled than those of their domestically bound consorts.[36] If, on the one hand, male sexual potency became in the nineteenth century 'a way of thinking about power, both of the public and the domestic variety' (and indeed, until 1945, male sexual capacity was a qualifying feature for full citizenship in France), the biological base of that political power was also understood to be fragile, in need of careful husbanding, menaced as it was by the dangers of impotence, degeneration and homosexuality.[37] More profoundly, Nye's book shows us how this particular, bioligized understanding of male honour contributed to the politicization of male sexuality in a nation where anxiety over the falling birth rate produced policies and rhetorics that addressed male heads of families at least as often (if not more frequently) as mothers. It is an interesting and, I think, significant difference with England, whose *fin-de-siècle* population policies addressed themselves to the 'feckless mothers' presumed responsible for poor children's ill-health and inadequate education.[38]

In the opening pages of *Masculinity and Male Codes of Honor*, Nye raises the question of how it is male sexual identity changes over time, and expresses the hope that his book will contribute to elucidating that process. As one reads through the pages of his book, however, the reader is more aware of that which endured than of that which changed. I wonder if this isn't an effect of Nye's methodological choices. For all his recourse to the more sociologically grounded work of Elias (which explores the interrelationship of social change, psychic structures and political culture) and Bourdieu (which focuses on the socially specific embodiments of sexual/gender identity), Nye's concept of honour is, ultimately, a discursive one, drawing its inspiration from Michel Foucault and the 'school' of cultural history he has inspired: 'The cultural sphere is the site of power struggles between competing representations that may not be reduced to, but must be somehow correlated with particular interests and social groups,' writes Nye. 'But because representations have a kind of independent and fluctuating status, the truths they assert and the dominion they seek may be tailored to a multitude of ends ... Cultural representations are thus both structures of meaning and discursive practices that are employed in contingent ideological strategies'.[39] In other words, history happens on the discursive plane, as a result of changes in these discursive domains that are 'contingent and mutually reinforcing'.[40] But how does change actually occur on a purely discursive plane? Although *Masculinity and Male Codes of Honor* sets forth realms of social practice and realms of discourse, the links binding the two are not always clear. And without some way of connecting discursive process to social experience, historians are hard put to explain how the meanings of masculine and feminine might shift over time.

For in the end, the problem – and challenge – of gender is that it is not merely a discursively constructed identity, but also a social and subjective one. Historians will be able to trace changing meanings of masculine and feminine only if they are able to grasp these three analytic levels simultaneously, as John Tosh seeks to do in his analysis of the specific appeal that a newly constructed and highly aggressive imperial masculinity held for late nineteenth-century clerical workers. Not only were these men precariously perched on the edge of the cliff separating middle class from proletariat, but they were also faced at this time with substantial – and growing – competition from women clerks: 'Male clerks protested at this slur on their manhood,' writes Tosh. 'A hearty, and above all a *physical* identification with the quintessentially masculine ethos of empire was one very effective way in which the slur could be countered... As a form of political identification... the empire served to underpin beleaguered masculinities at home'.[41] Tosh thus identifies the emergence of a distinctly imperial form of masculinity at the end of the nineteenth century – one that was quite different in both content and social reach from the 'expressive manliness' of Britain's mid-Victorian elite – and links its widespread purchase on lower middle-class male clerical workers (who seized on the new jingoism with alacrity) to the shifting contours of class and gender that shaped their social, economic and subjective worlds at the turn of the twentieth century.

Historians of gender have often noted that one of masculinity's defining traits in the modern west is its very invisibility. If women have been marked as 'the sex', creatures possessed of a singular, unitary and essentially maternal nature that suffuses their entire being and defines both 'feminine' character and women's social position, masculinity has managed to remain discreetly 'out of sight', since the identity of men as a sex has never been so thoroughly bound up with their reproductive function. As Rousseau memorably put it: 'The male is only male at times; the female is a female all her life and can never forget her sex'.[42] This asymmetrical vision has proved remarkably enduring; one need only consult the tremendous outpouring of Victorian scientific comment on women's distinctive biology, and the character traits that were believed to flow from it, compared with the utter silence on men's. Indeed, as John Tosh has pointed out, men's distinctive nature was vested more in their reason than in their bodies. 'A profound dualism in Western thought has served to keep the spotlight away from men. In the historical record, it is as though masculinity is everywhere but nowhere.'[43] By patiently uncovering the distinctive sufferings that shaped bourgeois masculinity in nineteenth-century France, Robert Nye has broken the pact of silence surrounding male sexuality and shown us male identity as both psychic and social reality, shaped by the twin constraints of bourgeois patrimonial necessity and the demands of public honour.

Endnotes

1 Joan Hoff, 'Gender as a Postmodern Category of Paralysis', *Women's History Review*, 3:2 (1994), 154.

2 Natalie Zemon Davis, '"Women's History" in Transition: The European Case', *Feminist Studies*, 3:3/4 (Spring/Summer 1976), reprinted in Joan W. Scott (ed.), *Feminism and History* (Oxford, 1996), 88. This is just as apparent when approached from the other, masculine side, as Robert Nye notes: 'there is something in men's experience that has provoked periodic reassessments of both women's nature *and their own*. How could it be otherwise if "man" and "woman" have been yoked together as complementary if fluctuating terms from time out of mind?' Robert Nye, *Masculinity and Male Codes of Honor in France* (Berkeley, CA, 1992), 12.

3 Jane Rendall, 'Uneven Developments: Women's History, Feminist History and Gender History in Great Britain', in Karen Offen, Ruth Roach Pierson and Jane Rendall (eds), *Writing Women's History: International Perspectives* (Bloomington, IN, 1991), 53.

4 Joan Hoff summarized women's history's 'rear-guard' position very well when she wrote: 'If experience cannot be based on socio-economic categories and on the diversity and variability of common gender identities

in different time periods, then there can be no political, visionary… history from which contemporary feminist activists can draw sustenance and advice for opposing and critiquing the obvious discrimination against women in the United States and other countries.' Hoff, 'Gender', 158.

5 Gisela Bock, 'Women's History and Gender History: Aspects of an International Debate', *Gender & History*, 1:1 (Spring 1989), 7–30.

6 Alain Corbin, 'Le "sexe en deuil" et l'histoire des femmes au XIXe siècle', in Michelle Perrot (ed.), *Une histoire des femmes, est-elle possible?* (Marseille, 1984), 152.

7 Corbin, 'Le "sexe en deuil"', 149–50. See also Gabrielle Houbre, *La Discipline de l'amour. L'éducation sentimentale des filles et des garçons à l'âge du romantisme* (Paris, 1997).

8 Alain Corbin, *Les filles de noce. Misère sexuelle et prostitution aux XIXe et XXe siècles* (Paris, 1978).

9 Corbin, *Les filles*, 95.

10 Corbin, *Les filles*, 96.

11 Corbin, 'Le "sexe en deuil"', 151, 148.

12 Corbin, 'Le "sexe en deuil"', 147.

13 In a recent interview with Michelle Perrot, Alain Corbin remarked that *Les Filles de noce* was less a history of sexuality than 'of the social condition of prostitutes and their clients'. 'Des hommes, des femmes, des genres', interview with Alain Corbin and Michelle Perrot, *Vingtième siècle*, 75 (juillet–septembre, 2002), 172. In gay and lesbian history, one might cite the pioneering work of Marie-Jo Bonnet, *Un choix sans équivoque. Recherches historiques sur les relations amoureuses entre les femmes, XVIe–XXe siècles* (Paris, 1981); Lillian Faderman, *Surpassing the Love of Men: Romantic Friendships and Love Between Women from the Renaissance to the Present* (New York, 1981); David Halperin, *One Hundred Years of Homosexuality: And Other Essays on Greek Love* (New York, 1990); John Boswell, *Christianity, Social Tolerance and Homosexuality: Gay People in Western Europe from the Beginning of the Christian Era to the Fourteenth Century* (Chicago, IL, 1980); and John d'Emilio, *Sexual Politics, Sexual Communities: The Making of a Homosexual Minority in the United States, 1940–1970* (Chicago, IL, 1983).

14 On the history of masculinity, see Robin Weigman, 'Object Lessons: Men, Masculinity, and the Sign *Women*', *Signs*, 26:2 (2001), 355–88; Mrinalini Sinha, 'Giving Masculinity a History', *Gender & History*, 11 (1999), 445–60; George Mosse, *Nationalism and Sexuality. Respectable and Abnormal Sexuality in Modern Europe* (New York, 1985); H. Brod, *The Making of Masculinities: The New Men's Studies* (London, 1987); Michael Roper and John Tosh (eds), *Manful Assertions: Masculinities in Britain Since 1800* (London, 1991); John Tosh, *A Man's Place: Masculinity and the Middle-Class Home in Victorian England* (New Haven, CT, 1999); and John

Tosh, 'What Should Historians Do with Masculinity? Reflections on Nineteenth-Century Britain', *History Workshop Journal*, 38 (1994), 179–202; Stephen Garton, 'The Scales of Suffering: Love, Death and Victorian Masculinity', *Social History*, 27:1 (January 2002), 40–58; Paul Seeley, 'O Sainte Mère: Liberalism and the Socialization of Catholic Men in Nineteenth-Century France', *Journal of Modern History*, 70 (December 1998), 862–91; Annelise Maugue, *L'Identité masculine en crise au tournant du siècle* (Marseille, 1987).

15 'If men have constructed an amatory and familial regime that has brought suffering to women, the historian would do well to regard those regimes as "signs of male suffering".' Nye, *Masculinity*, 12. For classic statements of the greater 'complexity' surrounding women's sexuality, see Peter Gay, *The Bourgeois Experience: Victoria to Freud*, vol. I, *The Education of the Senses* (New York, 1984), 144; and of course, Sigmund Freud himself, notably his 1933 lecture on 'Femininity'. Feminist scholarship often reproduces this structure, not because feminists agree with Freud's view, but simply because such scholarship has tended to devote the lion's share of attention to female sexuality.

16 Corbin was not the first historian in France to address the history of sexuality; that honour belongs to Jean-Louis Flandrin, whose *Les Amours paysannes. Amour et sexualité dans les campagnes de l'ancienne France, XVIe–XIXe siècles* (Paris, 1975), appeared three years before Corbin's *Filles de noce*.

17 The concept of *mentalités* officially entered into the *Annaliste* tool kit with the publication in 1942 of Lucien Febvre's magisterial *Le Problème de l'incroyance au XVIe siècle. La religion de Rabelais* (Saint-Amand, Cher, 1942).

18 Indeed, since the 1960s, cultural analysis has moved increasingly to centre stage in France and has assumed a more reciprocal relation with social and economic analysis, as Roger Chartier noted in 1982: 'the relationship thus established is not one of dependence of the mental structures on their material determinations. The representations of the social world themselves are the constitutents of social reality'. (Roger Chartier, 'Intellectual History or Sociocultural History? The French Trajectories', in Dominick LaCapra and Steven L. Kaplan (eds), *Intellectual History: Reappraisals and New Perspectives* (Ithaca, NY, 1982), 30.

19 An important exception here is the work of British Marxist Edward Palmer Thompson, whose *Making of the English Working Class* rejected the material base/cultural superstructure metaphor in favour of studying what he called 'cultural and moral mediations... the way these material experiences are handled... in cultural ways'. Thompson, quoted in Ellen Kay Trimberger, 'E.P. Thompson: Understanding the Process of History', in Theda Skocpol (ed.), *Vision and Method in Historical Sociology* (Cambridge, 1984), 219. For all his interest in cultural mediation, however,

Thompson remained within Marxism's materialist model of historical explanation: 'class experience is largely determined by the productive relations into which men are born – or enter involuntarily'. Edward palmer Thompson, *The Making of the English Working Class* (London, 1963), 10.

20 Indeed, writing a history of sexuality was quite simply unthinkable within the more narrowly materialist paradigm of social history as it was practised in the Anglophone world in the 1960s and 1970s.

21 Patricia O'Brien, 'Michel Foucault's History of Culture', in Lynn Hunt (ed.), *The New Cultural History* (Berkeley, CA, 1989), 26. On the ongoing and pervasive polarization of cultural and social forms of analysis, see Antoinette Burton, 'Thinking Beyond the Boundaries: Empire, Feminism and the Domains of History', *Social History*, 26:1 (January 2001), 60–71.

22 Jane Rendall, 'Uneven Developments', 49.

23 Nye, *Masculinity*, 3–4 (original emphasis).

24 Nye, *Masculinity*, 5.

25 Nye refers to this as 'the need to consider sex and gender dialectically'. Nye, *Masculinity*, 5.

26 Nye, *Masculinity*, 6 (original emphasis).

27 Pierre Bourdieu, *The Logic of Practice*, trans. Richard Nice (Stanford, CA, 1990), 73 (original emphasis). Cited in Nye, 6–7.

28 Nye, *Masculinity*, 7.

29 Nye, *Masculinity*, 8.

30 Nye, *Masculinity*, 40. Norbert Elias, *The Civilising Process*, 3 vols (New York, 1983).

31 Michel Foucault, *The History of Sexuality. An Introduction*, trans. Robert Hurley, vol. I (New York, 1980), 124–5, cited in Nye, *Masculinity*, 9.

32 Nye, *Masculinity*, 13.

33 Nye, *Masculinity*, 7, 9.

34 David Gilmore, *Manhood in the Making. Cultural Concepts of Masculinity* (New Haven, CT, 1990), 4–5. Cited in Nye, *Masculinity*, 10.

35 Nye, *Masculinity*, 13.

36 Nye, *Masculinity*, 13–14.

37 Nye, *Masculinity*, 67, 69.

38 Anna Davin, 'Imperialism and Motherhood', *History Workshop*, 5 (Spring 1978), 9–65.

39 Nye, *Masculinity*, 11.

40 Nye, *Masculinity*, 148.

41 Tosh, 'What Should Historians Do with Masculinity?', 194.

42 Jean Jacques Rousseau, *Emile*, Book V, 'Sophie, or the Education of Woman', trans. William Payne (London, 1893).

43 Tosh, 'What Should Historians Do with Masculinity?', 180. Nye's research suggests French doctors may have been rather more forthcoming on the subject of male biology than their British counterparts.

7

Gender, poststructuralism and the 'cultural/linguistic turn' in history

By now I hope it is clear that the arrival of gender as a tool of historical analysis contributed mightily to the displacement of feminist history's attention, away from women's experiences (especially of work) and towards the construction of masculine and feminine identities across the social spectrum. This shift in object – from experience to the social construction of gendered identities – would be confirmed and extended by the arrival of poststructuralist theory in departments of women's studies and history across the USA and the UK at the turn of the 1990s.[1] But what exactly is poststructuralist theory and why did its 'invasion' into the human sciences cause such upheaval in the US and UK academies?

Poststructuralism: a very short introduction

Poststructuralism is one aspect of the broader phenomenon of postmodernism, which first took shape in the late 1960s and 1970s as a form of art that refused modernist understandings of art and the artist's role in society. 'Modernism was based on the premise that the artist, a gifted individual standing outside society, could use the special skills of painting or writing to access hidden truths about the human condition,' writes Kevin Passmore in his illuminating article 'Poststructuralism and History'. 'Impressionist painters, rather than merely reproducing the appearance of landscape, claimed to evoke the feeling aroused by looking at it. By extension, "conventional" history is modernist too, in that expert techniques are used to access truths not visible to the lay person.'[2] Postmodernist artists rejected the proposition that the artist (or anyone else, for that matter) can uncover underlying meanings – indeed, some went so far as to suggest that no such meanings are out there to be uncovered – and insisted that artists abandon such vain hopes and focus instead on drawing attention to the various techniques of representation that construct their work.

Philosophers and sociologists were quick to seize on the postmodern concept and extend it to the realm of social analysis. Here, it seemed, was a useful way to characterize our contemporary, post-capitalist 'society of the spectacle', where the production of images has overtaken the production of mere goods. French philosopher Jean Baudrillard thus argued that in the postmodern capitalist condition, the 'over-production' of images has rendered reality inaccessible; our perceptions are shaped entirely by the images purveyed by advertising, television and the internet.[3]

Poststructuralist thought shares with postmodernism the conviction that artists and intellectuals must focus on representation, rather than futilely chasing after that will-o'-the-wisp that is an inaccessible reality. But poststructuralists focus more precisely on language. Taking the insights of structural linguistics, and especially the work of Ferdinand de Saussure, as their point of departure, poststructuralists understand language as an unstable system of signs in which meanings can shift about with disconcerting slipperiness. Hence, Saussure's *Cours de linguistique générale* (1916) stressed the gap that yawns between the sound or appearance of a word (which he called the signifier) and the concept that it evokes in our minds (the signified). The signifier (word) is by no means identical with the signified (mental concept); indeed, the relation between them is utterly arbitrary, fixed by the rules of grammar rather than by any direct relation of correspondence. Worse yet, neither signified nor signifier can provide any direct access to reality, for both are mere constructions of language; their significance derives from their position in a larger grammatical structure that is built of binary oppositions – a cat is a cat because it is not a dog; a woman is a woman because she is not a man – and not from any intrinsic, privileged relation that word or concept enjoys with the object it represents.

By underscoring the hiatus between words and the things they represent, Saussure's work suggests that language cannot give us direct access to any kind of reality that dwells outside it. Yet human beings are so constructed that language is the sole medium by which we are able to order the hodgepodge of perceptions that arrive via our five senses into some kind of meaningful datum. One consequence of Saussure's work, then, was to shift linguists' attention away from the study of what words denote in the real world and toward the analysis of their interrelation with one another within the larger structures of a particular language's grammar (hence the term 'structural' linguistics). But structuralism soon spilled over the boundaries of linguistics into adjacent disciplines, such as literature and anthropology. In the latter case, the adoption of structuralist approaches by cultural anthropologists in the 1950s opened up the possibility of interpreting cultures as if they functioned like language. Claude Lévi-Strauss thus argued that cultures could be analysed as closed systems that (like language) are based on an underlying structure of binary oppositions that lend meaning to social classification (male versus female, high versus low) as well as to the everyday acts of ordinary life. For Lévi-Strauss, the notion that different aspects of social life, including art and religion, could be studied with the help of concepts similar to those employed in linguistics was not merely a methodological breakthrough, but also an insight into the very structure of culture itself, whose various aspects, he speculated, 'constitute phenomena whose inmost nature is the same as that of language'.[4] As we have seen (above, chapter 4), the structuralist analogy between language and culture would pave the way, 20 years hence, for Clifford Geertz's famous notion that cultures could be 'read' like texts, that cultural anthropologists could gain access to the underlying meanings that lend coherence to a particular society by analysing semiotically its symbols, rituals, belief systems, historical artefacts and social organization.[5]

In the hands of structuralist researchers, whether linguists or anthropologists, meaning was increasingly coming to be understood as the product of human convention (language, symbolism), rather than the spontaneous creation of an external reality. Poststructuralists took these insights into the culturally/linguistically constructed nature of reality and pushed them yet a step further. Hence in 1967, philosopher Jacques Derrida argued in his famous book, *Of Grammatology*, that even within language, meaning is not the fixed outcome of a stable relationship between signifier and signified. On the contrary, the internal structure of language (the binary relations linking signs, the relationship between signifier and signified) is shot through with instability. Hence, if the structuralists had already cast radical doubt on our ability to access 'reality' via language, they nonetheless saw language itself as an internally stable system in which meaning is produced through difference, through the binary oppositions that underpin all language. Poststructuralists, by contrast, argued that while binary oppositions are in fact essential to the operation of language, such relations are by no means fixed and unchanging; rather, they are unstable and have a tendency to collapse inward on each other, thus rendering meaning itself a slippery, shifting, uncertain entity.[6]

In order to come to grips with the eternal uncertainty of textual meaning, Derrida developed a technique of reading that he called 'deconstruction', which sought to reveal how all texts must repress as much as they express in order to uphold the 'logocentric' illusion that they convey a stable and coherent meaning. The deconstructive method thus demonstrated that texts could be interpreted in multiple (though not infinite) ways, precisely because the link between signifiers and signified is neither stable nor expressive of any essential 'truth'. For Derrida and his disciples, then, all texts are mere linguistic constructions, and to uphold the idea that words might convey the truth of reality is merely to indulge in the futile illusions of 'logocentrism'.[7]

Though equally esteemed as a poststructuralist thinker, philosopher Michel Foucault took the structuralist heritage in a somewhat different direction from that taken by Derrida. *Madness and Civilization* (1961) thus uses the structuralist contention that phenomena are constructed through language to argue that insanity has been understood in radically different ways at different times in history. Far from being a simple, self-evident 'fact' of biology, Foucault argued, insanity is a socially and linguistically constructed phenomenon whose significance has shifted dramatically over time and from one society to another. Moreover, the unhappy tale of the mad includes no upbeat ending, no pretty story of progress towards a more humane treatment, for as Foucault tells it the language and practice of psychiatry worked to construct mental illness as a form of social deviance. Psychiatric practice thus marginalized the voices of the insane, constructing medically/scientifically grounded mechanisms of social control whose reach would only be extended with the development of welfare state-based forms of social assistance in twentieth-century Europe. Foucault's later work would continue in a similar vein, analysing language in relation to social and institutional practices and power. In Foucault's own words, this constituted a sharp contrast with the work of Derrida, which focused on language alone and (famously) saw 'nothing outside the text'.[8] Foucault nonetheless preserved the poststructuralist emphasis on language in his readiness to see social relations as structured by binary oppositions, much like language. He thus tended to textualize social relations, which then opened those relations up to semiotic versus social analysis.[9]

As my very brief and highly schematic survey suggests, poststructuralist thinkers mounted a powerful critique of historical practice, focusing in particular on historians' reliance on written texts ('primary sources') as a guide to events and experiences past. Borrowing various techniques of deconstructionist analysis from their neighbours in literary criticism, poststructuralist historians (with feminist poststructuralists often leading the way) turned to the analysis of historical documents as literary artefacts, placing at the heart of their work an exploration of the internal structure of these texts and the construction of the categories on which their internal logic is based.[10]

Rather than seeking to reconstruct the past 'as it really was', then, poststructuralist historians preached the analysis of discourses, of representations and of the often-gendered construction of social categories. If nothing else, this had the salutary effect of renewing and expanding techniques for the critical reading of sources. But in asking that historians turn their attention to the textual construction of social categories, poststructuralists also called into question the very epistemological base of the new social history, namely the logical chain that bound experience to identity, and from there moved to politics.[11] The relationship between structure and agency that had animated so much of the new social history, including women's and gender history, was thus supplanted by a new concern with the relationship between culture and politics, and the ways that language serves to mediate that relationship.[12] Those scholars who remained faithful to the project of social history would henceforth try to marry their narratives of social and economic structures with new stories of the 'cultures' of work, that is, the representations and discourses that surround work, and notions of production and the economy more generally.[13] But historians in general, and feminist historians in particular, would continue to move away from the world of labour, so cherished by the new social history, and towards a newly renovated cultural and political history that focused on such things as the gendered and raced construction of categories like citizenship and representations of nation and empire.[14]

Gender, poststructuralism and feminist historical analysis

'It seems significant that the use of the word "gender" has emerged at a moment of great epistemological turmoil,' wrote US historian of modern France, Joan Scott in 1986. This turmoil

> takes the form, in some cases, of a shift from scientific to literary paradigms among social scientists (from an emphasis on cause to one on meaning)... and in other cases, the form of debates about theory between those who assert the transparency of facts and those who insist that all reality is construed or constructed, between those who defend and those who question the idea that 'man' is the rational master of his own destiny.[15]

With these words Joan Scott introduced her understanding of the concept of gender as a category of historical analysis in what is perhaps her most influential, and certainly her most widely cited article on the subject, 'Gender: A Useful Category of Historical Analysis'. This article marks a key moment in the diffusion to a wider public of a larger, ongoing conversation among poststructuralist feminists about gender, sexuality, politics and identity. Over the next five years or so, feminist historians would become acquainted with poststructuralist thought through a variety of intermediaries, including British philosopher and poet Denise Riley, whose widely read works disseminated to a broader public the sustained reflections of poststructuralist feminists on the constructed nature of such fundamental categories as 'woman/women' and 'gender'.[16] Scott's article nonetheless stands out as one of the very first translations of poststructuralism – and of feminist reflection on the relevance of poststructuralism to feminist scholarship and politics – to a wider audience of historians and social scientists, including but by no means limited to scholars of gender history.

Scott's article offers a two-part definition of gender, whose two wings are interrelated but analytically distinct from each other. First, gender is a 'constitutive element of social relationships based on perceived differences between the sexes'. Second, and equally vital, gender is also a 'primary way of signifying relationships of power... one of the recurrent references by which political power has been conceived, legitimated and criticized'. Moreover, 'gender both refers to and establishes the meaning of the male/female opposition'.[17] Poststructuralist feminists were thus taking up once again the question of power, though this time (following Michel Foucault on the power/knowledge nexus) the focus was less on the micropolitics of power in the household than on gender as a metaphor for social and political power. Hence, relations between the sexes constitute a 'primary aspect of social organization' (and not simply of class formation, as Davidoff and Hall would have it), for 'the differences between the sexes constitute and are constituted by hierarchical social structures'.[18]

Scott then offers a gloss on her two-part definition in the four 'subsets' to her definition that follow, which are, essentially, four aspects of gender in its operation as a constitutive element of social relationships. Only two of the four subsets need detain us here, for it is they that are most intimately bound up with the theory and practice of poststructuralism.[19] First, Scott emphasizes that 'normative' concepts of gender are generally expressed in 'religious, educational, scientific, legal and political doctrines and typically take the form of a fixed binary opposition'. While particular ideas of gender might at one time or another be contested, one position will ultimately emerge triumphant and will then be proclaimed 'the only possible one'. Such a triumph depends, of course, upon the repression or refusal of alternative notions of gender, which repression is subsequently written out of a historical record that presents normative ideas about gender as the product of 'social consensus rather than conflict'. As a consequence, binary representations of gender difference have a tendency to assume the appearance of a 'timeless permanence', which illusion stems from the fact that all debate over the meaning of masculine and feminine, that is, the *politics* of gendered representations and categories, has been effaced from the record. It is the task of the feminist scholar to restore this politics to view.

The merits of such a position are obvious: by recovering repressed struggles over the meanings of masculine and feminine, feminist historians retrieve the gendered politics of history and demonstrate the centrality of gender to the actual and metaphorical constitution of power relations. But for historians who are concerned with women's agency, the problems raised by this way of framing things are equally evident. Hence, tracing out the implications of the proposition that ideas about gender typically take the form of a fixed binary opposition leads inexorably to the conclusion that femininity can only be expressed as the negative term of a binary opposition. Women are thus seen as imprisoned within discursive structures, and women's agency (or male agency, for that matter) becomes but a linguistically created illusion.[20]

Yet Scott's musings on gendered subjectivity, which constitute the second 'subset' that I will discuss here, potentially reopen a space for female agency via her doubts before the 'universalist claim' of psychoanalysis. Hence, an equally crucial 'aspect' of gender is 'subjective identity,' writes Scott, and yet psychoanalytic understandings of the construction of gendered identity clearly give Scott pause precisely because of the ahistoric nature of a theory (psychoanalysis) that is grounded in timeless and universal structures (the human psyche, unconscious mental process).[21] 'Even though Lacanian theory may be helpful for thinking about the construction of gendered identity, historians need to work in a more historical way', cautions Scott.

> Moreover, *real men and women do not always or literally fulfill the terms of either their society's prescriptions or of our analytic categories*. Historians need instead to examine the ways in which gendered identities are substantively constructed and relate their findings to a range of activities, social organizations and historically specific cultural representations.[22]

The idea that 'real men and women do not always or literally fulfill the terms of their society's prescriptions' implies that whatever the dogma of patriarchal discourse may prescribe, things are always more complicated in real life. Indeed, the subordinate might go so far as to seize hold of those same identities that position some (men) as possessors of power and use them to constitute their own identities and thereby challenge the dominant discourses.[23] As we will see in the next chapter, on gender and colonialism, many feminist historians have adopted some version of this approach, blending certain insights of poststructuralism into the ways that language constructs social experience with ongoing fidelity to the notion that historical subjects possess some degree of agency, however limited or constrained it may be by social or cultural circumstance.

Whether feminist historians chose to adhere to the more radically discursive path, or to pursue their research in light of some notion of female agency, one thing was perfectly clear: henceforth, 'gender' in its social-historical incarnation (social relations of the sexes, the sexual division of labour) would undergo serious conceptual transformation as poststructuralist feminists displaced the accent from the social to the discursive construction of categories, including gender identities and the category of 'women' as a self-evident collectivity; and the goal of gender history would no longer be that of recovering or reconstructing the experiences of women in the past, but rather that of tracing the process by which discourses about masculinity and femininity have been produced over time. The category of experience, on which reposed the narratives of social and gender history, was thus dismissed as part and parcel of a worn-out and positivist social history that had (since 1989) been deprived of all Marxist legitimation. Indeed, for some of the more radical partisans of poststructuralist feminism, experience does not really exist as such. Rather, the notions of experience, and of subjectivity itself, are themselves a product of discursive processes that position individuals in relation to discursive formations, and so produce both their 'experiences' and their sense of possessing a 'true' inner self. The real objects of historical research are therefore constituted by the discourses that organize experiences, and not by the experiences themselves.[24]

The turn towards cultural history and discursive modes of analysis met with a sharply divided reaction in history departments of the early 1990s: on the one hand, a defensive rejection of what was perceived by some to be a perverse deconstruction of the entire historical enterprise; on the other, considerable enthusiasm from those historians who, since the late 1970s, had been living uneasily with the growing 'crisis' of social history.[25] This crisis was an epistemological one, rooted in historians' increasing discomfort with the determinist vision of the individual-experience-to-social-identity link on which so many narratives of social history rested.[26] After all, it is by no means clear that a particular experience will inevitably give rise in individual consciousness to one social identity and not another. Indeed, once one relinquishes all notion of a fully determined relation between the two, then a troubling explanatory gap opens up between individual self-perception and the 'objective' structures of society and economy. So long as scholars were prepared to presume that the move from inner cognitive process to outward social identification was a fully determined one, no such gap was visible. By the late 1970s, however, historians were no longer so sure, as debates over problems such as 'false consciousness' (a way to account for those workers who, in an apparent failure to grasp the political consequences of their class position, vote conservative) led scholars increasingly to question the determinist nature of the epistemological chain binding individual consciousness to larger collective identities.

Well before the arrival of poststructuralist theory, then, social historians already entertained serious doubts about the explanatory power of categories like 'experience'.[27] Small wonder that the poststructuralist message found receptive ears in British and North American history departments.[28] Indeed, for some (ex-)social historians, the study of discourse became the sole possible way to do history, a history that focused on the 'discursive aspects of experience', and on analysing the discursive logic within which individual identities were produced: 'the events, structures and processes of the past are indistinguishable from the forms of documentary representation, the conceptual and political appropriations, and the historical discourses that construct them,' wrote British historian Patrick Joyce in 1991. 'Once this is conceded, the foundations of the social history paradigm are greatly weakened... New approaches and new kinds of history are now on the agenda'.[29] In place of the naturalism of social structure that undergirded the new social history, poststructuralists thus proposed to install a naturalism of language.

Feminist historians were likewise divided in the face of the poststructuralist onslaught on the certitudes of experience. Thus, on the one hand, poststructuralist historians' 'refusal of the real' presented genuine practical problems for scholars (feminist and non-feminist alike) who had been raised inside the highly empiricist traditions that have long shaped social historical research. In addition, many feminist scholars were frankly suspicious of the claim that our understanding of the intersection between gender and power had arisen exclusively from poststructuralist thought. After all, remarked Catherine Hall, hadn't feminist consciousness-raising groups, with their stress on the personal as political, generated just as much insight into the power/knowledge couplet as had the rarified debates of poststructuralism?[30] But in the end, it was the profound anti-humanism of poststructuralism's most extreme claims that stirred the sharpest reaction from feminist historians, for whom an approach that preached the analysis of discourse rather than of human activity and consciousness was deeply off-putting. Though powerfully drawn by the prospect of broadening gender's analytic reach to include the gendered analysis of the foundations of social and political organization, many feminist scholars remained ambivalent before poststructuralists' radical demand for a complete abandonment of the study of social phenomena and experiences in favour of a kind of cultural history that seemed utterly turned in on itself, circularly self-referential and absorbed by linguistic wordplay.[31]

Despite these reservations, however, poststructuralism and the crisis around the 'linguistic turn' have left durable traces in the methods and objects of historical research, placing the analysis of representations and discourses firmly on the agenda while turning historians' eyes from the analysis of social experience *tout court* towards more cultural histories of political and national identity, of citizenship and of the multiple and sometimes competing forces of race, class and gender in shaping those identities.

The impact of the methodological debates around poststructuralism and the role of discursive analysis in historical narrative registered quite powerfully in the work of the generation of historians that came of age in the USA and the UK at the turn of the 1990s. Indeed, poststructuralist critiques of social history's epistemological certitudes often travelled hand in hand with history's famous 'cultural turn' at the turn of the 1990s, at least in the Anglophone world (French historian, Roger Chartier, though a prime exponent of cultural history, has been very critical of what he calls the 'American linguistic turn').[32] A quick glance at the concerns and methods that have animated recent work on women and the Great War, published since the mid-1990s, shows the rich possibilities that cultural and deconstructive analysis holds for opening up new fields to historical analysis: the deep anxieties over wartime social change, expressed in the post-war era as a 'crisis' in gender identity; the effort to re-anchor society in a redoubled valorization of motherhood.[33] But a closer look at one of the strongest examples of this literature, Mary Louise Roberts' *Civilization Without Sexes*, also reveals the weaknesses inherent in a purely cultural analysis of an event whose powerful material and political consequences did not confine themselves solely to the realm of public cultural expression.

World War I and the 'crisis' of gender identity in France, 1917–1927

'This civilization no longer has clothes, no longer has churches, no longer has palaces, no longer has theatres, no longer has paintings, no longer has books, no longer has sexes,' thundered Great War veteran (and future fascist collaborator) Pierre Drieu la Rochelle in 1927.[34] With this emblematic quotation, Mary Louise Roberts opens her influential study *Civilization Without Sexes*, a resolutely cultural analysis of the war's impact on gender relations in France. Drawing on a broad range of literary sources – magazine articles, parliamentary speeches, militant pamphlets, educational manuals (on vocational guidance, but also on sex), fashion commentaries and novels of every sort – Roberts reveals the deep preoccupation with gender in post-war France, a fear that natural gender hierarchies had been reversed by a war in which women not only took over men's jobs, but became the 'insiders' on a home front from which soldiers felt excluded, exiled to the 'death-ridden no-man's land' of the trenches. At the level of discursive output, then, *Civilization Without Sexes* challenges the widely accepted notion that the war constituted a moment of progress for women. For the voice that Roberts hears speaking across the period 1917–27 is that of male domination, anxiously reasserting itself against the war's presumed 'fragilization' of their sex.

The author traces this post-war 'backlash' against women back to the way that wartime writers confused shifting gender roles with a more general sense that the war had brought on a veritable 'crisis of civilization' in France. Debates about the sexes thus became a key site on which the impact and significance of the war were evaluated. Moreover, the conflation of gender anxiety with a broader sense of 'cultural despair' would continue to shape the way the war's impact was understood after 1918, so that debates over the changing roles of women became one crucial way that people talked about the meaning of the war.[35]

The bulk of the book dwells on three images of femininity that were repeatedly worked over in the political, journalistic and literary production of post-war

France: the mother, the single woman and the 'modern' woman, embodied in the androgynous figure of the *garçonne.* The mother represented unalloyed goodness and purity itself, contributing to the reconstruction of France through her reproductive and educative labours in the home. Equally important, she constituted a living link to the pre-war world, an icon of continuity whose timeless and unchanging maternal labours offered a comforting sense that all bridges to the past had not been burned in the violent upheaval of war. At the opposite end of the spectrum stood the *garçonne*, whose 'unnatural' way of life, organized around the heedless consumption of 'American' commodities (movies, cigarettes, dance halls, cars), became a vehicle for expressing profound ambivalence in the face of a rapidly developing consumer culture. Through her cheerful refusal of motherhood and her equally dangerous embrace of those masculine freedoms whose practice desexed and denatured her (sport, smoking, unentangled love affairs, sexual autonomy), the *garçonne* literally embodied the decline of France. Post-war novelists left their readers in no doubt as to the devastating consequences of this decline: rather than basking in the joys of her new-found freedom, the *garçonne*, was portrayed as a genderless, sterile and desperate being, lost in the unnatural pleasures of sex and drugs – and therefore lost to the natural joys of maternity.

In between the antithetical poles of motherhood and 'flapperdom' stood the single woman, barred from marriage and motherhood by the tragic loss of male life in the trenches and so condemned to earn her living in the wider world. 'Poised at the frontier of changing female identities, the single woman symbolized the war's impact on the social organization of gender,' notes Roberts. 'If the single woman could not be a mother, would she be a modern woman? How could she live up to traditional domestic ideals and yet still be independent and support herself?' In Roberts' estimation, the image of the single woman constituted the vehicle by which French women and men negotiated their way between past and present, tradition and change, the mother and the modern woman. Out of these tensions would come a 'new notion of gender identity, a "synthesis" of old and new'.[36]

Civilization Without Sexes is one of the most thoughtful and carefully shaded examples of the 'new' cultural history of the war, revealing as it does the conflicting and, ultimately, limited possibilities for imagining the female (or male) self in post-war France. By the same token, however, the book exemplifies some of the genre's weaknesses, notably a tendency for the written sources to float in their own discursive space, more or less disconnected from their larger social, economic and political contexts. Of course, Roberts is quite careful to clarify the limits of her study, which confines itself to an exploration of the images of female identity available to women in post-war France, at the expense of any effort to connect those images to actual women's lives (for example, by seeking to determine how individual French women may have assimilated or resisted such images). Nonetheless, readers are left with what Christine Bard characterized as an 'exaggerated sense of the gender anxieties that lay at the origin of the cultural "crisis" of the 1920s'. Indeed, Bard comments, the 'crisis' in gender identity, analysed as pure discursive product, ends up turning in its own discursive universe, with no demonstrated effects either on individual gendered identities or on the gendered structures that shaped social, political and economic life after 1918.[37] As a result, there is a curious circularity linking argument and evidence, as if the 'crisis' in gender identity was produced by, and confined to, the literary sources that Roberts analyses with such flair.

In 1999, two of cultural history's most enthusiastic exponents in the USA, Lynn Hunt and Victoria Bonnell, reflected with some ambivalence on the wild success of cultural analysis in 1990s North America, a success that, until quite recently, both scholars had ardently sought. In particular, the authors voiced the increasingly widespread sentiment that the cultural turn, at least as it had been taken in the USA and the UK, represented too radical a rupture with the social history from which it had emerged: '[we] have all been profoundly influenced by the cultural turn,' wrote Bonnell and Hunt; nevertheless we have 'refused to accept the obliteration of the social that is implied by the most radical forms of culturalism or poststructuralism. The status or meaning of the social may be in question … but life without it has proved impossible'.[38] As the twentieth century gave way to the twenty-first, historians like Hunt and Bonnell seemed to be searching for a kind of golden mean between social and cultural forms of analysis. For in rejecting social history as an outmoded and hopelessly naïve form of analysis, cultural historians had let go of techniques and approaches they could ill afford to lose, notably, a clear sense of and means of describing the socio-economic and political structures that shape hierarchies of power and distribute wealth and resources unequally among the different classes, races and genders that inhabit the planet.

My brief discussion of the cultural turn in the historiography on women and the Great War, as exemplified in the work of Mary Louise Roberts, supports this sense of unease. For in order to grasp the multiple effects that the war had on women, men and the gendered meanings attached to both self and society, we need tools of analysis that will allow us to move back and forth between the social and the cultural with some clear sense of the underlying structures that connect the two realms. We need tools of analysis that will allow us to describe the structures of power and wealth that engaged the world in such a conflict and set so many of its terms, and a means of conveying how the transformations in self-understanding that the war entailed – as well as its attendant upheaval of social, political, economic and family life – were understood by those who lived through it.[39] In other words, we need to refuse the radical separation between social and cultural forms of analysis that has so strongly marked Anglo-American historical practice, a separation that, ironically, has continued to plague British and American historians even after the linguistic and cultural turns. For as I argued above (chapter 6), UK and US historians, unlike their French colleagues, have tended to view social and cultural analysis as distinct approaches that are grounded in opposing epistemologies – a stance which implies that social and cultural analysis cannot be harmonized within the pages of a single historical narrative. But if historical research over the last 30 years has shown us anything, it is that culture and society are, in fact, mutually constitutive of one another, that individuals and social groups seize hold of particular images and identities and use, refuse or reshape those images and identities in an effort to comprehend and actively refashion their social worlds. Rather than confining our analysis to the dissection and deconstruction of the range of images and identities available to women and men, then, we should be striving to understand how women and men have used cultural materials, including language, to grasp and indeed transform the world they lived in.

In the wake of the often violent debates around poststructuralism, feminist historians have turned to a rather differently constituted range of subjects and are drawing their techniques from an increasingly eclectic tool kit.[40] For if the basic epistemological differences between poststructuralists and anti-poststructuralists have found no real resolution (nor could they, being grounded in fundamentally opposed ontologies), the sound and fury that attended these debates over the period 1988–94 has since abated, leaving historians to continue their work as they may. Yet even in this more theoretically heterodox era, some of the issues that divided poststructuralist feminists from their non(or anti)-poststructuralist colleagues continue to find expression, though in less polemical and more historically grounded terms. Hence, those historians of gender who would like to take the more purely constructivist route continue to face some very real epistemological difficulties, notably the fact that gender, understood as a purely discursive construct, cannot in and of itself explain change. If, for example, sexual identities are understood to be produced solely through discursive processes, then how are we to account for changes in said identities over time? Without some way of linking discursive process to social experience, historians cannot account for the changing meanings of masculine and feminine. This is doubtless the most serious problem that the radically constructivist posture – which focuses on the performative rather than the representational aspect of language – has left to historians of gender.[41] For while endless performativity and subjectivities that are the pure product of discursive positioning pose no a priori problem for literary analysis, they are of limited use to historians, who need tools that will allow them to account for change in time.[42]

I have argued that if historians wish to resolve this problem, they should refuse the disconnect between cultural and social forms of analysis and focus instead on understanding how social and cultural forms are mutually constitutive of one another. The final three chapters of this book take up, in turn, three different 'post-poststructuralist' historiographies in which scholars have striven to do just that: to understand cultural and social forms of analysis as complementary aspects of a seamless whole. I look first at recent colonial and postcolonial scholarship, in which historians have applied some of the insights of poststructuralist analysis to analysing colonial and postcolonial relations. I then turn to the literature on the 'gendering' of public and private, and hence of citizenship, in the modern west. Finally, the book closes with an exploration of some recent work that seeks to marry discursive understandings of gender to psychoanalytic frameworks for understanding human subjectivity. What I hope will emerge across the discussion in these final three chapters is a clearer sense of what has been most fruitful in the debates over language and agency that so shook the Anglo-American academy at the turn of the 1990s.[43]

Endnotes

1 There is an enormous literature on poststructuralist feminist theory. Some useful starting points include Linda Nicholson (ed.), *Feminism/ Postmodernism* (London, 1990); Judith Butler and Joan W. Scott (eds), *Feminists Theorize the Political* (London, 1992); Seyla Benhabib and Drucilla Cornell (eds), *Feminism as Critique: On the Politics of Gender* (Minneapolis, MI, 1987); and Alison Assiter, *Enlightened Women: Modernist Feminism in a Postmodern Age* (London, 1995).

2 Kevin Passmore, 'Poststructuralism and History', in Berger, Feldner and Passmore (eds), *Writing History. Theory and Practice* (London, 2003), 119.

3 Passmore, 'Poststructuralism', 120.

4 Lévi-Strauss as quoted in Terrence Hawkes, *Structuralism and Semiotics* (Berkeley, CA, 1977), 33, as quoted (in turn) in Victoria Bonnell and Lynn Hunt, *Beyond the Cultural Turn: New Directions in the Study of Society and Culture* (Berkeley, CA, 1999), 8.

5 Clifford Geertz, *The Interpretation of Cultures: Selected Essays* (New York, 1973).

6 Jacques Derrida, *Of Grammatology*, trans. G. Spivak (Baltimore, MD, 1976). My discussion of structuralism and poststructuralism draws heavily on Passmore, 'Poststructuralism'.

7 There are those (including Derrida himself) who deny that he intended to undermine the category of truth so radically. But as Kevin Passmore has observed, 'what Derrida "really" meant to say concerns us less than the fact that many critics of history have interpreted Derrida thus, and not entirely without reason'. Passmore, 'Poststructuralism', 123.

8 Michel Foucault, 'My Body, this Paper, this Fire', *Oxford Literary Review*, 4:1 (1979, first published 1972), 9–28, cited in Passmore, 'Poststructuralism', 122.

9 The work of Russian literary critic Mikhail Bakhtin (1895–1975) provides an intriguing route past the apparent impasse created by deconstructionism's deep scepticism about the possibility of meaning. By turning the attention from *langue* (the abstract structures and rules that allow language to function, on which structuralist and poststructuralist alike have focused) to *parole* (the actual utterances that language-users produce), Bakhtin produced an alternative theory of language as inherently social or 'dialogic'. Meanings are therefore generated in the context of intersubjective communication, as speakers (and writers) address their words towards a 'future answer word': 'The word in living conversation is directly, blatantly oriented towards a future answer word. It provokes an answer, anticipates it and structures itself in the answer's direction' (Mikhail Bakhtin, *The Dialogic Imagination* (Austin, TX, 1981) 280, cited in David Lodge, *After Bakhtin: Essays on Fiction and Criticism* (London, 1990), 57). The speaker therefore constructs her discourse through a series of dialogues, not only with her interlocutor, in anticipation of her response, but with a broad range of materials and languages produced by others. While this material is always re-shaped in accordance with the speaker's purposes, it nonetheless carries (and is, indeed, constructed of) a 'host of languages' – of masculinity and femininity, for example – which are, in Bakhtin's formula 'half someone else's'. Further, the 'multivocality' of discourse implies that the interlocutor can interpret the speaker's words in unexpected ways. Rather than worrying about instabilities inherent in the structures of binary opposition that produce meaning through difference (*langue*), the Bakhtinian approach analyses meaning as the product of a process of intersubjective communication (*parole*), an approach that privileges the kinds of close contextual analyses (including the status of and relations between the speaker, listener and the object under discussion) that are the bread and butter of the historian's trade. Historians have not (yet) rushed *en masse* to apply Bakhtin to historical writing. There are, nonetheless, several excellent examples of Bakhtin's theories being put to good use in such writing, notably: Kevin Passmore, '"Planting the Tricolour in the Citadels of Communism": Women's Social Action in the Croix de feu and Parti social français', *Journal of Modern History*, 71 (1999); S.H. Rigby, *Chaucer in Context* (Manchester, 1996); and Gabrielle Spiegel, 'History, Historicism and the Social Logic of the Text in the Middle Ages', *Speculum*, 65 (1990).

10 For a classic example of this kind of work, see Joan W. Scott, 'A Statistical Representation of Work: La Statistique de l'Industrie à Paris, 1847–1848', in Joan Scott, *Gender and the Politics of History* (New York, 1988), 113–38.

11 See Joan Hoff, 'Gender as a Postmodern Category of Paralysis', *Women's History Review*, 3:2 (1994), 149–68, for a critique in which post-structuralist feminists are seen to be engaged in no less than the wholesale destruction of the fruits of their foremothers' labours.

12 As early as 1983, then, Gareth Stedman Jones argued that it was political language that endowed political behaviour with meaning: 'we cannot therefore decode political language to reach a primal and material expression of interest since it is the discursive structure of political language which conceived and defined interest in the first place'. Gareth Stedman Jones, *Languages of Class: Studies in English Working-Class History, 1832–1982* (Cambridge, 1983), 22.

13 See Sonya Rose, *Limited Livelihoods: Gender and Class in Nineteenth-Century England* (Berkeley, CA, 1992) for a good example of a feminist labour history that took the cultural and linguistic turn.

14 As we will see in the following chapter, the rise of postcolonial studies would only reinforce this trend.

15 Joan W. Scott, 'Gender: A Useful Category of Historical Analysis', in *Gender and the Politics of History*, 41 (this article was first published in the December 1986 issue of *American Historical Review*).

16 Denise Riley, *Am I that Name? Feminism and the Category of Women in History* (Minneapolis, MI, 1988). As I have argued elsewhere, both Scott and Riley explore the internal instabilities that riddle the category 'woman/women'. Riley, however, does so across time, using an approach that is reminiscent of Foucault's genealogical analysis of the 'descent' of words, concepts and identities. (See Michel Foucault, 'Nietzsche, Genealogy, History', in D.F. Bouchard and S. Simon (eds and trans.), *Language, Counter-Memory, Practice; Selected Essays and Interviews* (Ithaca, NY, 1977).) Riley's historical-genealogical examination of the category 'woman/women', of the 'sedimented forms of previous characterisations on which new outcroppings flourish', enables us to see gender shape-shift in time; a temporally specific category produced by specific historical relations and 'possessing their full validity only for and within those relations'. (Riley, *Am I that Name?*, 166, paraphrasing Marx's *Grundrisse*.) See Laura Lee Downs, 'If "Woman" is Just an Empty Category, Then Why Am I Afraid to Walk Alone at Night? Identity Politics Meets the Postmodern Subject', *Comparative Studies in Society and History* (April 1993), 416. Riley is also the author of a very fine and subtle history of social policy regarding working mothers in 1940s and 1950s Britain, *War in the Nursery: Theories of the Child and Mother* (London, 1983).

17 Scott, 'Gender', 42, 48–9. For an insightful analysis of the functionalist logic that lies at the heart of Foucault's power/knowledge nexus, in particular of its residual structuralist logic that runs in curious parallel to that of 1970s Marxism ('its substitution of power in the place of relations of production'), see Gareth Stedman Jones, 'The Determinist Fix: Some Obstacles to the Further Development of the Linguistic Approach to History in the 1990s', *History Workshop Journal*, 42 (Autumn 1996), 19–35.

18 Scott, 'Women's History', in Scott, *Gender and the Politics of History*, 25.

19 The other two subsets are: (1) Gender operates through culturally available symbols, such as Eve and Mary, that evoke 'multiple (and often contradictory) representations'; and (2) Feminist scholars must look outside

the family and household in their pursuit of gender, for if gender is in part constructed through kinship, 'it is constructed as well in the economy and the polity, which, in our society, at least now, operate largely independently of kinship'. Both of these propositions follow unproblematically from the accumulated researches of women's and gender history up to this point.

20 Scott herself pursued this angle in a subsequent book on French feminism. Scott thus argues that French feminists, whether or not they believed in gendered differences themselves, were forced to articulate their demands from a discursively constituted subject position that lay outside the universal subject position that liberalism (and republicanism) accorded solely to men. French feminists were thus discursively locked into a logical contradiction that feminism could not resolve. Joan W. Scott, *Only Paradoxes to Offer: French Feminists and the Rights of Man* (Cambridge, MA, 1996).

21 This was Scott's position in 1986. There are hints in her preface to the 1999 reissue of *Gender and the Politics of History* that she may be looking once again in the direction of psychoanalytic theory.

22 Scott, 'Gender', 43–4 (my emphasis).

23 This approach is reminiscent of the later work of Michel Foucault. I am indebted to Kevin Passmore for this point. See Kevin Passmore, 'Introduction', in Passmore (ed.), *Women, Gender and Fascism in Europe, 1919–45* (Manchester, 2003), 4.

24 In other words, recourse to 'experience' as a category of analysis presupposes the system of signification that must itself be analysed. Joan W. Scott, 'The Evidence of Experience', *Critical Inquiry*, 17:4 (1991), 773–97.

25 See Richard Evans, *In Defence of History* (London, 1997) for a detailed summary of the opposition to poststructuralist 'nihilists'.

26 As Gareth Stedman Jones remarked, this logical chain is an expression of the larger 'determination of thought by social being' that lies at the core of historical materialism and 'all the different versions' of Marxist history. Gareth Stedman Jones, 'The Determinist Fix', 20.

27 Stedman Jones, *Languages of Class*.

28 As we saw above (chapter 6), French social historians, in particular those grouped around the *Annales*, had never drawn such a hard-and-fast distinction between social and cultural history. Concern with the determinist vision of the individual-experience-to-social-identity link that is embedded in macro-structural analysis thus tended to express itself in the turn to micro-history rather than in any radical assertion of the superiority of cultural and linguistic forms of analysis.

29 Patrick Joyce, 'History and Postmodernism', *Past and Present*, 133 (November 1991), 208–9. See also Joyce, 'The End of Social History?', *Social History*, 20 (1995).

30 Catherine Hall, *White, Male and Middle-Class: Explorations in Feminism and History* (Oxford, 1992), 15.

31 Hall, *White, Male and Middle-Class*, 15.

32 Roger Chartier, *On the Edge of the Cliff. History, Language, and Practice* (Baltimore, MD, 1997), 4.
33 Susan Grayzel, *Women's Identities at War: Gender, Motherhood, and Politics in Britain and France During the First World War* (Chapel Hill, NC, 1999).
34 Pierre Drieu la Rochelle, *La Suite des idées* (Paris, 1927), quoted in Mary Louise Roberts, *Civilization Without Sexes: Reconstructing Gender in Postwar France, 1917–1927* (Chicago, IL, 1994), 2.
35 Roberts, *Civilization*. Here, Roberts puts into practice Joan Scott's observation that, in the modern period, at least, gender often serves as a primary way of signifying identity and relations of power.
36 Roberts, *Civilization*, 11.
37 Christine Bard, 'Review of Mary Louise Roberts, *Civilization Without Sexes: Reconstructing Gender in Postwar France, 1917–1927*', *Journal of Modern History*, 69:2 (June 1997), 365–8.
38 Bonnell and Hunt, *Beyond the Cultural Turn*, 11. The 'we' refers to the ten contributors to the edited volume as well as the co-editors.
39 There is some evidence that more recent scholarship is striving for just such a synthesis between material and cultural forms of analysis. See, for example, Belinda Davis, *Home Fires Burning: Food, Politics and Everyday Life in World War I Berlin* (Chapel Hill, NC, 2000).
40 There are those who would agree with Stedman Jones in seeing the demolition of the barriers that once separated social from political and cultural history as one of the achievements of British history's linguistic and poststructuralist turn. Gareth Stedman Jones, 'The New Social History in France', in Colin Jones and Dror Warhman (eds), *The Age of Cultural Revolutions: Britain and France, 1750–1820* (Berkeley, CA, 2002), 101–2.
41 See, for example, Judith Butler, *Gender Trouble: Feminism and the Subversion of Identity* (New York, 1990), which argues that identities and differences do not arise from a group's objective socio-political location but rather are discursively constructed and performatively elaborated through cultural processes. See also Joan W. Scott, 'Evidence of Experience'.
42 For a stimulating analysis of the problematic relationship between feminist politics and poststructuralist philosophy, see Michele Le Doeuff, *The Sex of Knowing* (trans. by Kathryn Hamer and Lorraine Code), London, 2003.
43 Of course each of the historiographical trends that I discuss here traces back to well before the linguistic and cultural turn in history. Unlike fields such as women's labour history, however, these three fields have seen rapid and extensive development in the aftermath of the linguistic turn.

8

Gender and history in a postcolonial world

'Until quite recently scholars of empire seemed to resemble the objects of their own inquiry,' wrote Frances Gouda and Julia Clancy-Smith in the introduction to their 1998 reader on race, gender and family life in the French and Dutch Empires.

> Empire was imagined as a global chess game whose players were almost exclusively European men, often hailing from elite backgrounds... Millions of different ethnic peoples populating colonized societies were virtually absent from conventional political or diplomatic narratives... [while] women, whether European or non-European, were rarely singled out as deserving special scrutiny in this older scholarly tradition. The historical narratives detailing international politics or the global dissemination of European culture, written before decolonization altered the map of the world, were regarded as immune to gender analysis.[1]

With these hard words, Gouda and Clancy-Smith sketched a grim portrait of colonial scholarship over the first three-quarters of the twentieth century, a field in which the predominant form of historical analysis – narrowly political and administrative, or military and diplomatic – placed the vast majority of colonial inhabitants outside the magic circle as the faceless objects of colonial policy. Even the morally outraged narratives of an angrily anti-imperialist generation (1960s and 1970s) tended to leave colonial subjects in a state of complete anonymity as they decried the relentless exploitation of vulnerable native populations by ruthlessly expansionist European states. Only with the gradual development of the multidisciplinary field of colonial studies over the 1980s – a somewhat 'unruly offshoot of cultural studies', in Gouda and Clancy-Smith's neat summation – did new voices and new social groups from the colonial past start to find their way into very differently shaped histories of various colonial enterprises, and of the complex social, economic, cultural and political relations that underpinned those enterprises, binding colonizer and colonized in a relationship whose benefits were anything but mutual.[2]

The tale of colonial/postcolonial studies' origins that Gouda and Clancy-Smith weave here is a familiar one to anyone who has read the recent literature on colonial and postcolonial studies. If Gouda and Clancy-Smith tell this tale with considerable clarity and eloquence, they are nonetheless recounting a story of origins that is widely shared across the field. And yet this account, which underscores the centrality of cultural studies in the founding of this new field, shows a curious amnesia regarding the deeper roots of colonial and postcolonial studies in vibrant traditions of Marxist social and economic history that flourished in both Indian and African history in the 1960s, 1970s and 1980s. Social and economic historians of the era thus explored such classic subjects as migration, industrialization (and de-industrialization), agrarian modes of production and peasant protest. As a result, they produced histories that reached far beyond the narrow confines of the imperial relationship, broad histories of pre-colonial and colonial India and Africa in which imperial history constituted but one axis of investigation. Moreover, the voices of the people were far from absent from this social history tradition, particularly in its 1970s 'history from below' incarnation. Colonial and postcolonial studies are thus more accurately and fully understood if they are seen as emerging out of this broader social history tradition, via critiques that arose from within; in particular, via feminist and nationalist critiques of the primacy of class as a category of analysis over those of gender or nation. These critiques, which took shape across the 1970s and 1980s, would eventually lead some historians of Africa and India to closer collaboration with postcolonial studies (which was, at the time, a literary discipline) and with cultural studies more broadly. Others would continue to work on national (versus imperial) history, using approaches that, while influenced by discursive methods and the cultural turn of the 1990s more broadly, remain fundamentally rooted in social historical practice.[3]

The process whereby colonial studies emerged from the predominantly Marxist social and economic history of the 1960s, 1970s and early 1980s resonates with similar developments in the UK, continental Europe and the USA, where (as we have seen) a crisis of confidence in the epistemological bases of social history led many historians to adopt a more discursive or culturalist understanding of social categories and phenomena. A closer look at the case of India, where a distinctive brand of Marxist social history from below flourished from the mid-1970s onwards, will allow us to consider some of the similarities and differences that marked Indian history's own linguistic turn, lending a particular shape to the multidisciplinary fields of colonial and postcolonial studies that emerged therefrom.[4]

Social and economic histories of the nation in India, 1947–1990

With the end of British rule, in 1947, Indian historians were concerned above all to 'decolonize' modern Indian history, a field of research that, in Dipesh Chakrabarty's estimation, came into being only after 1947:

> In its early phase, this area of scholarship bore all the signs of an ongoing struggle between tendencies which were affiliated to imperialist biases in Indian history and a nationalist desire on the part of historians in India to decolonize the past. Marxism was understandably mobilised in aid of the nationalist project of intellectual decolonization.[5]

Nationalism and colonialism soon emerged as the two major areas of research in the new field of modern Indian history, with much of the earliest work focusing either on nationalist elites or on the struggle between the broad and rather abstract forces of nationalism and colonialism.[6] By the 1970s, however, a new generation of social historians, imbued with the mission of restoring the voices of the people to history, began disrupting earlier narratives of a unified nationalist struggle with fine-grained accounts of local nationalist movements that were, in fact, split along class lines. Hence, the very elites who had mobilized masses of poor peasants and urban workers in the nationalist cause did not shrink from cruelly repressing strikes or any other protest from below that threatened to 'exceed the self-imposed limits of the nationalist agenda' and turn its furies against the social, political and economic domination of those same elites.[7] It was from among this younger generation of social historians, with their emphasis on history from below, that the Subaltern Studies group drew its first recruits. Ranajit Guha's famous call to arms, published in the first issue of *Subaltern Studies* (1982) announced the group's intellectual agenda with a stinging critique of 1960s-style national and colonial history for its relentless focus on elites and concomitant inability to explain

> the contributions made by people *on their own,* that is, *independent of the elite* to the making and development of this nationalism...What is clearly left out of this un-historical historiography is the *politics of the people...* [which] was an *autonomous* domain, for it neither originated from elite politics nor did its existence depend on the latter.[8]

Guha's insistence on the autonomy of popular politics from the movements of India's elites draws our attention to the Subaltern school's distinctive understanding of the nature of peasant activism. Indeed, it was at this point that Guha and the Subaltern school parted company with the Thompsonian brand of 'history from below' as it was then practised in Europe and North America. Hence European historians have tended to treat peasant activism as a kind of 'pre-political' protest, the inevitably atavistic and backward-looking resistance of people who refuse to enter into capitalist relations. But in the case of India, Guha argues, peasant protest cannot simply be dismissed as mere atavism; indeed, Marx's rigid typology of stages – where, in the passage from a pre-capitalist to a capitalist economy, feudal forms of domination give way to bourgeois liberalism – simply does not hold true for India. For in India, landlord domination of a type associated with pre-capitalist and feudal relations in Europe actually harmonized quite well with the arrival of capitalism. Peasant protest in India against ongoing landlord domination thus cannot be relegated to the category of pre-political protest against capitalism, for over the past several centuries, such peasant revolts have erupted (and continue to erupt) within a larger framework of increasingly capitalist relations. Hence, concludes Guha, the exercise of power, which is bound up with bourgeois domination in Europe, must in the case of India be distinguished from capitalism. In other words, 'capitalism' and 'power' must be treated as analytically separable categories.[9]

It was the distinction between power and capitalism that would ultimately lead the Subaltern school (or at least certain members within that school) to take its own linguistic turn around 1985.[10] For with power emerging as a distinct object of investigation, new tools of analysis had to be found in order to understand relations of domination that operated independently of capitalist relations and logic. Clearly the work of Michel Foucault would play an important role here. But as we shall see, the single key text that exercised decisive influence in the form and content of Subaltern Studies' discursive and linguistic turn was literary critic Edward Said's *Orientalism.*[11] Its publication in 1978 marked what Homi Bhabha would later describe as the 'inauguration of the postcolonial field' in literary studies.[12] Small wonder, then, that as the Subaltern historians began to question the epistemological bases of their fundamentally Marxist categories of analysis (class, agency, subjecthood), Said's pioneering analysis of the binary oppositions underpinning colonial rule and imperial ideology – Orient/Occident, colony/metropole, tradition/modernity, feminine/masculine, savage/civilized should have exercised such decisive sway. Convinced that these same binary oppositions had also shaped Marxist historical practice (which was, after all, a western derivative), and must therefore be deconstructed if the historical discipline were ever to throw off the weight of imperial ideology, the Subaltern school eagerly embraced the tools of deconstructionist analysis then current in colonial and postcolonial literary studies, with Said's *Orientalism* constituting the prime conduit by which such techniques passed from literary criticism and over into history.

But what of women's and gender history in all this? First of all, it is worth noting that in its earliest incarnation, the Subaltern school did not concern itself in the least with the problem of gender inequality/oppression; nor did any women scholars figure among those gathered in the collective in 1982. The first woman scholar to be published in the pages of *Subaltern Studies*, Gayatri Chakravorty Spivak, lambasted the collective on this very point in her 1985 article, 'Deconstructing Colonial History', which launched a broad critique of the Subalterns' ongoing attachment to what she characterized as a kind of unreconstructed Marxism, that is, a Marxism that had failed to turn the deconstructive lens on its own categories of analysis.[13] Despite the Subalterns' utter lack of interest in the issue, however, gender history was alive and well in India, and was engaged in a series of highly productive debates with the dominant Marxist models, Thompsonian and otherwise, for their privileging of the category of class over that of gender.[14] KumKum Sangari and Sudesh Vaid's widely read volume, *Recasting Indian Women*, brought together much of this work at the end of the 1980s in a collection that reflects the sub-discipline's overall orientation: a prudent caution regarding patriarchy as the universal key to all female oppression, combined with a deep concern to render social and economic history more gender-conscious. One important source of *Recasting Indian Women*'s critical distance from the concept of patriarchy lies in the authors' concern to come to grips with the many kinds of difference that divide women. As Sangari and Vaid point out in their very useful introduction to the volume, deploying a single, universal analytic category like patriarchy inevitably produces a single, unified category woman/women, as scholars bulldoze merrily across the differences among women in search of the common, overarching evidence of patriarchal violence that must *perforce* unite them. Their introduction thus stresses the need to develop new analytic tools that will allow scholars to grasp and express the interactions among gender, caste, class, religion, race and region in colonial and postcolonial India, interactions that have produced far more complex social relations than can be conveyed by the simple notion of patriarchy. By the late 1980s, this critical perspective on patriarchy (or patriarchy-plus-capitalism) had turned many feminist historians of India towards a more eclectic methodology that embraced cultural as well as social and economic approaches in order to better appreciate the intrinsically gendered nature of social and economic relations, institutions and practices.[15]

Recasting Indian Women thus reflects the state of the art in feminist research in India at the turn of the 1990s: a sub-field that was grounded in social history yet informed by more cultural and discursive approaches as scholars sought to place gender within an analytic grid whose multiple axes included race, caste, religion, region and ethnicity without privileging any one over the others. The commitment to a culturally informed social history finds ample reflection in the broad spectrum of subjects and approaches taken in the articles that make up the volume. These range from discussions of women's participation in agrarian and industrial production, including analyses of their progressive relegation to the most backward and ill-paid sectors as the economy modernized, to analyses of Britain's 'invention of tradition' in the matter of *sati* (widow-burning) and how that colonial invention cast Indian women as both emblems of tradition and its perpetual victims.[16] This kind of research, emerging directly out of the practice of social and economic history and yet transforming that practice from within via a gendered critique, would exercise a profound influence over the kinds of questions and subjects approached by gender historians working within the fields of colonial and postcolonial studies across the late 1980s and early 1990s.

Gender and colonial/postcolonial studies

Gender emerged early on as a crucial axis of inquiry in the new colonial studies, for not only were women present and active on all sides of the colonial relation, but that relationship itself was often expressed and legitimized through gendered and/or familial metaphors. Understanding the politics of colonial domination clearly demanded that historians subject those metaphors to some kind of sustained gender analysis. After all, European colonizers themselves had long placed issues of gender at the heart of colonial relations. This can be seen, most basically, in their tendency to view the management of sexuality and reproduction as the *sine qua non* of colonial governance, a tendency that grew ever more visible from the late nineteenth century onwards. But the centrality of gender to colonial rule can also be read in the gendered metaphors that saturated European (and perhaps indigenous) understandings of the colonial relationship, which was cast either as a paternal/maternal relation between parental metropole and 'protected' colony or, perhaps less predictably, as a kind of marital relation binding virile European states to fragile, effeminate and/or childlike native populations.[17]

Gendered analyses of colonial relations have most recently unfolded in the larger context of poststructuralism, for as we have seen, scholars in colonial studies, whether they were specifically concerned with gender or not, were among the first to deploy deconstructionist analysis, not only in their analysis of documents, but also in their reading of the colonial relationship itself.[18] Hence, when metropolitan citizens looked abroad with satisfaction on their colonial acquisitions, they saw not only the great wealth of mineral and agricultural resources contained therein; equally important, they saw their own faces, mirrored negatively in a colonial world peopled by what they represented as a range of barbarous 'others' – societies whose manifold deficiencies both defined metropolitan civilizations and justified their conquest of such backward colonial 'others'. Nowhere was this dichotomous European vision more pithily expressed than in the widespread European conviction that the condition of indigenous women, which Europeans generally perceived as abject, constituted the ultimate indicator of native barbarism, thanks to the widely popular idea that the surest measure of a people's level of civilization is the 'elevation or debasement' of its women.[19]

This tendency to textualize the socio-political relationships of colonialism (that is, to understand social relationships in literary terms, for instance via metaphor) owes much to the work of Edward Said, for as we have seen, Said's widely read *Orientalism* profoundly influenced the way that scholars in colonial studies have understood the relationship between western knowledge and colonial domination. Hence, Said argues, from the late eighteenth century onwards, Europe's imperial enterprise, though fundamentally an economic and political venture was, crucially, accompanied by a massive cultural project (which he calls 'orientalism') that literally reconstructed what Europeans knew about the Orient so as to facilitate the exercise of imperial rule. The orientalist cultural project was therefore both a product of the economic and political demands of modern imperialism and the condition of its success.

The orientalist project was premised on a dichotomous vision of western self and oriental 'other', in which the latter was consigned to the static position of 'eternal Orient', and so situated firmly outside the stream of history. Europe's imperial conquest of the non-western world thus produced what would be figured as 'the Orient' in western scholarship, an unchanging backdrop against which the dynamism of the west might be measured. It is here in his emphasis on the fact that the representation of 'oriental' culture as 'other' was itself a product of western epistemology and colonial projects of power that Said's considerable debt to the work of Michel Foucault becomes visible: 'So far as Orientalism in particular and European knowledge of other societies in general have been concerned, historicism meant that one human history uniting humanity either culminated in or was observed from the vantage point of Europe, or the West,' wrote Said in 1985. Here he was expressing the conviction (widely taken up since) that this 'unifying' notion of history was based on a binary model that sharply dichotomized west and non-west, and that furthermore recounted a so-called 'universal' history of civilization in purely western terms.[20] Western observation and knowledge of the non-western world were thus, in Said's influential formulation, discursively related to imperialism. Among other things, this meant that western historical perspectives (including the 'history from below' that had flourished in the 1970s and 1980s) were incapable of recounting the history of colonial subjects. After all, these perspectives were inextricably bound up with the colonial enterprise, as they were constructed on the basis of the same binary oppositions that underwrote imperial ideology (Occident/Orient, civilized/barbaric, masculine/feminine, modernity/tradition etc.). Far from offering 'objective' categories by which histories of pre-colonial and colonial subjects might be written, western history constituted nothing less than an instrument of colonial domination, an object to be deconstructed rather than an instrument of genuine historical analysis.[21] Hence, the disciplinary consolidation of history in the nineteenth-century west was predicated on denying that Africa or 'the east' even had a history. Rather, these societies were set up as 'timeless' sites of pure culture, in opposition to western dynamism and technological superiority, both of which were understood to be the products of a particular, western history – or so the Subaltern critique goes. If such an 'epistemological annihilation' of the non-western other has been the condition of the west's self-definition through history, then the best that the postcolonial scholar can do is to deconstruct the binary oppositions underpinning those corrupt instruments of western analysis, rather than turning them back against his or her own society.[22]

Said's orientalist paradigm has exerted enormous influence over the shape and direction of colonial studies since 1978. And yet his extreme binary vision, in which the west creates and imposes on Asian societies a kind of totalizing vision/knowledge of the Orient, has come in for strong criticism from colonial and postcolonial historians who are concerned with the way that Said's understanding eliminates all space for agency on the part of the colonized. Indeed, within the polar oppositions of Said's analytic perspective, Asians figure as mere 'inert objects of [western] knowledge', curiously passive in the face of orientalist representations that, paradoxically, seem to possess 'an extraordinary power to elicit recognition and acceptance' from the colonized.[23] As Rosalind O'Hanlon and David Washbrook have argued for the case of India, there is a danger in pressing Said's argument so far that colonial officials are assumed 'virtually to have invented what they "knew" about India, or merely transposed onto it ideologies and imaginings from the metropolitan context'. Among other things, this leaves hanging the important question of Indians' apparent readiness 'not only to recognise aspects of the "essentialized" identities associated with Orientalist knowledges, but to claim and defend them vigorously as their own'.[24] O'Hanlon and Washbrook explain this paradox of self-recognition by arguing that far from being the mere products of colonial officials' imagined vision, the 'essentialized knowledges' of early colonialism were in fact the product of a collaboration between European officials of the East India Company and south Indian Brahman informants. Hence, at the end of the eighteenth century, Brahmans at the old centres of orthodox learning participated directly in the redaction of the Company's legal codes.

> To overlook their participation in projects of colonial knowledge not only ignores a considerable body of evidence; it also deprives us of important insights into continuities from the pre-colonial period, and hence into reasons why the 'essentialized knowledges' of early colonialism appeared to find such ready recognition among at least some of their Indian audiences.[25]

Some 12 years after the publication of *Orientalism*, O'Hanlon and Washbrook's detailed historical research into the early years of colonial rule deconstructed the polar opposition Occident/Orient on which Said's stark vision of absolute cultural domination rested, replacing it with a more nuanced sense of the circulation and negotiation of power/knowledge in colonial India.

By underscoring the ways in which metaphor and representation functioned to justify and naturalize European rule, making it seem at once natural and inescapable, Said's work turned the eyes of an entire generation of colonial studies scholars to examining the semantics of imperial politics.[26] And this, in turn, led to the famous 'textualization' of socio-political relations that characterizes so much of the scholarship in colonial studies. But as Israeli historian Billie Melman has caustically observed, Said's work, as well as that of other critics of orientalism, is actually quite gender-blind: 'Even when, occasionally, it allows women a part in the culture of empire, it hardly recognises the role of gender in the construction of colonial identities,' wrote Melman in 1996. 'It is ironic, then, that feminist scholarship has embraced an analysis of culture which has excluded gender'.[27] An ironic choice, perhaps, and yet Said's work remains an important reference in the most recent work on gender and colonialism, suggesting that feminist scholars in the 1990s have been willing to try and reformulate Said's theories so as to take gender into account, or at least to make use of those aspects of his argument that illuminate the cultural predicates of colonial rule.

In order to see how Said's legacy would acquire its feminist edge, we must step back to the mid-1980s, when a group of Third-World feminist scholars (mostly literary critics) drew on Said's work in order to develop a critique of the 'latent enthocentrism' that lies at the heart of western feminism. One of the most influential pieces to emerge from this moment in Third-World feminism is Chandra Talpade Mohanty's 'Under Western Eyes: Feminist Scholarship and Colonial Discourses', first published in 1986 and often reprinted since. Mohanty takes Said's 'predominantly discursive' understanding of colonization as the point of departure for her own critique of western feminism, which stands accused of 'discursively colonizing the material and historical heterogeneities of the lives of women in the Third World', thus producing a vision of the 'Third-World Woman' as a singular, 'monolithic' subject.[28] Put simply, western feminists' insistence on the universal nature of women's oppression collapsed the differences among colonial women, pressing a variegated lot of individuals (and experiences) into the single, suffocating category of 'non-western women'.

In an analysis that parallels that of historians KumKum Sangari and Sudesh Vaid, Mohanty insists on the manifold differences among colonial women. and so takes apart the falsely unified subject of the 'Third-World Woman' even as she decentres the unified notion of gender/gender oppression expounded in western feminist theory. She thus analyses how western feminists have constructed their own (collective) identity at the expense of their non-western 'sisters' through the creation of a deceptively universal analytic tool: patriarchy. This tool produces the falsely unified analytic category of 'woman/women', and erases all differences among women in the process. Like the African-American feminists whose work we discussed above, Chandra Mohanty sees the white, western feminist privileging of patriarchal dominance above racial or class-based divisions as constructing a falsely unified socio-political identity 'woman/women', based on a sociological notion of the '"sameness" of their oppression'.[29] To this insight, Mohanty adds the Saidian observation that the projection of this unified feminist political identity onto the world stage has followed the dictates of western orientalist thought (which she calls 'humanism'), creating a falsely unified non-western 'other' in order to preserve the shaky unity of a western feminist political identity.[30] The consequence has been an unbridled condescension on the part of western feminists, whose own gendered brand of orientalism allows them to cast themselves as the impeccably credentialled feminist representatives of their oppressed 'little sisters' in Africa and Asia.

Mohanty was by no means the first Third-World feminist to have identified western feminist theory's own, home-grown brand of orientalism. Indeed, two years earlier, Valerie Amos and Pratibha Parmar had already summarized quite succinctly the very negative consequences that western feminist insistence on shared forms of oppression had on their interactions with non-western women: 'Feminist theories which examine our cultural practices as "feudal residues" or label us "traditional", also portray us as politically immature women who need to be versed and schooled in the ethos of western feminism,' observed Amos and Parmar in 1984.[31] Mohanty develops this analysis further, explaining precisely how it is that western feminist insistence on the unity of the category 'woman/women' produces an account in which Third-World women are inevitably understood to be *more* oppressed than their western sisters. For western feminist discourse, 'by assuming women as a coherent, already constituted group that is placed in kinship, legal and other structures, defines Third World women as subjects *outside social relations*, instead of looking at the way women are constituted through those very structures'.[32] By refusing to explore the radically different meanings that being a woman might have in various class, racial, ethnic or religious contexts, western feminists have no choice but to arrange the singular entity 'woman/women' on a scale of socio-economic development ranging from Third-World underdevelopment to the First-World standards that the Third World may one day achieve. Rather than seeing a wide range of identities that women might possess, including identities in which gender plays a less important part, western feminist theory takes an already known being, 'defined in a particular way prior to [her] entry into social relations', and plugs her into the existing, evolutionary narratives on development.[33] The parallels with black feminist critiques of white middle-class feminists' presumption that all women are 'white under the skin', that is, fundamentally the same despite their often extraordinarily divergent conditions, should be obvious.

Western feminist theory thus fails (or refuses) to analyse the power differentials between the First and Third Worlds, preferring instead to regard the Third World as merely 'underdeveloped', trudging along that single, linear and narrowly teleological path towards western-style social, economic and political institutions: 'Legal, economic, religious, and familial structures are treated as phenomena to be judged by Western standards,' writes Mohanty in a particularly revealing passage.

> It is here that ethnocentric universality [by which she means the projection of a particular, Western subjectivity into the space of an allegedly universal humanity] comes into play. When these structures are defined as 'underdeveloped' or 'developing' and women are placed within them, an implicit image of the 'average Third World woman' is produced. This is the transformation of the (implicitly western) 'oppressed woman' into the 'oppressed Third World woman'. While the category of 'oppressed woman' is generated through an exclusive focus on gender difference, 'the oppressed Third World woman' category has an additional attribute – the 'Third World difference'... [which] includes a paternalistic attitude toward women in the Third World.[34]

The result of this mental process is a series of images – the veiled woman, the obedient wife, the chaste virgin – images that dwell in universal, ahistoric splendour, 'setting in motion a colonialist discourse that exercises a very specific power in defining, coding and maintaining existing First/Third World connections'.[35] And these images, in turn, conjure into being an orientalist politics of feminism, based on a familiar couple – Occident and Orient, but this time garbed in feminist dress. The result is a politics of western feminist *self*-presentation and western feminist *re*presentation of women in the Third World, with the haplessness of the latter serving as the mirror in whose reflection the former can enjoy the spectacle of their own relative liberation. Mohanty does not mean to imply by this that western women are in fact liberated and in control of their own lives. On the contrary, what Mohanty exposes here is the 'discursive self-presentation' of western feminism. For if western women's liberty and autonomy had any actual material basis in reality, all need for feminist movements would have long since withered away.[36]

It has perhaps not escaped your notice that in this Third-World feminist account, western feminist thought looks eerily reminiscent of John Stuart Mill's insistence on women's status as the marker of a society's location on the civilization-barbarism scale. I think this is no accident, for what has particularly exercised Third-World feminists is their western 'sisters' uncritical adoption of the orientalist mode of thinking, whose underlying binary logic (western self, non-western other) flattens the multiple differences among real humans and presses them into a pair of abstract categories arranged in such a way that the first term (western, male, universal) is 'privileged over' and 'colonizes' the second (eastern, female, particular): 'In other words, it is only insofar as "woman/women" and "the East" are defined as others, or as peripheral, that (Western) man/humanism can represent him/itself as the center'.[37] But as Robert Young has pointed out, the Third-World feminist critique of western feminists' 'latent ethnocentrism' has in fact tended to homogenize western women in the history of colonialism.[38] And this, in turn, suggests that the postcolonial critique has, paradoxically, left the orientalists' primary east–west divide unshaken, and merely shifted the attention to events on the non-western side of the curtain.

Masculinity in the *fin-de-siècle* imperial formation

In order to assess the success of feminist efforts to recuperate Said's *Orientalism* as a tool of historical analysis, I would like to turn to the work of Mrinalini Sinha, whose *Colonial Masculinity. The 'manly Englishman' and the 'effeminate Bengali' in the Late Nineteenth Century* draws heavily from Said in its understanding of the discursive aspects of colonial rule.[39] Yet Sinha presses beyond the limits of Said's homogenizing, binary vision, in which colonial rule looks pretty much the same at all times and in all places: the western domination/imaginative annihilation of its non-western 'other'. For if Sinha draws on Said's primarily discursive understanding of colonial rule, she nonetheless strives to locate those discursive forms in a specific historical context: Bengal in the 1880s and 1890s. By using what she calls a 'historical materialist perspective', Sinha seeks to ground the imperialist discourses which Said 'rightly identified as "Orientalism"' in the socio-economic and political imperatives of imperialism, notably in the imperative to restructure colonial (and metropolitan) societies in keeping with the needs of extraction and transfer of surplus that governed late nineteenth-century imperial economics.[40] Sinha thus takes as her object the entire 'imperial social formation', by which she means both India and Britain, bound as they were in a relationship of unequal, yet interdependent development, and argues that this formation shifted at a key moment in the late nineteenth century, recasting social, cultural and racial relations between colonizer and colonized. Her focus on local politics enables her, moreover, to demonstrate that European colonialism on the ground tended to be a negotiated relationship, a two-way street in which relations were shaped in part by indigenous traditions, even as Europeans strove to recast native customs and practices in their own image. It further allows her to show how this local process of negotiation could then export back to the metropole altered understandings of class and gender relations, thus illustrating the interactive character of metropolitan–colonial relations and the proposition that important aspects of those relations were in fact reshaped on the imperial periphery.

Colonial Masculinity focuses on the 'processes and practices' whereby, in the final decades of the nineteenth century, two 'differently positioned elites' in colonial Bengal were constituted, respectively, as 'manly Englishmen' and 'effeminate Bengalis'.[41] For, as the author notes in her introduction, colonial masculinity 'points toward the multiple axes along which power was exercised in colonial India: among or within the colonisers and the colonised as well as between colonisers and colonised', neither of which constituted a homogeneous group.[42] Her interest in the problem of colonial masculinity has its roots in her critique of Said's homogenizing vision of the colonizer–colonized relationship, for Sinha wishes above all to stress that the categories of colonizer and colonized were not in fact fixed or self-evident; rather, there was a 'constant need... to define and redefine the coloniser and the colonised. Moreover, since the coloniser and the colonised were themselves two historically constructed categories, the relations between the two were neither fixed nor given for all time', for such relations were constantly shifting in accordance with the ever-changing political and economic imperatives of colonial rule.[43] Such identities can only be explored, then, in relation to '"specific practices of ruling" rather than as products of a universalised or generalised colonial condition'.[44] The contours of colonial masculinity were thus shaped by an imperial social formation that included both Britain and India, which means that the 'manly Englishman' and 'effeminate Bengali' took shape not only in relation to the societies of late nineteenth-century India, but also in relation to that of *fin-de-siècle* Britain, including the late nineteenth-century 'remaking' of the English working class, the emergence of the so-called new woman, and the anti-feminist backlash of the 1880s and 1890s.

Across the four chapters of her book, Mrinalini Sinha explores the refiguring of colonial masculinity as it emerged in a series of debates over the extension of legal equality to (male) Indian British subjects. The backdrop to each of these debates was the longer-term shift in colonial ruling strategies from an 'Anglicist' to a more 'orientalist' mode of rule in the wake of the 1857 rebellion and transfer (in 1858) of political authority in India from the East India Company to the

British Crown. The Anglicist system, which arose in the early nineteenth century, rested on rationalizing the existing colonial administration in keeping with evangelical and utilitarian ideals of good government. This, in turn, had entailed considerable restructuring of Indian society, as well as the Anglicization of a class of Indians who, educated in English 'tastes, in opinions, in morals and in intellect', might collaborate with the British colonial elite in the administration and rule of India.[45] The 1857 rebellion sounded the death knell of this policy in favour of a more cautious 'orientalist' strategy of indirect rule through the very indigenous elites (large landholding classes and the leaders of urban Indian communities) who were deemed responsible for fomenting the rebellion in the first place.

The 'orientalist' system that gradually took shape over the second half of the nineteenth century was, thus, a mode of indirect rule through supposedly traditional means, which 'traditions' had, of course, been reconstructed by late eighteenth-century orientalist administrators-cum-scholars, whose tireless scholarly pursuit of 'traditional' society and codifications of indigenous laws helped to construct a 'specifically colonial understanding of indigenous tradition'.[46] As the author points out, this colonial construction of indigenous practice had, in the late eighteenth century, allowed the East India Trading Company to exercise what was in fact a new form of authority in the name of continuity with Indian traditions. These were the allegedly traditional Indian forms of rule to which the colonial administration returned over the second half of the nineteenth century. Hence, at the very moment when the western-educated corps of native officials that the British administration had created was starting to demand a greater share in the exclusive privileges of the British colonial elite (with whom they had long collaborated), that administration turned its face from them altogether in favour of indirect rule, based on collaboration with India's traditional powers-that-be. Sinha intriguingly suggests that the Bengali elites' struggle to retain their hold on positions of authority in the colonial administration, and the ultimately successful efforts of British colonialists to contain those ambitions, took place not on the terrain of arguments for establishing racial exclusivity in the colonial public service, but was rather cast in terms of establishing a more 'natural' gender hierarchy between 'manly' and 'unmanly' men. Bengali 'babus' (i.e. educated men) were therefore not chased out of the colonial administration altogether but were simply confined to the inferior ranks.[47]

As we shall see, this conflict would play itself out around four debates: first, the Ibert Bill (1883/4), which proposed to give a small number of native officials in the colonial administration limited criminal jurisdiction over European subjects living in India's country towns; second, the Native Volunteer Movement (1885/6), in which men from different regions (Bengal, Madras, Punjab) proposed to create armed native volunteer corps; third, the Public Service

Commission (1886/7), which was called in order to reorganize employment in the Indian Civil Service, ultimately to the detriment of native demands for an increased role therein; and, fourth, the Age of Consent Controversy, which erupted in the aftermath of an 1891 bill proposing to raise the age of consent for sexual intercourse for Indian girls from ten to twelve years. In each of these struggles, the issue of the Bengali babu's defective or deficient masculinity occupied a central role in the debate; indeed, Sinha argues, it came to constitute the very heart of the matter.[48]

'The physical organization of the Bengalee is feeble even to effeminacy,' wrote Thomas Babington Macaulay in a mid-1830s description of the entire Bengali people.

> His pursuits are sedentary, his limbs delicate, his movements languid. During many ages he has been trampled upon by men of bolder and more hardy breeds... though voluble in dispute and singularly pertinacious in the war of chicane he seldom engages in personal conflict, and scarcely ever enlists as a soldier. There never perhaps existed a people so thoroughly fitted by habit for a foreign yoke.[49]

British colonialists had long accused the Bengali people of 'feeble effeminacy' *vis-à-vis* other hardier, more warrior-like tribes in India – the Punjabis, for example, or the Sikhs. It was a characterization that very conveniently justified British rule of the province. Moreover, Sinha argues, this designation grew far more widespread and virulent in the late nineteenth century. Equally important, it came to settle on the shoulders of a specific sub-group of the Bengali population, namely, western-educated middle-class men. Finally, this occurred at the very moment that the shift in colonial ruling strategies, from Anglicist to orientalist, marginalized those same educated Bengalis, deposing them from their previous role as mediators between the colonial administration and the rest of the Indian population to the position of 'an unrepresentative and artificial minority' who represented nothing more than the 'anomalies' of their own situation, a situation that was summarized in the late nineteenth-century concept of the 'effeminate babu'.[50]

Significantly, the Bengali male's notorious effeminacy was not merely a matter of British colonial propaganda but an issue of deep concern to the Bengali middle classes, who read in their own alleged emasculation the dreaded proof of Indian society's decline.[51] Bengali men were thus equally invested in the issue of their alleged effeminacy, and participated vigorously in the discussions and debates that proliferated around that 'enfeebled' masculinity after 1880. This is perhaps most visible in Bengali men's involvement in the Native Volunteer Movement of 1885. For over the course of their struggle for the right to bear arms, these men accused the colonizing power of having emasculated the Bengali male through its strategies of rule, thus articulating an entirely new critique of the colonial administration within the terms of colonial masculinity. In this debate, at least, Bengali men appear to have accepted the proposition that their masculinity had indeed been damaged, but then laid the blame for that decline at the feet of the colonial administration. The best way to recuperate some of that wasted masculinity was to participate in the military exercises of volunteer troops, argued Bengali proponents of native volunteering.

But colonial officials ultimately refused to alter existing statutes, whereby certain members of India's landed and martial elites had always participated in such volunteer militias, to the exclusion of educated elites. They had a range of complex reasons for rejecting the idea of creating more broadly recruited native volunteer reserves in India, among them the fear that Britain's colonial policy of divide-and-rule by region would be overcome by a structure of native volunteering that would promote unity among diverse Indian elites.[52] Hence, the ultimate resolution of the controversy was to continue as they had been doing for decades, and draw their reserves primarily from resident Anglo-Indian (i.e. British and mixed descent) populations, adding only the occasional Indian warlord ('wealthy landlords and scions of aristocratic families with a martial tradition').[53] This effectively excluded Indians on what were racial grounds, though the explicit regulations remained coy about this fact, invoking participation (by blood) in manly and upper-class Indian martial traditions as the main criterion for Indian admission to the volunteer corps. This was undoubtedly a blunder from a purely Machiavellian point of view, as indigenous elites, including those whose main form of capital was a western education, were genuinely enthused about participating in the volunteer corps, and had, moreover, their own parallel interest in enforcing social order. But British fears of an armed and unified colonial population prevailed, and Bengali hopes for recuperating their compromised masculinity via military exercise came to naught.

Bengali criticism of the colonial administration's 'demartialization' of native educated elites in the native volunteer movement thus remained very much within the framework of colonial masculinity, accepting terms that were, ultimately, laid down by the rulers, and seeking privileges and recognition within those terms. Yet within that larger framework, the entire native volunteering debate ended up shifting the terms within which Bengalis understood their own emasculation. Henceforth, it was the colonial administration that was to be held responsible for the Bengali male's humiliating lack of martial virtue. The Volunteer Movement thus represented another step in the struggle for hegemony by Indian elites, a struggle that, at the end of the nineteenth century, was engaged in the language of colonial masculinity. Hence, concludes Sinha, 'at a time when the Bengali elite still eschewed direct criticism of colonial rule, it expressed its hegemonic aspirations not so much by assuming economic and political leadership of colonial society, but by attributing to itself – specifically to the elite male physique – all the ravages and despair of colonial rule'.[54]

Sinha's effort to marry gender analysis with imperial history is shown to best advantage in her discussion of C.P. Ibert's proposed amendment to the Code of Criminal Procedure of the Indian Penal Code. This amendment would have extended to certain classes of native officials in the colonial administration limited criminal jurisdiction over European British subjects living in the country towns (*mofussils*). In Sinha's analysis of the controversy that erupted around Ibert's Bill, we hear not only the voices of Bengali and European men, we are witness, also, to European women's involvement in the affair, an involvement that leaves little doubt as to their active role in upholding the racist structures of British domination. Far from being the victims of an imperial government policy in which white women's sole role was as breeders of the imperial race, European women emerge in the Ibert controversy as utterly complicitous in maintaining the racist ideologies and practices that underpinned British rule in India.

In January 1883, C.P. Ibert, who was the Law Member of the Government of India, proposed to abolish the special legal status of European subjects in India, whereby the latter enjoyed the right to be tried not before the native district magistrate but rather by a European joint magistrate, even if the European magistrate was of lower rank than the district's native magistrate. Native district magistrates were thus obliged to call upon their European inferiors each time a European was scheduled to appear before them in court, an anomaly in terms of civil service ranking that occurred ever more frequently as natives in the elite Indian civil service gained enough seniority to be appointed as district officers in the *mofussils*. Ibert's effort to end this anomaly unleashed a storm of protest from the Anglo-Indian community, a veritable 'white mutiny', the goal of which was to protect the special legal status of the European British in India. So fierce was Anglo opposition that Ibert was ultimately forced to back down. Rather than extending to native magistrates full powers over all who dwelt in their districts, the compromise bill of 25 January 1884 preserved the Europeans' special legal status, granting them the right to demand a trial by a jury of whom at least half were European British subjects or Americans.

How was it that the Anglo-Indian community prevailed over the Law Member of the Government of India? Once again, the unfitness of effeminate Bengali babus played a key role in the defence of Anglo racial privilege. In this case, the babus were condemned for their presumed inability to stand in judgement over a more 'manly' people. Opponents of the bill thus argued that the 'constitutional timidity of the race' made Bengali civilians unfit to exercise authority of any kind over the 'manly Englishman'; their inherent physical weakness and consequent lack of physical or moral courage (the two were held to be inextricably linked), rendered them incapable of fulfilling their duties as district officers where European subjects were concerned. Thus far, the arguments are familiar, as are the parties to the debate – 'manly' Englishmen versus 'degenerate' and 'effeminate' Bengali babus. But the affair then lurched off in an entirely new direction when, in a rhetorical flourish intended to mobilize opposition by portraying the worst-case scenario, Anglo-Indian defenders of racial privilege imagined these weak and therefore vindictive men sitting in judgement over European women as well: 'Natives who practice polygamy, [who] treat their wives as caged birds, kept in the dark chiefly for the creation of sons... who immolate infants of tender age to marriage, who compel infant widows to remain widows till death – are as such competent to try European men and women?' asked a British Deputy Commissioner in Assam.[55] It was every European woman's worst nightmare, being subjected to the authority of men whose sense of masculine self was so fragile and warped that they could buttress it only through the bullying maltreatment of their own wives and daughters. Worse yet, lurking behind the Deputy Commissioner's words was the widespread fear that Bengali magistrates would deliberately abuse their powers over European women in order to get back at their husbands: 'One's wife may be walked off for an imaginary offence,' wrote one Anglo-Indian gentleman in February 1883. 'What would more please our fellow subjects than to bully and disgrace a wretched European woman? The higher her husband's station and the greater her respectabilities, the greater the delight of her torturer'.[56] Bengali babus, acutely conscious of their inadequate masculinity, would thus square off with the manly white conqueror not on the equal terms of man-to-man combat, but rather on the abject terrain of his 'wretched' wife, dragged before the judge on some trumped-up pretext in order to avenge the Bengali's wounded sense of male pride.

Anglo-Indian women seized upon these arguments with alacrity, casting cultural/racial difference in moral and juridical terms and highlighting the alleged ill-treatment of Indian women as evidence that native magistrates were completely unfit to sit in judgement over European women: 'In Bengal the men are notoriously destitute of manliness,' wrote one Anglo-Indian woman, for they are 'most harsh and cowardly in their treatment of the weaker sex'. Male opponents of the Ibert Bill initially welcomed the staunch support of Anglo-Indian women in their campaign. But when, in early spring of 1883, the Anglo-Indian women of Calcutta went so far as to abandon the strictures of Victorian domesticity (which were far more vigorously upheld in colonial India than in the metropole, Sinha tells us) and mobilize politically in defence of white privilege, Anglo-Indian men grew anxious. For in the independent 'Ladies Committee' that met in Calcutta to draft a separate women's petition against the bill, Anglo-Indian men saw the dreaded spectre of something which they had thought they had left safely behind them in the metropole: the 'new' woman, independent, wage-earning, university-educated and demanding a voice in the public world of politics. When chastised by the men for adopting such unseemly, unwomanly tactics, the Ladies Committee immediately denied all political ambition; their sole interest was defence of white womanhood against the dire prospect of being sullied at the hands of native magistrates.

And indeed, the men needn't have worried, for the terms in which the Ladies Committee framed their petition left no doubt as to the hierarchical understanding of gender that underpinned their demands. Hence, on 6 March 1883, one member, Annette Ackroyd-Beveridge, wrote of the 'ignorant and neglected' women of India, who testify to the 'justice of the resentment which English women feel at Mr Ibert's proposal to subject civilized women to the jurisdiction of men who have done little or nothing to redeem the women of their race, whose social ideas are still on the outer verge of civilization'.[57] If gender relations among Indians were based on an 'uncivilized' and abusive form of patriarchy, where weak-kneed males shored up their feeble masculinity in acts of terror and abuse towards their own women, the benevolent, 'civilized' patriarchy of Englishmen showed itself in the masculine arm of chivalry that stretched itself protectively over the threatened heads of white women. In framing the issues this way, the women of the Ladies Committee blunted the political edge of their demand, claiming not the right to speak in public on their own behalf, but merely the appropriately feminine right to male protection.

The Ibert controversy thus pitted two 'races', two forms of civilization, two forms of patriarchy, against one another: one based on the enfeebled and perverse masculinity of an abusive Bengali babu; the other based on the chivalric instincts of the manlier English race. When framed in such terms, the outcome seemed incontrovertible (at least to the English): it was utterly unreasonable, if not downright immoral, to ask that European women, accustomed to the 'respect' and 'protection' of European men, bow their heads and accept the judicial authority of men who were content to see their own women 'degraded, ignorant and enslaved'.[58]

By recasting the debate in these terms, women's participation in the struggles over the Ibert Bill set what Lady Beveridge called 'the pride of (white) womanhood' against the extension of legal equality to native men. Moreover, Sinha observes, even as women like Beveridge 'invited white men to serve as the benevolent protectors of white women from native men', they excluded native women altogether from the logic of the argument.[59] In a curious coda to the episode, then, Sinha explains that, while the actual voices of native women were not to be heard throughout the affair, Indian men, incensed by the negative stereotypes of Indian women (and of themselves as Indian women's abusers) that underwrote Anglo-Indian opposition to the Ibert Bill, 'ventriloquized' Indian women's voices in a 'native female memorial' that contested the Calcutta Ladies' petition to the Queen. This document, which was allegedly signed by members of the Bengali *bhadramahila* (women of the Bengali middle class), protested that Indian women were by no means 'ignorant and enslaved'; in fact, Indian women were far better educated than their white counterparts (Indian women had been admitted to university degree programmes in 1878, earlier than any of the English universities). Though a complete forgery, the memorial nonetheless suggests that, by 1883, Indian men were beginning to recognize the importance of mobilizing women's voices in the national struggle, if for no other reason than that the politics of colonial masculinity placed male–female relationships at the heart of the matter, the criterion by which the society's level of civilization was to be judged.

The other two debates analysed over the course of Sinha's book – the Public Service Commission and the Age of Consent controversy – both unfolded along analogous lines, with struggles over what were essentially matters of political control in a colonial context being fought out on the terrain of colonial masculinity. In other words, social order in colonial India was to be secured through the establishment of a proper gender hierarchy between manly Englishmen – endowed with the military virtues of valour, good sportsmanship, chivalry and sexual self-discipline – and the effeminate Bengali babus, whose timorous lassitude and unchivalrous failure of sexual self-restraint were manifested not only in their lack of a heroic military tradition, but also – perhaps more profoundly – in the custom of child marriage, testament to the moral depravity of an enfeebled, emasculated manhood. On this particular issue, the colonial government chose to break with the post-1857 practice of reserving to local custom all matters associated with private and domestic life. Citing grounds that were at once humanitarian and eugenic, the government presented its Age of Consent Bill, intended to raise the age of female consent to sexual intercourse from ten to twelve. The bill, which was signed into law in 1891, did not in fact interfere with the practice of child marriage per se, for such marriage bore the sacred imprimatur of 'tradition' in India, and was therefore treated with great circumspection by Anglo-Indian officials. Rather, it drew a distinction between child marriage, as practised by the 'manlier' tribes of India, and the premature consummation of such marriages by the effeminate – hence sexually uncontrolled – Bengalis. In the case of the former, fathers married off their young daughters in keeping with ancient custom, but kept them at home until they were of an age to bear children. The degenerate Bengalis, by contrast, threw themselves upon their child brides with such savagery that the results could be read not only in the degeneration of the entire 'race', but, more tragically, on the broken bodies of the young girls who paid the price. (British medical science was convinced that there was a link between physical deterioration of the 'race' and early sexual intercourse/childbirth.) Yet the interests of these young girls were hardly present in the controversy that raged around the Consent Bill. On the contrary, Sinha tells us, agitation against the bill recentred the issue squarely on the recurrent problem of native masculinity. Such protests found fertile soil in an unexpected intersection between the Indian nationalist movement's perception of a 'crisis' of Indian/Bengali masculinity and a growing perception in Britain of a 'crisis' of British masculinity. 'The responses to these crises were different and even contradictory in India and Britain, but they intersected – albeit in uneven ways – to reframe the Consent controversy as a referendum on native masculinity'.[60]

It is here, in her discussion of the nationalist opposition to the Age of Consent Bill, that Sinha delivers most consistently on her promise to reveal the links binding metropolitan and colonial politics. For the nationalist defence of the conjugal rights of an unreformed indigenous Hindu patriarchy found echoes of support among British men whose own sense of domestic authority had been shaken by the renewed feminist challenges of the 1880s, notably by the mobilization of middle-class women in various crusades against prostitution and the so-called white slave trade.[61] Swept up in the anti-feminist backlash of the 1880s, British pundits rose to the defence of the Hindu patriarch, whose family life was, in the words of one journalist, 'of a very high order'. One retired colonial official even went so far as to assert that in matters of marriage and the control of women, 'England had as much to learn from India as she has to teach that country'.[62] In the storm of protest that this unholy alliance of Indian nationalist and British patriarchs raised, the British viceroy hastened to issue an executive order that made it virtually impossible to bring cases of premature consummation of child marriage to trial under the Consent Act. The bill thus remained a dead letter, and another 40 years would pass before the British government sought to take any further initiatives in the matter of child marriage (Child Marriage Restraint Act of 1929).

Colonial Masculinity thus offers its readers a sustained reflection on the discursive links binding imperial, nationalist and patriarchal politics, for as Sinha herself puts it, 'the history of colonial masculinity... reveals not only the patriarchal politics of the nationalism of indigenous elites, but also the limits of a nationalist politics based on the defence of indigenous patriarchy'.[63] More profoundly, Sinha's analysis of colonial masculinity joins that of a host of other recent scholars of gender and empire in demonstrating that although gender is a key axis along which colonial power was constructed, the category of gender itself was never distinct from national, class, racial and caste categories, but rather interacted with them in a range of ways, depending on the political structure. Indeed, Sinha finds that 'the widely dispersed arena for the construction of colonial masculinity disrupts any stable equation between gender identity and sex difference: it demonstrates that masculinity had as much to do with racial, class, religious and national differences as with sex differences'.[64] From this, she concludes that the 'expanded politics of gender' practised by a number of scholars (including, as we shall see, Lora Wildenthal) – 'one that recognises the imbrication of gender in a variety of axes of power' – is in fact inadequate to the task of feminist critique of the politics of colonial masculinity. She therefore urges feminist scholars to abandon all forms of analysis that give gender priority in favour of a more global enquiry into 'the entire domain of social relations', conducted from a 'feminist-materialist' perspective.[65]

Sinha's effort to recuperate Saidian analysis for feminist purposes thus ends in the radical move of abolishing gender's privileged status within feminist analysis in favour of a feminist-materialist mode of enquiry whose outlines remain, alas, studiously vague. Among the most obvious victims in this approach are the voices of native women who, though notably active in the struggle to raise the age of consent, are nowhere to be heard from in Sinha's account of that struggle. But native women did speak 'and spoke furiously, acted rapidly, formed organizations, lobbied the government sometimes with and sometimes without the help of British feminists of the time,' writes Padma Anagol of native women's activism in the Age of Consent controversy as it unfolded in Maharashtra. 'They created counter-discourses privileging the historical context-over-text based arguments of those who opposed the age of Consent and privileging their experiences, demonstrated clearly that early marriage stunted the psychological and physical development of girl-brides'.[66] In Anagol's view, the absence of native women from analyses such as Sinha's owes not to any actual silence on the part of native women at the time but rather to the theoretical and methodological tools of the postcolonial American academy. Hence the very techniques of deconstructive reading that Sinha deploys so effectively in order to analyse the dominant discourses of imperial rule prove far less well suited to recovering the voices of women that have long since been silenced. After all, as Sumit Sarkar has observed, the colonial government and its institutions (notably the law) were important resources for Indian women. At no time was this more visible than in the case of the Age of Consent Bill, when Indian women had recourse to the institutions of an 'alien' government and 'aligned themselves on its side in their search for justice and equality'.[67] Small wonder that the voices of native women, who took political action with the aid of the British government and against the practices of their own menfolk, are no longer audible in nationalist narratives of liberation!

When viewed in this broader context, the debates over masculinity become simply one aspect of a far broader range of arguments invoked over the course of the Age of Consent controversy. Anagol thus concludes that

> if the Hindu patriarchal system felt it was under siege this was so, not so much from the claims of unreserved masculinity of the foreigner but from the threat of real actions taken by their own womenfolk. If, as Tanika

> Sarkar points out, defence of tradition was now a 'political strategy' being fashioned by male elites then it should be equally seen as a combative weapon against... the assertive actions of women who had been made bold by the Raj to claim status as 'agents'.[68]

The Age of Consent controversy was thus at least as much about conflicts within Indian society as it was about divisions between Indian and European male British subjects.

Hence, revealing though it is of the displacement of questions of colonial power onto the grid of masculinity, not to mention of the intricate interweavings that bound colonial and metropolitan histories in the '"uneven and combined development" of the global political economy', *Colonial Masculinity* remains problematic as a work of history. For in the end, its mode of analysis is more discursive than historical, and purely discursive analysis, however sensitive to the location of those discourses in specific historical and material contexts, has a problem with explaining (rather than merely asserting) change. Hence, in the introduction to her study, Sinha *asserts* the importance of change in her insistence that 'the Orientalist enterprise was not a simple intensification of ancient prejudices; it marked a crucial break in the strategies by which "knowledge" about cultures and civilizations was constructed'.[69] But she never actually *explains* precisely how these 'constructions of knowledge' actually changed. Nor is she in a position to do so, for her fundamentally discursive analytic perspective lacks any concrete way of connecting discourses to their socio-economic contexts. As we shall see, Lora Wildenthal's social-historical analysis is far more successful in this regard, as it able to identify the shifting constellation of forces in German colonial Africa that produced a radical reorientation of policy *vis-à-vis* mixed marriages and the broader question of social stratification by race. Wildenthal is thus able to give us race, class and gender as mutable categories, while, moreover, demonstrating precisely how their political saliencies shifted.[70] Sinha, by contrast, gives us mutable categories without being able to link those categories back to the social experiences of particular human agents, whose shifting interests and affiliations shaped and reshaped political choices in specific places and times.

Let us conclude this chapter, then, with a discussion of Lora Wildenthal's *German Women for Empire, 1884–1945*, a book that succeeds admirably in historicizing colonial discourses and techniques of rule, placing women's particular colonial interests and dreams within the broader context of nationalist, feminist and imperial politics in Germany at the turn of the twentieth century. It offers, moreover, the additional advantage of focusing on a country that is not Great Britain. For as scholars in colonial studies are first to point out, the field of colonial studies has from its origins been shaped around the single, and in many ways singular, case of Great Britain, which accounts for a staggeringly large proportion of scholarly production within the field.[71] Much of the theoretical literature in the field is thus written with the particularities of the British Empire (notably British India) in mind, and scholars in colonial studies have only recently begun to redress this imbalance through studies of the French, Belgian, Dutch and German colonizers, who gobbled up great stretches of Africa and East Asia from the mid-nineteenth century onward.

Out of Africa: German women and the imperial enterprise, 1884–1945

German Women for Empire opens in the aftermath of Germany's unification by arms, achieved under the direction of Chancellor Otto von Bismarck, who, in his first ten years of service under King (later Emperor) Friederich II, masterminded a profound transformation of the map of central Europe, replacing a congeries of medium-sized German states and principalities with a single and quite powerful federal empire, unified under Prussian leadership. No sooner had the continental empire taken shape than German eyes began to turn abroad in search of as-yet-unconquered terrain in Africa and East Asia that might serve the interests of both German business and national prestige (overseas empire being a condition of Great Power status in late nineteenth-century Europe). By the mid-1880s, when Wildenthal's story begins, Germany already claimed four colonies in Africa – German Southwest Africa, German East Africa, Togo and Cameroon – as well as German New Guinea in the Pacific, to which the island of Nauru was annexed in 1888. Over the next 12 years, Germany would add the Chinese city of Qingdao (which Germany occupied and then leased in 1897, along with its hinterlands on the Shandong Peninsula), the Mariana, Caroline and Palau Islands (purchased from Spain in 1899), and the islands of Savaii and Upolu, which became German Samoa in 1900. On the eve of World War I, then, Germany had acquired an empire that was third in territorial size and fifth in population among the British, French, Dutch, Belgian, US, Portuguese, Italian and Spanish empires.[72]

In some of these territories, notably in German Southwest Africa, Protestant missionaries had been busily converting and ministering to the resident populations, both 'native' and Dutch (Boer), while occasionally intermarrying with said populations, particularly in the mission station of Rehoboth. But with the formal acquisition of African territory after 1884, German society at large seems to have thrown itself into the imperial adventure with a vengeance. The nation's two existing colonial societies (the German Colonial Association and Carl Peters' Society for German Colonization), dedicated to the promotion of German settlement in what they hoped would become a vast overseas empire, soon found themselves flanked by a host of new organizations that sprang up almost overnight in the enthusiasm for spreading German culture, and German humans, across the seas. One of the first such new societies was the Women's Association for Nursing, founded in 1886 with the express purpose of providing rough imperial outposts with adequate health care in the form of skilled and well-trained nurses. As Wildenthal explains, these women were meant to be single (women nurses were barred from marriage), and to devote themselves selflessly to the well-being of others, both German and native (but Germans first), in the conquered territories. Only ten years later would new associations appear whose express purpose was to promote the emigration of Germany's 'surplus' population of young, single women to colonial lands where they might find work (generally as domestics) and, ultimately, husbands among colonial populations that would remain overwhelmingly male throughout Germany's brief colonial era (1884–1919).

The story of these feminine settlement associations and their complicated links to various nationalist, feminist and racist agendas lies at the heart of Wildenthal's tale. But she begins by setting the colonial stage with those intrepid nurses who were among the first German women to depart for Africa, in the 1880s. Along with missionary work, nursing constituted German women's primary social role in the colonies, 'predating even marriage and motherhood'.[73] In certain ways, these women broke with traditional models of female deference to male authority, managing to detach their occupation not only from male nursing but from male missionary authority and from religious justification in general, carving out a purely secular professional role for themselves in the colonialist movement and in the various colonial states. The Women's Association for Nursing was, moreover, the first colonialist organization run by and for women, overseeing the dispatch of women nurses to all parts of the empire, where they laboured in the name of the state and conservative nationalism. Yet the break with male authority was a strictly circumscribed one, as nurses (who were in theory 'desexualised' by the marriage bar) served for only limited periods of time in the colonies (generally two to four years), and always under the strict oversight of the colonial administration's doctors. 'Like frontline nurses in wartime, they were permitted to bring certain feminine qualities to an intensely masculine space,' notes Wildenthal in a neat summation of the contradictions that shot through a profession that was at once imbued with the quintessentially feminine quality of service to others and yet permitted a certain female autonomy from male authority, granted in the name of those very conservative national ideals that preached the inequality of the sexes.

But if the colonial nurses' overall profile – single, submissive, self-sacrificing – produced one powerful model of German women's 'saving presence' in Africa, this model did not go uncontested. Hence, the remarkable Frieda von Bülow began her colonial career under the conventional auspices of colonial nursing in Zanzibar, in 1887. Just months later, she threw off the encumbering demands of this feminine mission in favour of individual adventuring on the wide open spaces of German East Africa, where she hoped, ultimately, to make an independent colonial career for herself.[74] No sooner had she arrived at the hospital where she was to serve, in Dar es Salaam, than Bülow began quitting its narrow and laborious confines in order to explore nearby Zanzibar Island and its cosmopolitan society, comprising Afro-Arabs, South Asians, Swahilis, Persians and Egyptians. She carried on a passionate and ill-concealed love affair with colonial explorer, Carl Peters, and shared her excitement at her exotic colonial adventures with German readers back home in a series of travel sketches, published in family magazines and in the Society for German Colonization's journal, *Kolonialpolitische Korrespondenz.* She did manage to find some time for the hospital, but in a purely administrative incarnation only, hiring new staff and planning the establishment of a convalescent centre in her own house just outside Zanzibar Town. (As it turns out, Zanzibar was a better place to organize medical care than the mainland city of Dar es Salaam.) From the very outset, it would seem that nursing, though an important part of the colonial project, could not easily contain colonialist women's ambitions.[75]

Bülow's brazen love affair, plus her refusal to conform to the pious image of the self-sacrificing nurse, did not win her any fans in Foreign Office circles, nor among her erstwhile collaborators back home in the German-National Women's League (who were, after all, financing her adventures). Increasingly ill at ease in the face of her scandalous behaviour, the League decided to pull the plug on Bülow in January 1888; she had no choice but to leave Zanzibar four months later. When she returned once again, in 1893, it would be to run her own plantation and pursue a successful career as a novelist – the first writer, male or female, to use the German colonies as a setting for fiction.

Bülow's tale is in most respects quite singular, linked to the very forceful character of the individual. And yet it illustrates beautifully the gendered contradictions that swiftly gathered on colonial terrain, most notably around the issue of constructing a new, freer German society in colonial space, far from the social conflict and stifling bourgeois norms that ruled the mother country. But if German men could escape those snares by plunging ahead into the uncharted wilderness, realizing a feminine version of that freedom was not quite so simple, as Bülow's chequered colonial career illustrates. For even the more conventional women, who accepted the reigning gender hierarchy and set sail for Africa in the hope of finding a husband and establishing a new life for themselves in the open fields (by farmsteading, for example), found that their freedom and opportunities might well clash with the kind of freedom German men sought in those same colonial spaces. After all, as far as certain colonial men were concerned, these spaces represented a site of freedom *from* German women: 'In the colonies, German men were able to represent German civilization yet leave "civilized" relations between the sexes behind,' writes Wildenthal. 'Sexual and other forms of coercion that were unacceptable in Germany were part and parcel of the apparatus of rule in the colonies'. Colonialist women, who arrived in ever greater numbers after 1890, thus landed in worlds where a 'special standard of colonial morality' had already taken hold, including widespread cohabitation with indigenous women and distressing levels of violence against them. Committed both to colonialism and to 'civilized' gender relations, German colonial women found standards of colonial sexual behaviour deeply troubling, to say the least. And yet placing African and Pacific Islander women on a plane of equality with German colonialist women was, in their eyes, no solution, 'for that would threaten their own authority as agents of colonial power'.[76] It was an authority that colonialist women would increasingly link to their capacity to produce white (hence fully 'German') offspring.

Wildenthal's study thus bears out what contemporaries and historians alike have observed, namely, that as more European women settled in the colonies, racial segregation and racial hierarchies grew more pronounced.[77] It was in this context that the old-style 'imperial patriarchs' of pre-colonial and early colonial days – those original colonial conquerors who had often married into elite indigenous families as a means of reinforcing their local dominion – found their way of life threatened by the strategies of a new generation of German liberal nationalists, whose *fin-de-siècle* campaign to build a regime of racial purity (read: complete segregation) in the colonies entailed banning racially mixed marriages while stepping up the pace of German women's migration.

The liberal nationalists launched their campaign in response to the conditions they found waiting for them in the colonies at the end of the nineteenth century. Gone were the days when individual explorers might engage in the orgies of military conquest and spectacular land-grabs on which an earlier generation of imperial patriarchs had built their power. The liberal nationalist johnny-come-latelys had to rest their hopes for land and access to a cheap, compliant labour force on the state-ordered expropriation of colonial subjects, not on political alliances and intermarriage with them. 'They argued for the proletarianization of colonial subjects and greater upward mobility and equality for deserving German colonists,' writes Wildenthal. 'In their view, sex was not a man's private decision, but a social marker of status'.[78] By eliminating intermarriage, then, liberal nationalists sought to build an all-white community of German farmers who enjoyed relations of equality among themselves. Whiteness would thus become the visible sign of citizenship in 'an idealized German community overseas'.[79] But that ideal community was premised on the exclusion, expropriation and exploitation of indigenous peoples.

Imperial patriarchs, on the other hand, had long practised a very different model of masculinity and, accordingly, held quite different notions of the interrelation of sex and political power. For these men, racial hierarchy did not require racial purity, for in their view, sexual relationships with colonized women, far from damaging German authority, actually expressed that authority through a gender relation in which the inferior, wifely position was, appropriately enough, occupied by a woman hailing from the inferior, colonized group. As Wildenthal recounts in some detail, these men were often loath to put aside their indigenous wives and concubines in the name of the differently raced (and gendered) strategy of rule being promoted by liberal nationalists. But the tide was running against the mixed-race families of the old imperial patriarchy, for by the end of the nineteenth century, the growing population of German colonial men began restlessly seeking greater rights of political participation through regimes of self-administration. And this, in turn, presumed sharpening the lines separating colonizer from colonized, lest the latter be drawn inexorably into the kinds of political participation that liberal nationalist colonizers sought to win for themselves. 'Families that crossed racial lines, once considered a normal part of precolonial and early colonial societies, were now described as threats to white German supremacy', for in the context of *fin-de-siècle* colonialism, 'issues of race, family, and sexuality provided a language for German colonists' self-constitution as free and autonomous political subjects'.[80]

Realizing the liberal nationalist ideal of an all-white German community entailed considerable intervention in existing private and political relationships. For if liberal nationalists claimed to be preserving supposedly natural racial differences, building the ideal white farmer community in fact demanded that women and men of African or Pacific Islander descent be forcibly detached from their locally recognized sexual, familial or political ties to German imperial patriarchs. 'Liberal nationalism's impact on colonial societies was therefore at once equalizing for some [men] and racializing for all,' concludes Wildenthal, for if liberalism ultimately created new categories of rights-holders, it also created new, racialized ways to organize exclusion from those same rights. Imperialist patriarchy and liberal nationalism thus pitted two forms of masculinity and two forms of racist political domination against each other, for if both models were racist, and both entailed male domination, sexuality and racism nonetheless interacted quite differently within each model.[81]

Not surprisingly, the ban on intermarriage, which ultimately passed into local, colonial law in the early twentieth century, aroused fierce opposition from those imperial patriarchs who were happily ensconced in such marriages.[82] After all, such a ban compromised these men's freedom to have sex with and marry whomever they liked, while gravely interfering with their basic right, as propertied male citizens, to pass their citizenship and property on to their children, whatever the colour of their skin might be. Their determined opposition underscored the extent to which turn-of-the-century campaigns against race-mixing clashed with male colonizers' interests, notably with their patriarchal sexual liberties. Over the course of this conflict, the solution to reconciling German men's freedom to choose sexual partners with the new demands of racial purity/hierarchy gradually took shape in the form of the white German settler woman, who would henceforth accompany the male colonist as his 'cultural, economic and political partner... wherever he might go'.[83] That 'wherever' was most popularly figured as a colonial farm, plantation or ranch, where German women would collaborate with German men in both the production of economic values and in the reproduction of white German children, while participating in the cultural life of local German communities.

The colonial agrarian idyll exercised considerable sway over nationalist and colonialist women in turn-of-the-century Germany, precisely because it promised to reconcile tradition (conventional family life) with recognition of women's economic contributions: 'The farm reunited production and reproduction and allowed women to cross boundaries between men's and women's labor, and between public and private activity,' writes Wildenthal.[84] Such boundaries were firmly etched into the more complex industrializing economy of the metropole, and middle-class women in particular found themselves consigned to the sidelines of the economy, to a strictly private realm where reproduction had been hived off from all productive and remunerative activity. Colonial emigration promised to transport such marginal, middle-class women to a 'mythical time and place where they would have a central role in the economy that industrialized Germany had denied them'.[85] Feminist leaders such as Minna Cauer thus welcomed the colonial enterprise with open arms, believing that women's emancipation would be more easily institutionalized in the colonial world. For not only was colonial society deemed to be more open and free than in the metropole, but the productive and reproductive labours of German women were openly acknowledged as central to the entire colonial venture.

The thousands of German women, feminist and non-feminist alike, who were mobilized into enthusiastic participation in the newly racialized German colonial dream, raised little protest about the terms of their involvement. On the contrary, such women were among the most militant upholders of racial purity in the colonies: 'The Europeans who take black women may well train good sick-nurses and dog-slaves for themselves, but we will never conquer Africa with the children,' wrote one colonialist woman, Grete Ziemann, in 1907.

> In my opinion, race pride – naturally only in the best and noblest sense – cannot be exercised strictly enough. *If Germany wants to conquer Africa, in no case may a mixed race arise there.* From that follows the compelling demand that, as much as possible, white women in ever increasing numbers be active there as true pioneers of European culture.[86]

That this was so should perhaps come as no surprise. After all, women's ability to 'sustain racial purity' constituted the basis for their political participation in colonialism. One might thus expect colonialist women to number among the most vehement proponents of racial purity in the colonies.

Lora Wildenthal concludes her book with a look forward into the post-imperial era, where she unblinkingly assesses the grim legacy of colonial politics in the interwar metropole. She takes great pains to underscore how the campaign against race mixing in the colonies ultimately gave colonialist women a new claim to citizenship in the 'extralegal, biologized polity of the white and German race, which they argued had a substantial reality behind the existing legal and social order of the German state'.[87] Long before such notions acquired any purchase in the metropole (which never legalized the interracial marriage ban promulgated in the colonies), this 'biologized polity' took shape on the colonial periphery. Only in the interwar years would such visions of a racially based political order find their way back to the metropole in the form of Nazi racist politics. And yet the very conditions that made colonialist women central to the construction of racially pure German communities also circumscribed the ambit of their activity, casting these women's worth in the very narrow, instrumentalizing terms of their simple biological capacity to reproduce white children. However much colonialist women sought to expand the terms of their mission to that of 'culture-bearers', promoting German culture overseas through the practice of domestic virtue and the transmission of German values to their offspring, they were nonetheless unable to escape the central condition of their existence in the colonies as the 'means to an end' (assuring racial purity as the basis of an all-male German political community) rather than as ends in themselves.[88]

Lora Wildenthal's combination of social-historical and discursive analysis thus lays bare a world in which gender, race and sexuality combined in various and conflicting ways to structure colonial politics from the pre-colonial period through to Germany's loss of empire, in 1919, and beyond, to the interwar years, when the racist practices of the colonial periphery came home to haunt an increasingly crisis-ridden metropolitan society. In an analysis that recalls Jacqueline Jones's *Labor of Love, Labor of Sorrow*, Wildenthal shows us how very mutable masculine and feminine identities can be in a context where sexuality, race and gender are being recombined to shape differently raced and gendered forms of rule. And this, in turn, reminds us of the centrality of gender, sexuality and the family to the construction of politics itself. Far from occupying 'separate spheres', the two are in constant interaction, and nowhere is this more visible than on the shifting landscapes of Europe's colonial acquisitions.

In important ways, then, *German Women for Empire* and *Colonial Masculinity* proceed from diverging theoretical vantage points, the one emphasizing social historical approaches, the other stressing the importance of discursive analysis. Nonetheless, both texts make important contributions to the larger project around which recent feminist research on gender and colonialism has turned, namely underscoring the ways in which matters of sexual practice and sexual order 'proved useful vehicles for both nationalist and imperialist agendas'; in the end, indeed, the linkage often proved 'indisseverable'.[89] After some 20 years of feminist research in the field, then, it is abundantly clear that some kind of gender analysis must stand at the heart of colonial and postcolonial history. For if feminist scholars are not always in agreement about the precise forms such analysis should take, there is little doubt that understanding the modalities of colonial rule, and the intricacies of the relationships binding colony and metropole, demands analytic perspectives capable of comprehending the ways that gender operates – both as metaphor and as lived social relation – to shape political structures and guiding ideologies.

Postscript: differences among women

By now it should be clear that poststructuralist and postcolonial emphasis on the differences that reside at the heart of the category woman/women has produced a subtle shift in the way that feminist scholars understand the concept of difference. For if feminist debates in the 1970s and 1980s tended to focus on difference as a matter of experiential diversity – my experiences as a white, middle-class American woman have shaped a 'me' who has precious little in common with the 'me' produced by Sudesh Vaid's experiences as a woman of the postcolonial Indian middle classes – the concept of difference that nestles at the heart of poststructural (and hence postcolonial) theory operates quite differently. Hence, as we have seen, the experiential concept of difference relies on a near-continuum between experience and identity, with the category of experience constituting a transparent entity whose political authority is rarely questioned. The poststructuralist concept of difference, by contrast, turns on deconstructing the category woman/women itself, using the Saussurean insight that meaning is constructed through linguistic opposition, rather than through a relationship of direct and absolute reference.[90] The arbitrariness of the signifier-signified link thus shows that meaning is in fact constructed by position and relationship, that is, by relationships of difference or opposition, rather than in terms of a model (signified) and its referent (signifier). The Derridean or deconstructionist analysis of texts took this insight as its point of departure, exposing the traces of those opposing meanings that the text must deny in order to exist as such.

When this kind of analysis is transposed from the textual to the social realm, the coherence and stability of individual identities is called into question, as is the possibility of acquiring any certain knowledge about the world, for poststructuralist thought refuses any sharp distinctions between objective phenomena and the concepts that we use to apprehend them. Feminist sociologist Michèle Barrett has shrewdly observed that during the period of the linguistic turn (*c.* 1987–94), these two ways of conceptualizing difference were often mingled together in the same texts, despite the fact that experiential diversity's valorization of experience and of a politics of identity is not easily combined with the poststructuralist refusal of 'identity' as a coherent, stable, inner-directed sense of self.[91] Nonetheless, feminist scholars in the early 1990s, already at home with the destabilization of suffocatingly narrow accounts of gender identity via the notion of social construction, were often drawn by poststructuralists' proclamation of the death of the subject. Here bloomed alluring visions of radical indeterminacy, a 'dizzying choice of identities, the death of centres, and postmodernism's eschewal of any form of authority, including masculine authority'.[92] Such radical indeterminacy allowed some to imagine that sexual difference might no longer be a prison from which one could not escape, but rather 'an ethereal substance, an endless play of light and shadow in which the intellect could delight'.[93]

Yet the death of the subject actually posed acute problems for the kind of politically committed scholarship to which many feminist historians aspired, a scholarship that was organized around the very real problems of flesh-and-blood beings for whom the painful limitations of gender were not to be escaped so lightly. Historians of women and gender have thus begun to ask themselves whether feminism among historians constitutes more of a politics than a theory – and if it is indeed a theory, then what kind of theory is it? There are, after all, some very real problems with the transportation of methodologies from one disciplinary context (literature) to another (history). Caught between two equally problematic ways of conceptualizing difference, historians of women and gender have had to pause and consider the material constraints that the practice of history offers to a structure of thought (poststructuralism) that was developed in a different discipline and out of very different kinds of textual sources. Hence, if the experiential view of diversity is constantly bedevilled by the fact that individual experience is in fact a very partial and limited guide to grasping the totality of social relations, let alone any vision of 'truth', the poststructuralist vision is rife with problems of its own, notably the fact that the textualization of social relations – their rendering as mere 'sites of difference' – tends to obscure the fact that these relations (of gender, race or class) are also relations of power.[94] For historians of women and gender, this is not a minor point. For as Carolyn Steedman long ago pointed out, 'the written history of women, prompted by no matter what feminist theory, cannot do the work that the feminist aesthetic has attempted to accomplish in literary studies: of writing polyvalency and fragmentation [of the feminine subject] as resistance and critique of an existing patriarchal order'.[95]

Endnotes

1 Frances Gouda and Julia Clancy-Smith (eds), *Domesticating the Empire. Race, Gender and Family Life in French and Dutch Colonialism* (Charlottesville, VA, 1998), 1.

2 Gouda and Smith, *Domesticating the Empire*, 2. Colonial studies is the fruit of interdisciplinary encounters among anthropologists, historians, literary critics and scholars from the Subaltern Studies school, itself an interdisciplinary enterprise founded in the early 1980s on the critique of western pretensions to 'know' the colonized.

3 For an excellent example of recent work in this vein, see Padma Anagol, 'The Emergence of the Female Criminal in India: Infanticide and Survival Under the Raj', *History Workshop*, 53 (2002), 73–93.

4 The course of events in Africa was rather different, for after very bright beginnings, in which Europeans, Africans and, eventually, Americans collaborated in the production of 'decolonized' histories (often based on Marxist social and economic history, but with an especially strong input from anthropology and oral history, cf. the work of Jan Vansina), economic constraints and political upheaval in the 1980s combined to drive history from a number of African universities altogether. As the IMF called in its loans to African states in the mid-1980s, funding for history and the humanities dried up, and states consecrated what money was left to the development of scientific and technological fields. Dictatorships merely 'added to the woes of academia', as tyrants like Mobutu drove historians into exile. By the end of the decade, university campuses, which were periodically subjected to terror, plunder and violence (at least 20 students were murdered at Lubumbashi by elite troops one night in 1990), had practically 'ceased to exist'. Jan Vansina, *Living with Africa* (Madison, WI, 1994), quoted in Peter Lambert, 'The Professionalization and Institutionalization of History', in Stefan Berger, Heiko Feldner and Kevin Passmore (eds), *Writing History: Theory and Practice* (London, 2003), 55. See also Nancy Hunt, 'Introduction', in Nancy Hunt (ed.), *Gendered Colonialisms* (Oxford, 1998). Vibrant schools of social and economic history at Ibadan and Dar es Salaam (to name but two of the most widely renowned) were thus destroyed not by internal crises but rather by the external force of politics. Reconstruction across the 1990s was a hesitant, painful and uncertain process in Africa, as historians continued to find themselves caught between rejection and emulation of European and North American historiography in an atmosphere where such historiography has been tarred by the brush of 'western corruption'. Lambert, 'Professionalization', 55.

5 Dipesh Chakrabarty, 'A Small History of Subaltern Studies', in Henry Schwartz and Sangeeta Ray (eds), *A Companion to Postcolonial Studies* (Oxford, 2000), 468–9. Most Indian historians in this period were working in universities in India, the UK, the USA and Australia.

6 Bipan Chandra, *The Rise and Growth of Economic Nationalism in India: Economic Policies of Indian National Leadership, 1880–1905* (Delhi, 1969); A.R. Desai, *Social Background of Indian Nationalism* (Bombay, 1966, first published 1948); Anil Sneal, *The Emergence of Indian Nationalism: Competition and Collaboration in the Later Nineteenth Century* (Cambridge, 1968). Some of the journals in which these issues were discussed include *Economic and Political Weekly* and *Indian Economic and Social History Review*.

7 Chakrabarty, 'A Small History', 470. For examples of this Marxist history from below, see Gyanendra Pandy, *The Ascendancy of the Congress in Uttar Pradesh, 1926–1934: A Study in Imperfect Mobilisation* (Delhi, 1978); Kapil Kumar, *Peasants in Revolt: Tenants, Landlords, Congress and the Raj in Oudh, 1866–1922* (New Delhi, 1984); David Arnold, *The Congress in Tamilnadu: National Politics in South Asia, 1919–1937* (New Delhi, 1977); David Hardiman, *Peasant Nationalists of Gujarat: Kkeda District* (Delhi, 1981). All these scholars except Kumar would later join the Subaltern Studies collective.

8 Ranajit Guha, 'On Some Aspects of the Historiography of Colonial India', *Subaltern Studies I: Writings on South Asian History and Society* (Delhi, 1982), 3, 4 (original emphasis). As Chakrabarty points out, the word subaltern itself is drawn from the writings of Antonio Gramsci, which offered a common fund of ideas and concepts to both the Subaltern school and to the British 'history from below' of E.P. Thompson, Eric Hobsbawm and Christopher Hill.

9 Ranajit Guha, *Elementary Aspects of Peasant Insurgency in Colonial India* (Delhi, 1983). See Eric Hobsbawm, *Primitive Rebels: Studies in Archaic Forms of Social Movement in the 19th and 20th Centuries* (Manchester, 1978), for a classic statement of the pre-political peasant argument. The early Subaltern school's contention that the Indian peasantry was autonomous has come in for considerable criticism. See Jim Masselos, 'The Dis/Appearance of Subalterns: A Reading of a Decade of Subaltern Studies', *South Asia* 15:1 (1992), 105–25, who argues that the linguistic turn was in fact a desperate bid for an alternative tool of understanding where none had existed previously. Even Partha Chatterjee casts doubt on the autonomy of peasantry (at least implicitly) when he states that Subaltern Studies can never be more than 'oppositional history'.

10 The decision to take the discursive turn or not divided the Subaltern school, and social historians of India more broadly, after 1985. For a perceptive critique of some of the epistemological problems with the extreme poststructuralism of colonial and postcolonial studies, see Sumit Sarkar, 'Orientalism Revisited: Saidian Frameworks in the Writing of Indian History', *Oxford Literary Review* 16 (1994), esp. 214, where he points out that if all attempts to reform Indian society are to be 'condemned as instances of surrender to Western values, we are really back to the crudest

and most obscurantist forms of nationalism'. See also Sumit Sarkar, *Writing Social History* (Delhi, 1997). Sarkar was a founding member of the Subaltern Studies collective and participated actively until 1992, when his name disappeared from the masthead.

11 Edward Said, *Orientalism* (New York, 1978).

12 Gayatri Chakravorty Spivak, too, defined Said's *Orientalism* as 'the foundational text in our discipline'. Homi Bhaba and Gayatri Spivak, cited in Maneesha Lal, 'Sexe, genre et l'historiographie féministe contemporaine: l'exemple de l'Inde coloniale', *Cahiers de genre* 34 (2003), 152. See also Ranajit Guha and Gayatri Chakravorty Spivak (eds), *Selected Subaltern Studies* (New York, 1988).

13 Gayatri Chakravorty Spivak, 'Deconstructing Colonial History', *Subaltern Studies*, IV (1985). She developed this critique more fully in her famous 1988 article, 'Can the Subaltern Speak?', which criticized the Subalterns for their failure to problematize the idea of the subject. (Not surprisingly, no one in the collective was writing as if he had the least doubt about the agency or subjecthood of his peasant rebels, at least not in 1985.) Gayatri Chakravorty Spivak, 'Can the Subaltern Speak?', in Cary Nelson and Lawrence Grossberg (eds), *Marxism and the Interpretation of Culture* (Urbana, IL, 1988.) 'Even today, there is no sense of the Subaltern School taking on board the criticism regarding the lack of gender and women in their works,' mourned Padma Anagol in a private communication with the author (March 2004). 'There is plenty of tokenism though ...'. On the Subaltern school's failure to take such criticism into account, see Barbara Ramusack, 'From Symbol to Diversity: The Historical Literature on Women in India', *South Asia Research*, 10:2 (November 1990), 139–57, esp. 147–8.

14 After the Subaltern school began taking the linguistic turn, Spivak joined the collective for a brief period. Another stinging critique of the Subaltern school's lack of attention to questions of gender came from the pen of Rosalind O'Hanlon in her important article, 'Recovering the Subject: Subaltern Studies and Histories of Resistance in Colonial South Asia', *Modern Asian Studies*, 22:1 (1988), 189–224.

15 Kumkum Sangari and Sudesh Vaid, *Recasting Indian Women. Essays in Colonial History* (New Delhi, 1989), Introduction. See also Radha Kumar, *The History of Doing: An Illustrated Account of Movements for Women's Rights and Feminism in India, 1800–1990* (London, 1993); J. Krishnamurty (ed.), *Women in Colonial India: Essays on Survival, Work and the State* (Delhi, 1989); and Ursula Sharma, *Women, Work and Property in North-West India* (London, 1980). Two useful surveys of the literature in Indian women's and gender history are Aparna Basu, 'Women's History in India: An Historiographical Survey', in Karen Offen, Ruth R. Pierson and Jane Rendall (eds), *Writing Women's History: International Perspectives* (Bloomington, IN, 1991) 181–209; and Barbara Ramusack, 'From Symbol to Diversity'.

16 See Nirmala Banerjee, 'Working Women in Colonial Bengal: Modernisation and Marginalization', and Lata Mani, 'Contentious Traditions: The Debate on *Sati* in Colonial India', in Sangari and Vaid, *Recasting Indian Women,* 269–301, 88–123. The term 'invention of tradition' is drawn from Eric Hobsbawm and Terence Ranger's now classic edited collection, *The Invention of Tradition* (Cambridge, 1983).

17 On possible convergences between European and indigenous understandings of the colonial relationship see Rosalind O'Hanlon and David Washbrook, 'Histories in Transition: Approaches to the Study of Colonialism and Culture in India', *History Workshop Journal* (Autumn 1991), 110–27.

18 As we have seen, not all work on gender and imperialism has unfolded within the deconstructionist embrace, and historians like Padma Anagol continue to do a more classic kind of culturally informed social and economic history that cannot really be characterized as postcolonial or poststructuralist. Padma Anagol, 'Emergence of the Female Criminal' and 'The Age of Consent Act [1891] Reconsidered: Women's Perspectives and Participation in the Child-Marriage Controversy in India', *South Asia Research*, 12:2 (November 1992), 100–18.

19 Hence, in 1869, John Stuart Mill wrote that 'the surest test and most correct measure of the civilization of a people or an age' is its 'elevation or debasement' of women. John Stuart Mill, *On Liberty, with the Subjection of Women and Chapters on Socialism* (Cambridge, 1989), 138. Here, Mill was merely giving voice to a widespread *énoncé collectif* regarding the superiority of European gender relations. As we will see, this article of faith provided the colonizing powers with a platform from which to impose western understandings of women as weaker than men and essentially destined for maternity, and to criticize the widespread employment of women in agriculture and commerce.

20 By 'historicism', Said means historical forms of knowledge. Edward Said, 'Orientalism Reconsidered', in Frances Barker *et al.* (eds), *Europe and its Others*, 2 vols (Colchester, 1985), vol. I, p 22. See also Said, *Orientalism*.

21 The Subaltern Studies school, which came together in 1982, rapidly took up Said's point and devoted much of its firepower to denouncing the empty explanatory pretensions of western historiography on postcolonial terrain. See Guha and Spivak, *Selected Subaltern Studies*.

22 I draw the term 'epistemological annihilation' from Billie Melman, 'Under the Western Historian's Eyes: Eileen Power and the Early Feminist Encounter with Colonialism', *History Workshop Journal 42* (1996), 150.

23 Gyan Prakash, 'Writing Post-Orientalist Histories of the Third World: Perspectives from Indian Historiography', *Comparative Studies in Society and History*, 32:2 (April 1990), 384, quoted in O'Hanlon and Washbrook, 'Colonialism and Culture', 115.

24 O'Hanlon and Washbrook, 'Colonialism and Culture', 115.

25 O'Hanlon and Washbrook, 'Colonialism and Culture', 115.

26 In this realm, Said's work shows the influence of Michel Foucault, in particular, his reflections on the connections between power and knowledge in colonial governance, and the importance of familial metaphors in rendering European social control 'recognizable, habitable, intelligible, and natural'. Terence Hawkes, *Shakespeare's Talking Animals: Language and Drama in Society* (London, 1973), 212, quoted in Gouda and Clancy-Smith, *Domesticating the Empire,* 10.

27 Billie Melman, 'Under the Western Historian's Eyes', 149. See also Billie Melman, *Women's Orients. Englishwomen and the Middle East, 1718–1918* (Ann Arbor, MI, 1995).

28 Chandra Talpade Mohanty, 'Under Western Eyes: Feminist Scholarship and Colonial Discourses', reprinted in Chandra Talpade Mohanty, *Feminism Without Borders. Decolonizing Theory, Practicing Solidarity* (Durham, NC, 2003), 17–42, 19.

29 Mohanty, *Feminism Without Borders*, 22.

30 For an astute analysis of the poststructuralist critique of humanism, see Michèle Barrett, 'The Concept of Difference', in Michèle Barrett (ed.), *Imagination in Theory. Essays on Writing and Culture* (London, 1999), 111–23.

31 Valerie Amos and Pratibha Parmar, 'Challenging Imperial Feminism', in *Feminist Review*, 17 (1984), 7. For a historical elaboration of this point in the context of British and Indian history, see Antoinette Burton, *The Burdens of History* (Chapel Hill, NC, 1994).

32 Mohanty, 'Under Western Eyes', 40 (my emphasis).

33 Mohanty, 'Under Western Eyes', 40.

34 Mohanty, 'Under Western Eyes', 40.

35 Mohanty, 'Under Western Eyes', 41.

36 Mohanty, 'Under Western Eyes', 42. There is an implicit critique of Marxist politics that winds throughout the article and finally shows its face in the last sentence, when Mohanty remarks of this couple 'self-presentation-representation' (of the non-western other): 'It is time to move beyond the Marx who found it possible to say: they cannot represent themselves; they must be represented.' Mohanty, 'Under Western Eyes', 42.

37 Mohanty, 'Under Western Eyes', 41–2. Mohanty concludes, therefore that 'it is not the center that determines the periphery but the periphery that, in its boundedness, determines the center'. Mohanty, 'Under Western Eyes', 42. Gayatri Spivak, too, has been highly critical of western feminists' latent ethnocentrism.

38 Robert Young, *White Mythologies. Writing History and the West* (New York, 1990), esp. 167: 'Nevertheless, the paradox of Spivak's own work remains: it seems as if the heterogeneity of the Third World woman can only be achieved through a certain homogenization of the First.' The term 'latent enthocentrism' comes from Mohanty, 'Under Western Eyes', 42.

39 Mrinalini Sinha, *Colonial Masculinity. The 'manly Englishman' and the 'effeminate Bengali' in the Late Nineteenth Century* (New Delhi, 1997), 13 (1st edn, Manchester, 1995).
40 Sinha, *Colonial Masculinity*, Introduction.
41 Sinha, *Colonial Masculinity*, 1.
42 Sinha, *Colonial Masculinity*, 1.
43 Sinha, *Colonial Masculinity*, 1. Here, Sinha follows Spivak and Bhabha in their shared contention that imperialism was not just a territorial and economic project, 'but inevitably also a subject-constituting project'. Young, *White Mythologies*, 159.
44 Sinha, *Colonial Masculinity*, 1–2.
45 Lord Macaulay, 'Minute on Education', 2 February 1835, quoted in Sinha, *Colonial Masculinity*, 4.
46 Sinha, *Colonial Masculinity*, 4.
47 Sinha notes that Bengalis made up a large proportion of India's educated middle class.
48 Sinha notes in passing that Bengali efforts to hang on to their place in the colonial public service were all the more determined as their global economic position was declining sharply over the second half of the nineteenth century. Sinha, *Colonial Masculinity*, 5.
49 Thomas Babington Macaulay, quoted in Sinha, *Colonial Masculinity*, 15–16. The passage concludes in the same vein: 'Courage, independence, veracity are qualities to which his constitution and his situation are equally unfavourable'.
50 Sinha, *Colonial Masculinity*, 17.
51 Sinha, *Colonial Masculinity*, 21.
52 Native volunteering applied only to the educated elites in India, who, after 1857, were slowly developing ideas of nationalist resistance to colonial rule.
53 Sinha, *Colonial Masculinity*, 87.
54 Sinha, *Colonial Masculinity*, 91. Sinha attributes this point to Tanika Sarkar, 'The Hindu Wife and the Hindu Nation: Domesticity and Nationalism in Nineteenth-Century Bengal', *Studies in History*, 8:2 (1992), 213–35.
55 Quoted in Sinha, *Colonial Masculinity*, 45.
56 Quoted in Sinha, *Colonial Masculinity*, 51.
57 Quoted in Sinha, *Colonial Masculinity*, 58.
58 Sinha, *Colonial Masculinity*, 59.
59 Sinha, *Colonial Masculinity*, 59.
60 Sinha, *Colonial Masculinity*, 153.
61 On the crisis of British masculinity at the end of the nineteenth century, see Judith R. Walkowitz, *City of Dreadful Delight: Narratives of Sexual Danger in Late Victorian London* (Chicago, IL, 1992); and John Tosh, 'What Should Historians Do with Masculinity? Reflections on Nineteenth-Century Britain', *History Workshop Journal*, 38, (1994), 179–202.

62 *The Times* correspondent W.W. Hunter and Sir George Birdwood (a retired Anglo-Indian official), both quoted in Sinha, *Colonial Masculinity*, 154–5.
63 Sinha, *Colonial Masculinity*, 181.
64 Sinha, *Colonial Masculinity*, 182.
65 Sinha, *Colonial Masculinity*, 182.
66 Padma Anagol, private correspondence with the author, March 2004. This is a summary of the arguments in the final chapter of Anagol's *The Emergence of Feminism in India, 1850–1920 (London, 2006)*. Anagol's case study is based on Maharashtra rather than Bengal, but she doubts very much that Bengali women remained silent on the subject.
67 Anagol, private correspondence with the author.
68 Anagol, private correspondence with the author.
69 Sinha, *Colonial Masculinity*, 13.
70 Here I am paraphrasing Susan Pedersen, whose superb article, 'National Bodies, Unspeakable Acts: The Sexual Politics of Colonial Policy-Making', *Journal of Modern History*, 63 (December 1991), 647–80, offers an excellent example of such fine-tuned situating of actors and discourses in very precisely specified political and economic contexts.
71 Gouda and Clancy-Smith (eds), *Domesticating the Empire*, 4. The authors suggest, moreover, that the Subaltern school's important critique of British imperialism may, paradoxically, have reinforced the 'paradigmatic stature of British colonialism rather than dismantling it'.
72 Lora Wildenthal, *German Women for Empire, 1884–1945* (Durham, NC, 2001), 2.
73 Wildenthal, *German Women*, 13.
74 She had, since March 1885, been fascinated by Carl Peters' reports from his first expedition, which were published in the Berlin daily, *Tägliche Rundschau*, and soon after (May 1886) joined the newly formed Evangelical Missionary Society for East Africa, where she sought to make secular nursing, rather than missionizing, the top priority. She ultimately succeeded in detaching nursing from evangelizing only by founding her own society, the German-National Women's League, in October 1886, which League ultimately sent Bülow to Zanzibar in April 1887. Before leaving Germany, Bülow had already observed that the ideology of feminine self-sacrifice that shrouded women's nursing was little more than a threadbare justification for working nurses to the point of exhaustion and paying them pitiful wages for the privilege of engaging in this maternal 'labour of love'. She therefore militated for better wages, shorter working hours and less physically taxing work for nurses, in the hopes that nursing might be transformed from debilitating drudgery to a meaningful form of patriotism, as well as an

attractive career option for middle-class women. But nursing would not see much improvement in conditions or pay before the early twentieth century.

75 Wildenthal, *German Women*, 3.

76 Wildenthal, *German Women*, 3–4.

77 On this point, see Margaret Strobel, *European Women and the Second British Empire* (Bloomington, IN, 1991), esp. 1–15; Ann Stoler, 'Carnal Knowledge and Imperial Power: Gender, Race and Morality in Colonial Asia', in Micaela di Leonardo (ed.), *Gender at the Crossroads of Knowledge: Feminist Anthropology in the Postmodern Era* (Berkeley, CA, 1991), 51–101; and Kumari Jayawardena, *The White Woman's Other Burden: Western Women and South Asia During British Rule* (New York, 1995).

78 Wildenthal, *German Women*, 82–3.

79 Wildenthal, *German Women*, 83. Wildenthal explains earlier in the text that liberal nationalists were often quite critical of the materialist and capitalist values that suffused the rapidly industrializing society back home, and saw in the colonies the opportunity to build an idealized agrarian community within which a 'truly German' set of cultural values might find expression.

80 Wildenthal, *German Women*, 4, 109.

81 Wildenthal, *German Women*, 84.

82 Moreover, the bans apparently had no impact whatsoever on race-mixing outside of marriage.

83 Wildenthal, *German Women*, 5.

84 Wildenthal, *German Women*, 152.

85 Wildenthal, *German Women*, 167.

86 Grete Ziemann, *Mola Koko! Grüsse aus Kamerun. Tagebuchblätter* (Berlin, 1907), 178, quoted in Wildenthal, *German Women*, 155 (original emphasis). Ziemann had spent several years in Cameroon in the early twentieth century, where she kept house for her brother, a colonial doctor and an advocate of racial purity and female settlement in the colonies.

87 Wildenthal, *German Women*, 10.

88 Wildenthal, *German Women*, 11.

89 Pedersen, 'National Bodies', 677.

90 See Denise Riley, *Am I that Name? Feminism and the Category of Women in History* (Minneapolis, MI, 1988) for a particularly stimulating discussion of these issues.

91 Barrett, 'The Concept of Difference'.

92 Carolyn Steedman, 'La Théorie qui n'en est pas une, or, why Clio doesn't care', *History and Theory* (1992), 34.

93 Lyndal Roper, *Oedipus and the Devil: Witchcraft, Sexuality and Religion in Early Modern Europe* (London, 1994), 14–15.

94 And indeed, Foucault, and poststructuralists more generally, have been widely faulted for their failure to theorize resistance.

95 Steedman, 'La Théorie qui n'en est pas une', 34.

9

From separate spheres to the public sphere: gender and the sexual politics of citizenship

Near the end of the 1980s, one very fruitful means of thinking about gender in relation to modern politics took shape alongside the poststructuralist solution. It took shape over the course of some very heated, but nonetheless productive debates with Jurgen Habermas over the gendering of public and private spheres across the passage from absolutism to the earliest forms of the modern state in Europe.[1] Habermas's basic idea, as expressed in his widely read (or at least widely cited) tome, *The Structural Transformation of the Public Sphere* (1962), is that a new kind of public space, which he calls the bourgeois public sphere (and which identified itself by the more neutral and all-embracing term 'civil society'), emerged in Europe over the course of the seventeenth and eighteenth centuries. In Habermas's telling, this third sphere of public citizen discourse mediated between the home and the state, constituting an arena in which individual citizens could meet on a terrain of equality in order to discuss rationally matters of public concern. The construction of a bourgeois public sphere thus rested on two conditions: first, all differences of class and status were to be left outside the door in this arena of free public discourse (though let it be noted that one had to have a certain independence of means in order to qualify for admission at all); and, second, all private interests had to be left outside that same door, in order to guarantee the disinterested, truly public nature of the discussions held therein. As a kind of mediator between state and society, the bourgeois public sphere constituted a public yet extra-political (or at least extra-state) plane from which state policies could be evaluated – criticized, even – and proposals for reform could be launched in the name of the common good. The bourgeois public was thus meant to constitute a counterweight to the absolutist state, a public arena whose legitimacy stemmed from its claim to represent public opinion and the common interest.

In an era when the utopian dream of social renovation through Marxist revolution has been definitively unmasked in the face of the dystopian reality of authoritarian communist states that ruled in the name of the people, rather than being ruled by the people, the importance of Habermas's dis tinction between state apparatuses and public arenas of citizen discourse and association is obvious. For such a distinction reminds us that subjecting the economy to the control of the Marxist state is *not* the same thing as placing control of the economy in the hands of the socialist citizenry (pace Marx); nor could it ever be.[2] But for feminist theorists who seized upon Habermas's theory as a tool for explaining women's collective fate in the passage from early modern to modern society in Europe, the importance of his theory lay elsewhere. For the bourgeois public that Habermas gives us is clearly an essential constituent in the construction of modern democracy. And while he does not dwell on the point, it is also, and no less clearly, a space of exclusively male interaction and participation.

This crucial arena of open debate, whose existence and function was so critical to the founding of modern democracy, was thus closed to women from the outset. Indeed, feminist scholars like Carole Pateman and Joan Landes find in the homosociality of the bourgeois public one of its definitional features, for the exclusion of women was the foundational gesture that created civil society's all-embracing brotherhood. Hence, the bourgeois and aristocratic men who met in this space of public discourse established equality among themselves by minimizing the political significance of those social differences that divided them. And this, in turn, seems to have entailed exaggerating the significance of gender difference; transforming women, marked by mere differences of sex, into 'the opposite sex', beings whose particular, feminine natures condemned them to a purely private and domestic existence, far from the newly created realm of public and political discussion.[3]

Now Habermas's bourgeois public was clearly based on exclusions other than those of gender. Indeed, as Evelyn Brooks Higginbotham and Geoff Eley remind us, *The Structural Transformation of the Public Sphere* idealizes a bourgeois public that, for all its rhetoric, was deeply marked by differences of class, race and status. Nonetheless, the most systematic exclusion practised by the 'practitioners' of civil society was that of women, for their exclusion was not merely a contingent one (the dependent peasant or artisan could always hope to enrich himself and thereby gain the necessary economic independence to participate); it was constitutive of the bourgeois public itself. Hence, 'the identity-building in which the practitioners of civil society engaged was based more self-consciously on gender than on "class",' writes Isabel Hull.

> The fiction of natural universals (such as gender) seemed a logical extension of natural law and thus could both dissolve the old social status groups and ground the new in a single, efficient stroke. Gender was therefore a powerful tool in the self-creation made necessary by and contingent on the larger moral-political endeavour of creating civil society.[4]

Whatever the various alibis that were offered at the time for women's exclusion – they're too hot-headed to engage in rational discourse, they're too dependent to generate autonomous opinions, they're inherently private beings, too bound up with the fate of home and family to transcend those private interests in the name of a higher public good – it would seem that the deep structure of this particular, categorical exclusion sprang fundamentally from the logical demands of recasting male identity in universal terms that cut across the traditional divisions of class and status. As those traditional markers of difference among men lost their former legitimacy, there remained only one candidate for the job of negatively defining the new, universal man according to what he was not: the newly universalized 'woman', possessed of a singular identity that was now shared across her sex and rooted in the barest biological account of womanhood as motherhood (socially specific accounts of actual women being too messy for such reductive reasoning). Civil society thus created itself as a brotherhood of all men, and sealed the deal by rigorously excluding all who were not men.

Debate over the gendered origins of the bourgeois public sphere was first launched in the late 1980s, when feminist political theorists began to lock horns with Habermas over the silence with which he passes over the question of women's exclusion from this, the foundational institution of modern democracy. These initial debates often unfolded on the terrain of the French Revolution, which numerous feminist theorists revisited in their search for the primal moment of exclusion; that moment when, in Joan Landes' influential formulation, the republic was gendered masculine and the *ancien régime* society against which the nation had revolted was deemed decadent and feminine.[5] Once the fatal gendered identifications had been made, the road to women's exclusion from republican democracy was an inexorable one, for masculine notions of public virtue, defined against the 'effeminate' degeneracy of aristocratic culture, were built into the very concept of the republican public sphere. Women's exclusion from politics thus flowed logically from the gendered oppositions that underpinned revolutionary politics; indeed, their participation in political life would henceforth be associated in French republicanism with conservative backlash, the rule of the clerics, a return to aristocratic decadence.[6]

One important outcome of these discussions was that the term 'public sphere' began to be used with greater precision by feminist theorists. Hence, under the old public/private divide that had shaped so much feminist research in the early 1980s, 'public' designated all that was not private and domestic, and so conflated the economy with the state, as well as with the arena of public citizen discourse. Over the course of their debates with Habermas, feminist theorists began drawing finer distinctions around the concept of the public sphere, deploying the term in a more narrowly political sense. This lent the term far greater analytic precision than it had ever possessed within the simple public/domestic binary, as feminist historians now had language which allowed them to distinguish women's categorical exclusion from politics and the (bourgeois) public sphere from the far more class-specific patterns of working women's ongoing participation in economic life (commercial, farm and factory labour) – activities which, though every bit as public, were not directly embroiled in politics.

A second consequence of these discussions has been the elaboration of a powerful feminist critique of liberalism, for in feminist analyses of Habermas's argument, both liberalism and the sphere of public discourse that underpins it appear to be hopelessly and inevitably bound up with the exclusion of women. Yet it would seem that the 'inevitability' of women's exclusion is less clearly a product of liberalism's foundational premises than it is the outcome of the powerfully teleological bent that characterizes so much of the feminist literature about liberalism. Hence, scholars like Carol Pateman and Joan Landes begin with the early nineteenth-century consequence – women excluded from politics, and from the public sphere of citizen discourse – and then work their way backward through the liberal heritage (social contract theory and Enlightenment philosophy more generally) in search of the cause. The answers that both authors find, though differing in their details, suggest that liberalism cannot exist as such without instrumentalizing women and excluding them from public power. After all, was not liberalism's essential basis – civil society – founded on the categorical exclusion of women? The outcome-oriented shape of most feminist analysis of gender, civil society and modern liberal politics thus produces a profound pessimism regarding the possibility of ever reformulating liberalism so that it might embrace the human interests of women as well as those of men. As we shall see, one of Isabel Hull's great contributions to this literature is to avoid any such hard-and-fast conclusions by writing a history of gender, state and civil society whose ultimate, misogynist outcome is not written in stone from the very beginning, when the brothers first struck a deal to share power among themselves. This outcome is, rather, analysed as the product of the contingent, not wholly predictable triumph of one set of discourses, and one form of civil society, over other, competing visions in the passage from early modern absolutism to the modern state. *Sexuality, State and Civil Society in Germany, 1700–1815* is thus an important intervention in the feminist debate over liberalism and the public sphere. I would therefore like to devote the remainder of this chapter to a closer analysis of its subtle, complex and historically sensitive arguments.

Separate spheres revisited: gender and modernity in central Europe, 1500–1800

Unlike other works analysed thus far in this book, *Sexuality, State and Civil Society in Germany* is not a work of social or cultural history per se, but rather an extended reflection on the ways that changing understandings of male and female, public and private, state and civil society were expressed in the language of political philosophy as an 'engaged' science, that is, as a practical form of reflection intended to change the world in which these men lived. It is, in other words, a work of intellectual history, an analysis of the various philosophical and legal discourses that circulated around the problem of distinguishing the realm of state power from that of civil society; a problem that was worked out largely on the terrain of moral and sexual regulation. As Isabel Hull demonstrates, one vital strand in these discourses took the form of a narrative, popular across Enlightenment Europe, that recounted our collective passage from the primitive equality (including gender equality) of a pre-social 'state of nature' to a more civilized world in which the male–female distinction became one of polar opposition, even as it acquired deeper social and political significance.[7] As we shall see, the shape of this story – from state of nature to civilized society via some kind of social contract among its members – was meant to remind men of those natural rights and capacities they had all possessed in the state of nature, and so provide the philosophic basis on which those natural rights might be restored to them. But this same story also contains a powerful subtext in which male–female difference is recast as *the* fundamental relation of opposition structuring human society. Hence, the social contract story also provided the philosophical basis for the systematic exclusion of all women, no matter what their social standing, from politics and the public sphere of citizen discourse. Indeed, it was this particular and highly gendered form of the 'state of nature to civil society' narrative that would ultimately underpin the foundation of more liberal and democratic states in early nineteenth-century Germany, ensuring that at the very moment that (some) men acceded to civil and political rights (with the promise that some day such privileges would be extended to all men), women would be categorically barred from ever acceding to such citizenship rights.[8] In order to understand how women's exclusion from political life was built into the very fabric of liberal democracy in German-speaking central Europe, we must look more closely at the process whereby the gendered logic of civil society, first elaborated in the philosopher's imagination as he recreated our passage from state of nature to civil society, was spun out in more concrete prescriptive texts and practices across the early modern period.

'The great transformation from absolutism to the earliest form of the modern state redrafted the "sexual system",' states Isabel Hull in the opening pages of *Sexuality, State and Civil Society in Germany*.

> By sexual system I mean the patterned ways in which sexual behavior is shaped and given meaning through institutions. It is not surprising that the new configurations of state and social institutions in German-speaking

> central Europe in the late eighteenth and early nineteenth centuries should have profoundly affected the sexual system; however, because sexual behavior is at the heart of social reproduction and is symbolically central to social classification and the interpretation of order, the sexual system also shaped state and society as both of these changed.[9]

In these few and deceptively simple phrases, Isabel Hull announces her intention to rewrite the birth of the modern state in such a way as to mark the utter centrality of sex and gender to its form and function. She does this by organizing her investigation around a pair of key and difficult questions: how did a recognizably modern sexual system take shape in the passage from absolutism to the modern states of early nineteenth-century Germany? And what can this development tell us about the larger contexts of government and society, law and culture, within which it occurred? The outcome of Hull's investigation is a remarkably convincing retelling of the emergence of the modern state as the fruit of a struggle between absolutist states and an increasingly independent civil society. The latter is quite precisely defined as the 'ever widening new form of social life characteristic of the literate strata, especially males, both bourgeois and noble, in towns and administrative centers', manifested in the plethora of reading groups, patriotic societies and journals in which local patriots traded expertise and opinions with their fellows in other regions.[10] At stake in the contest between this nascent civil society and the absolutist state, Hull tells us, was nothing less than the power to define the society's sexual system. Over the 400-plus pages that follow, Hull recounts in fascinating (and, at times, prurient) detail the history of 'the changing public interest in sexual behavior at the moment of fundamental transformation toward the modern'.[11]

The overarching frame of Hull's argument is simple: in the passage from the absolutist to the modern state, which stretched across the seventeenth and eighteenth centuries and into the nineteenth century in central Europe, the state gradually ceded to a new entity – civil society – the responsibility for regulating the sexual system and policing sexual behaviour, via the redoubtable force of public opinion. In the process, Hull finds (contra Habermas) that something entirely new appeared – a private, domestic sphere – that had hitherto never existed as such. Hull thus reverses the causal order of Habermas's argument, making domestic privacy the *result*, rather than the origin of civil society's 'project' to recast the public sphere. Far from constituting the private springboard from which reformers posited civil society as a third, intermediary space, the private sphere, 'tailored to the presumed needs of the new male citizen was one of the most successful ideological creations of late Enlightened discourse. It was a product, not a cause, of the larger project to redraft the "public" according to the requirements of civil society'.[12]

State, civil society and the sexual system were thus bound up in a reciprocal and mutually constitutive relationship,

> for when the absolutist state reformed itself by relinquishing its monopoly over public life, encouraging and indeed presiding over the creation of a civil society independent of it, the state also purposely relinquished its previous, theoretically unlimited responsibility to police sexual behavior and granted to the active citizens of civil society, again theoretically, the right to define large sections of the sexual system [hitherto defined and upheld by the state] themselves.[13]

One crucial axis along which the distinction between civil society and the state was drawn thus ran along the boundary of regulating acceptable versus unacceptable sexual expression. In the gradual realization of the liberal vision of civil society, the civic and the sexual would be progressively reshaped through a relation in which each worked to constitute the other.

Why did the regulation of sexual behaviour so obsess early modern bureaucrats? What stake did they have in structuring private life along a single, heterosexual and reproductive line of desire? The thought of Michel Foucault resounds in the very questions themselves. And indeed, Isabel Hull embraces Foucault's understanding of sexuality as a product of the very socio-political structures whose evolution she examines. Her analysis is thus based on the Foucauldian insight that the sexual system and specific sexual behaviours have no intrinsic meaning in and of themselves; rather, such behaviours are endowed with specific meaning in relation to a given socio-political structure. In the early modern organization of sexual life, then, 'sex was completely embedded in the socioeconomic circumstances of people's lives; it was not a thing-in-itself, nor did it have value or meaning except in its different contexts'.[14]

Yet Hull nonetheless ultimately rejects the Foucauldian social disciplinary model, in which absolutist states simply impose their centralizing norms on local society, in favour of a more interdependent model of local/national interaction. For, as the tales she recounts in her earliest chapters so tellingly underscore, the German absolutist territorial states worked in much closer 'symbiosis' with their subjects than the social-disciplinary model allows, enforcing norms that were largely shared by the population: 'The central state did not impose alien or elite sexual views onto the populace,' observes Hull. Rather,

> there appears to have been a very broad basis of often unarticulated and unreflected agreement between officials and subjects on a whole range of sexual matters, especially rape; sodomy; bigamy; incest between close family members; female promiscuity; the assumption of a basic heterosexual drive; the assumption that sexual activity was not a human right, but a *ständisch*

> privilege (that is, dependent upon status, age, gender, condition); the assumption that a general sexual nature was and ought to be expressed somewhat differently by men and women, hence the expectation of male sexual aggression with its danger to society and the need to protect women from it; and the assumption that marriage was the best, most orderly place for sex to occur. Such broad agreement was doubtless the product of previous centuries of negotiation between church and parishioners and between governors and subjects...[15]

It is hardly the portrait of a ruthlessly disciplinary state imposing its norms willy-nilly on the locals. At the same time, however, interventions by state officials in local matters sexual did significantly undermine the greater harshness of customary law *vis-à-vis* women's sexual transgressions in the name of administrative efficiency. Hence, if local custom tended to treat individuals differently before the law, based on a complex calculation of sexual propriety that was constructed along the multiple axes of social class, marital status and gender, officials from the absolutist states worked to rationalize this multiplicity of unequal standings before the law in the direction of interchangeability, hence, of equality. For as Hull underscores, 'the old bureaucratic habit of regarding the objects of administration as interchangeable units... tended to produce fairly even-handed treatment of men and women, and, in a framework of rights, it encouraged a tendency toward equal rights'.[16] But the absolutist movement towards a more even-handed treatment of male and female sexual transgression would be reversed once again as the power to regulate norms of sexual propriety passed into the hands of civil society, at the turn of the nineteenth century. In order to see why this was so, we must look more closely at the several phases of Hull's argument.

In early modern Germany, Hull tells us, marriage exercised a kind of 'conceptual monopoly' over sexual expression, not only because it was the only framework for legitimate sexual activity, but also because illicit sex (out of wedlock, by force of violence, with members of the same sex, with prostitutes, or with members of different species) was understood and judged in relation to marriage – more specifically, in terms of the threat it posed to marriage. And yet marriage was by no means universal; rather, it was an estate that was restricted to those who could afford it. Marriage was thus 'the key sexual/social institution of the early modern period. It organized the basic units of economic production and ownership: the farmstead, the workshop, the estate. None of these could be operated by the labour of a single person.' He who would inherit a farm or workshop was thus obliged to seek a spouse who could share in the labour and in the oversight of servants. The inverse was also true, that is, only those with economic prospects – an inheritance, the promise of entrance into a guild, a tidy sum saved from his or her servant's wages – were in fact permitted to marry. The link between marriage and property, marriage and subsistence, thus meant that legitimate sex was a marker of social privilege. Servants and other dependants were relegated to the margins of this system, to lifelong celibacy, accompanied, perhaps, by episodic and furtive acts in the shadows. Far from constituting a basic human right or an expression of one's personhood, legitimate sex in early modern Germany was the province of those who were in a position to marry.

While the austere discipline imposed by such a system might suggest that early modern people's sex lives were rather impoverished by comparison to our own, Hull reminds us (following Foucault) that the present-day criteria used to evaluate such things, organized along the simple binary 'repression' versus 'free choice' is 'wholly inadequate' to comprehend a world that is so distant from ours, a world in which not only economy and society, but individual subjectivity, including sexual feelings and experience, were organized very differently. Hence, 'then as now, sexual desire and its possible modes of expression were fashioned within the contours of one's particular life condition. These conditions were material, mental, physical, social, and accidental, and they differed by *Stand*, wealth, gender, age and so on.' The Freudian conceptualization of sexual desire as a universal and unstoppable biological drive that rushes like a river through each of us, and is dammed up (or 'repressed') only at the cost of compromising our mental health, is thus put into perspective as a peculiarly modern understanding of sex that was not necessarily shared by our early modern ancestors. For as Hull is careful to insist, 'desire is not a "force" that must be constrained, but something that actually comes into being with a set of circumstances. It is an act of will, but it is never free.'[17] For the twenty-first-century heirs to a Freudian conception of self that is utterly bound up with the often subterranean movements of sexuality – the prime expression of self, the basis of individual identity – the world described in these words seems forbiddingly alien, which is precisely Hull's point: 'Absolutist traditional sexual ordering was not more or less disciplined or repressed, more or less erotic, more or less open to choice, more or less satisfying than our own; it was merely different.'[18]

By emphasizing the importance of marriage as a social relationship, a means of linking persons and families, as well as the only legitimate framework for sexual expression, Hull demonstrates that marriage was a 'colossally over-determined institution', one that carried an 'unsurpassed density of social meanings. Wealth, social standing, adulthood, independence, livelihood, communal responsibility, (for males) political representation, and sexual expression were all joined symbolically in this one estate, which meant that any one of these social meanings might stand in for any other'.[19] This 'unsurpassed density' of social meanings placed marriage and sexuality at the very heart of politics in early modern Germany. And there they would remain once the absolutist state had passed the regulatory baton on to civil society. For politics was understood to encompass 'fundamental social relations and duties which [late eighteenth-century reformers] interpreted in a moral framework'. This conviction granted sexual behaviour 'important political status and meaning' within the nascent liberal system.[20] Central to the reformist vision, then, was the promise to extend the privilege of marriage across the society, so that all men might enjoy that rulership of a household that constituted their indispensable apprenticeship to a life of political engagement in civil society and, eventually, politics itself: 'The coincidence in traditional society of legitimate sexual expression with independence and emancipation meant that civil society (which its eighteenth-century practitioners assumed would one day include almost all males as independent, emancipated, active citizens) considered sexual expression virtually a male right,' observes Hull. 'Sexual self-determination thus expanded to apply to more males exactly as, and because, self-determination generally had expanded.'[21] The sexual system thus constituted the terrain on which the enlightened practitioners of civil society would speculate about the social, biological and psychological causes of sexual behaviour. In so doing, they sought to work out what the proper balance of relations among state, law, social custom and the individual should, ideally, be.

But why did the absolutist states relinquish their regulatory control over sexual behaviour in the first place? In Hull's telling, it was in large measure because those states' enlightened bureaucrats (some of whom were themselves practitioners of civil society) were ultimately persuaded by civil society's critique of absolutist regulation as an inefficient and ineffectual system. Hence, in mid-eighteenth-century Germany, none doubted that absolutist sexual regulation was a sorry failure. For despite the web of laws and codes erected to enforce sexual propriety, immodesty and perversion still abounded. Moreover, argued the practitioners of civil society, the absolutist solution – imposing from the outside a single, centralized set of norms – was simply not adequate to the task of regulating a mass of sexual behaviours that were often inextricably wound into the texture of local social relations – a task that one Swiss pastor had likened to the disagreeable (and clearly futile) task of supervising a 'sieve of fleas'.[22] Enlightened bureaucrats thus listened attentively when the practitioners of civil society pointed out that it would be far more efficient, and more in keeping with the dignity of man, to turn such regulation over to civil society itself. The practitioners of civil society thus urged the state to rely on the capacity of its subjects (recast here as citizens) to police themselves and their dependants according to a set of duly internalized norms, rather than continuing to impose sexual propriety from without, as if the beneficiaries of absolutist state tutelage were mere children rather than fully autonomous adults, capable of moral self-regulation.

It has perhaps not escaped your notice that the citizens whom the practitioners of civil society had in mind were adult men, householders responsible not only for their own moral welfare but for that of their wives, servants and children as well.

For if the practitioners of civil society expressed their reformist vision in terms of abstract individuals, their understanding of the term 'individual' never in fact extended beyond the adult male householder; the only individual who, in theory, possessed the necessary economic and moral capital to sustain the political and policing duties that the practitioners of civil society sought to load onto his shoulders in his role as autonomous 'citizen'. Indeed, the link between masculinity and citizenship was overdetermined in the Enlightenment vision, for the practitioners of civil society promised that the male self-determination that lay at the heart of their system would not only deliver a more effective auto-regulation of sexual propriety, it would also unleash that wellspring of male energy that was grounded in men's sex drive. And this energy, newly released from the stifling confines of absolutist regulation, would, in turn, redound to the benefit of society, fuelling productivity and economic expansion.

Male sexual drive, properly managed and directed, was thus reconceived by Enlightenment thinkers as a source of general social dynamism (versus mere social disorder) that was, under absolutism, being choked off by the heavy hand of state regulation. Within this vision, an appropriately channelled sex drive became, moreover, the source of (male) independence, autonomy and freedom. Hence the growing interest in male sexual functioning and in its use as a metaphor for male power, individualism and creative productivity. Hence, too, the growing anxiety over the wastage and/or dispersal of such a precious social and economic resource through the antisocial practices of masturbation and infanticide, twin dangers that the practitioners of civil society reconceived as problems of uncontrolled male sexual drive. Indeed, Hull tells us, masturbation and infanticide constituted a pair of 'thought experiments' through which the practitioners of civil society explored the potential dangers of releasing male drives from the trammels of state regulation. In the case of masturbation, the problem was essentially one of unbounded and egoistic consumption, for masturbation was by definition 'a form of sex without society'; it created no social relations, but merely consumed the individual in the sybaritic pursuit of his own pleasure.[23] In the case of infanticide, the practitioners of civil society cast the problem as one of ruthless seduction and betrayal of lower-class girls by noblemen. Never mind that in actual fact infanticide was not a widespread practice in early modern Germany, and that most parents of illegitimate children were of the same social origins. By setting a scene in which numerous aristocratic Lotharios heartlessly used and then cast aside lower-class girls, leaving a trail of fatherless children in their wake, the practitioners of civil society imaginatively compounded gender inequality (male sexual freedom versus female dependence) with social inequality, thus casting the former in extreme terms, and so dramatizing the dangers that 'pure, unlimited (male) desire', unbounded by social obligation, posed for social order.[24] Both masturbation and infanticide thus constituted antisocial uses of a male sexual drive now freed from the weight of absolutist regulation. And in both cases, the solution proposed was marriage. For marriage was the institution that would harness sexual drive and transform it into love, thus 'preserving and ennobling' the sexual drive's useful qualities while protecting society from its destructive potential.[25]

But how had male sex drive come to be privileged over female as a source of creativity and autonomy in the first place? After all, Christian conceptions of female sexuality had traditionally emphasized the force of women's unbridled passion, equally a match for, if not, at times, overpowering male passion. How had Enlightenment thinkers managed to redefine male and female sexuality as utterly distinct in nature, recasting pleasure-seeking women as the sexually passive and submissive recipients of male drives? For Hull makes no bones about the negative consequences that such an extreme bifurcation of male and female sexual energy had for women in the passage to nineteenth-century modernity. Hence, she shows how the practitioners of civil society drew upon the same gendered understandings of male and female sexuality that governed traditional society: 'whereas early moderns were in awe of women's putative sexual *capacity* [seen as a passive entity, in that it accepts – often eagerly – but does not actually initiate sex], they nonetheless identified males with sexual *energy* and *desire*'.[26] In the context of 'traditional' (read: early modern) society, these constituted distinct, but roughly equivalent forces that met and were channelled within the confines of marriage: 'hence the strongly gender-specific traditional views of sexual honor: fidelity for women versus sexual potency for men'.[27] In Hull's reading, these traditional differentials were reined in by the strong social embeddedness of marriage, and of sexual behaviour in general in early modern society. 'But the practitioners of civil society were out to change the world, so to speak, at least conceptually', and in order to achieve this aim, they seized upon the gendered sexual assumptions of traditional society, sundered them from their social context, reified them – that is, they treated them as *natural* rather than *social* facts – then used these socially constructed 'facts' to define the essence of male and female in civil society.[28]

Now Enlightenment thinkers were increasingly concerned with sexual desire as a willed activity, Hull tells us, versus a mere animal-like drive. Male sexual drive was thus positively recast within a larger dynamic of sexual/political/economic energy – a kind of sexually driven male individualism that, moreover, received the all-important imprimatur of 'willed desire'. Within this same context, however, women's putatively passive sexual role, and the lack of identification of their gender with energy and (sexual) violence, worked subtly to undermine all notion of autonomous female desire, which latter force was increasingly cast into the shadows: 'As the expression of sexual desire came to be considered increasingly a male attribute, it became more and more socially dangerous for women to exhibit it'.[29] Sexual self-determination thus became the foundation of individual political self-determination, which was based on a desiring, potent, self-determining individual fit to assume the burdens of active citizenship, including the political representation of dependants. Women were accordingly redefined as the complementary opposite – beings who could not express their own will, whose public face consisted entirely of the collective identity/function 'wife and mother'. In the passage from savage state of nature to that of civil society, it was women who had tamed and channelled the force of male sexuality through their submissive and modest demeanour, or so the story went. Compelled by their economic dependence on men to transform the impermanence of sexual desire into a permanent domestic relation, women had developed their sexual modesty (a gift of nature, intended to counter the wild force of male sexual drive), and so tamed male desire and suited it for domesticity: 'By disguising their own, equal desire for sexual satisfaction, women subject men's sexual desire to social necessity,' writes Hull in a neat summary of the Enlightenment tale of progress from nature to civilized society.[30] Women are thus credited in the Enlightenment narrative (Rousseau, Kant, Hippel and others) with pressing men to take the first step towards civilization, that is, with containing male sexual energies within the domestic relation. But it was through no virtue of their own that women started the species down the long road of this civilizing process, for as Immanuel Kant hastened to remind his readers, feminine modesty is a 'gift' of nature in the service of culture: 'The purpose of nature in setting up femininity', wrote Kant, was 'the maintenance of the species, and... the culture of society and the refinement of the same through femininity'.[31] Whereas the state of nature to civil society narrative would have men eventually taking charge of channelling their sexual energies themselves, thanks to that exclusive male property that is reason, women would remain forever mired in their own thwarted natures, passive, modest, awaiting the impulse of male desire that would impart some direction to their own lives.

The passage from savage nature to civil society, as recounted by that society's practitioners, thus created civilized man as a self-realizing and active agent, endowed with the force of sexual energy, and his partner, civilized woman, strangely reduced from her natural state into a passive, submissive and domestic being. The institutional location of this dichotomy was, unsurprisingly, the family, recast by civil law as the sphere of male domination over women, a private realm that, for the first time, was placed beyond the reach of state intervention in the name of giving free rein to the energies of men. The consequences for women were, predictably, unhappy ones: 'Inside that sphere of privacy, the state, by refusing to extend there the equal protection of law, created more complete male domination than had been true under late Enlightened absolutism,' concludes Hull.

> This negative act of creation, undertaken to achieve the conditions necessary for civil society, emancipated the man (husband) from subjection

> (to his father and to state scrutiny) at the same moment that it made him the subjugator of his wife. Her unfreedom created his freedom; his position as private dominator qualified him to participate in the wider, public sphere of equals, in civil society. The key relation that qualified a citizen was therefore a sexual relation of domination...[32]

There were, of course, dissenting voices among the enlightened reformers of state and civil society, Theodor Gottlieb von Hippel, for example. Hence, like Immanuel Kant (and, later, J.G. Fichte), Hippel believed that women were the 'natural motor' of civilization, because they made men moral by attaching them to marriage and domestic life. 'Like most other civil practitioners, Hippel therefore deemed marriage the key institution in the moral completion of citizens and the civil advancement of society.'[33] Yet Hippel did not reason from the 'putative nature of the sexual drive or gender to domestic arrangement'.[34] Rather, his experience as lawyer and administrator seems to have inclined him to view men and women as equal objects of a uniform system of law (remember administrative law's equalizing tendency, above, p. 154). Ascriptive characteristics, whether of status, gender or putative sexual biology, were thus 'largely irrelevant' from this standpoint. And this conviction undermined any 'easy deduction' of domestic power from sexual or gender stereotypes.[35] Hull suggests that Hippel's gender egalitarianism is the product of his having started his reasoning from the perspective of the state, rather than from that of civil society (in other words, of conventional morality), and that this was the 'main difference between him and his opponents [Kant, Fichte] on the issue of the civil equality of women'. Hence, 'civil society, not nature, had caused female subjection', and Hippel hoped that legal reform might reverse civil society's gender-inegalitarian dynamic.[36]

Hippel's remarkable freedom from conventional misogyny clearly owed to his statist perspective, in which relations between all subjects (women included) and the state are, ideally, direct and unmediated. Nonetheless, this 'statist' perspective allowed him to conceive of a 'differentiated society composed of incommensurate contributions by different kinds of people, all equally deserving the title and rights of the active citizen'.[37] But as Hull points out, Hippel was the exception; the views of his more conventional fellow, Fichte, were becoming the rule. Henceforth, views of liberal democracy would be inextricably bound up with the vision of political society as a congeries of identical (adult male) units, making identical, or at least commensurable, contributions to the larger society.

You are perhaps beginning to suspect that *Sexuality, State and Civil Society in Germany* is not an easy read. And indeed, this is a book that demands a great deal of the reader, most notably, a patient attentiveness across its 411 densely packed pages, if one is to extract the basic argument from a welter of often overwhelming detail. But the journey is well worth the effort it demands. For in the rather crowded field of books on the gendered origins of liberal democracy and its bourgeois public sphere, *Sexuality, State and Civil Society in Germany* alone manages to escape the teleological pull that has bedevilled feminist writing on women and the public sphere. Hence, the abundant literature on the gendered and distinctly misogynist origins of liberal democratic politics in the modern west has tended to take as its point of departure the very negative nineteenth-century result: women excluded categorically from liberal, democratic politics. From there, this literature works its way backward in time, beating the early modern underbrush in search of that negative outcome's determinants. Such a teleological rendering of the problem inevitably leads to the unsurprising conclusion that sexism is inherent in liberalism, and that women would therefore be better off abandoning the liberal project in favour of other, more woman-friendly political formations. Isabel Hull's dense intertextual reading of discourses allows her to avoid the relentless circularity that has too often characterized this literature, which reads of modern liberalism as if the exclusion of women from politics were its necessary and inevitable condition, the sole foundation on which a liberal polity could ever have been built. Indeed, Hull's intertextual method establishes in all its micro-variety the dense web of discourses that surrounded the questions of state and civil society, and male and female sexuality, in early modern and Enlightenment Germany. The reader is thus exposed to several possible routes to the modern democratic polity other than the deeply misogynist one that was ultimately taken. That proposed by Theodor von Hippel, for example. And this plurality of competing liberal discourses is important for those feminist scholars who seek to reformulate liberalism so that it embraces women's freedom and human interests as much as men's.[38] For by re-placing the gendered origins of liberal democracy in their discursive context, Hull suggests that the gendering of the public sphere, and of the liberal and democratic politics that sprang therefrom, were contingent developments rather than necessary and inevitable outcomes. She thus underscores the fragility of the associations that bound male sexuality to active citizenship in the vision that ultimately prevailed: 'the association of sexual maturity, sexual potency, solidity of character, citizenship, marriage and social stability formed a tightly wound tautology, in which each term flowed ineluctably into the other'.[39]

And yet the attentive reader might still be left wondering why it was that the misogynist vision ultimately prevailed. This question, alas, is left pending, for in an approach that privileges discursive analysis, words and arguments are too often shorn of their socio-political context. And the answer to why one discourse, one philosophical underpinning for a particular (misogynist) political arrangement won out over another does not lie in the force of its arguments, its appeal to sweet reason, but rather in the socio-political forces that arrayed themselves around and behind that discourse, redoubling its weight in the court of public opinion.[40]

Endnotes

1 I say 'alongside' because although these debates shared some features with poststructuralism, notably a tendency to focus exclusively on discourses, the form of analysis deployed was nonetheless the classic close reading typical of political philosophy, rather than the deconstructive reading of texts advocated by poststructuralists.

2 For this point, I am indebted to Nancy Fraser's lucid article, 'Rethinking the Public Sphere. A Contribution to the Critique of Actually Existing Democracy', in Nancy Fraser, *Justice Interruptus. Critical Reflections on the 'Postsocialist' Condition* (London, 1997), 69–98, esp. 69–70.

3 Carole Pateman, 'The Fraternal Social Contract', in Carol Pateman, *The Disorder of Women* (Stanford, CA, 1989), 33–57; Joan Landes, *Women and the Public Sphere in the Age of the French Revolution* (Ithaca, NY, 1988).

4 Isabel Hull, *Sexuality, State and Civil Society in Germany, 1700–1815* (Ithaca, NY, 1996), 225.

5 Landes, *Women and the Public Sphere.*

6 Landes, *Women and the Public Sphere*; see also Lynn Hunt, *The Family Romance of the French Revolution* (Berkeley, CA, 1992); Pateman, *Disorder of Women*; Dorinda Outram, *The Body and the French Revolution. Sex, Class and Political Culture* (New Haven, CT, 1989); Geneviève Fraisse, *La Raison des femmes* (Paris, 1992). See Joan W. Scott, *Only Paradoxes to Offer: French Feminists and the Rights of Man* (Cambridge, MA, 1996) for the working out of this argument across the nineteenth and early twentieth centuries. For a rather different take on women's exclusion from republican politics, see Harriet B. Applewhite and Darlene Gay Levy, *Women and Politics in the Age of the Democratic Revolution* (Ann Arbor, MI, 1990), which argues that Robespierre and his allies identified the increasingly active and well-organized 'Société des femmes révolutionnaires' with the sans-culottes, against whom they were preparing to move in the fall of 1793. Shutting down the Société and restricting women's participation in political assemblies was thus a prelude to the Jacobins' broader move against the sans-culottes.

7 The ur-text for this particular, gendered version of the state of nature to civil society tale is surely that of Jean-Jacques Rousseau, as recounted in his *Second Discourse on the Origins of Inequality*, *Social Contract,* and *Emile.* As Isabel Hull demonstrates, these texts were widely circulated in late eighteenth century Germany, and clearly exerted enormous influence over the shape that social contract theory took in German-speaking central Europe.

8 Alternative versions of the state of nature to civil society narrative had circulated in Europe since the mid-seventeenth century, notably Thomas

Hobbes' *Leviathan*, in which the social contract that moves humans out of the state of nature has no particularly negative consequences for women.

9 Hull, *Sexuality, State and Civil Society*, 1.
10 Hull, *Sexuality, State and Civil Society*, 3.
11 Hull, *Sexuality, State and Civil Society*, 6.
12 Hull, *Sexuality, State and Civil Society*, 207.
13 Hull, *Sexuality, State and Civil Society*, 1.
14 Hull, *Sexuality, State and Civil Society*, 44.
15 Hull, *Sexuality, State and Civil Society*, 55–6, 90.
16 Hull, *Sexuality, State and Civil Society*, 408. See also 56. Another article of faith in the social-disciplinary model, namely, that the absolutist state exercised its disciplinary and repressive powers with far greater weight against women, tumbles in the face of Hull's extensive research into the minute realities of state/local interaction in the key realm of sexual regulation.
17 Hull, *Sexuality, State and Civil Society*, 47.
18 Hull, *Sexuality, State and Civil Society*, 49. Compare this with Alain Corbin's account, in which male sex drive stands outside history, an unchanging, trans-historical force whose shape and content is perfectly recogizable over time. Alain Corbin, 'Le "sexe en deuil" et l'histoire des femmes au XIXe siècle', in Michelle Perrot (ed.), *Une histoire des femmes, est-elle possible?* (Marseille, 1984), 142–54.
19 Hull, *Sexuality, State and Civil Society*, 31.
20 Hull, *Sexuality, State and Civil Society*, 4.
21 Hull, *Sexuality, State and Civil Society*, 409.
22 Hull, *Sexuality, State and Civil Society*, 52.
23 Hull, *Sexuality, State and Civil Society*, 275.
24 Hull, *Sexuality, State and Civil Society*, 81, 284. Regarding the discrepancy between the actual reality of infanticide in Germany and the tales spun about it by civil society's practitioners, Hull shrewdly points out that this discrepancy 'shows again that public discussion of fashionable topics does not primarily aim at a painstaking analysis of actual practices, but serves to organize cultural preoccupations in an efficient and symbolically resonant manner.' Hull, *Sexuality, State and Civil Society*, 281.
25 Hull, *Sexuality, State and Civil Society*, 240.
26 Hull, *Sexuality, State and Civil Society*, 410 (original emphasis).
27 Hull, *Sexuality, State and Civil Society*, 410.
28 Hull, *Sexuality, State and Civil Society*, 410.
29 Hull, *Sexuality, State and Civil Society*, 253.
30 Hull, *Sexuality, State and Civil Society*, 304.
31 Immanuel Kant, *Anthropologie*, part, 2, 53, cited in Hull, *Sexuality, State and Civil Society*, 304–5.
32 Hull, *Sexuality, State and Civil Society*, 411.
33 Hull, *Sexuality, State and Civil Society*, 324.

34 Hull, *Sexuality, State and Civil Society*, 325.
35 Hull, *Sexuality, State and Civil Society*, 326.
36 Hull, *Sexuality, State and Civil Society*, 329.
37 Hull, *Sexuality, State and Civil Society*, 330–1.
38 For a particularly compelling example of this project, see Martha Nussbaum, *Sex and Social Justice* (Oxford, 1999).
39 Hull, *Sexuality, State and Civil Society*, 242.
40 For a social-historical argument that accomplishes on the ground of social history aspects of that which Isabel Hull explains through discursive analysis, see Clare Haru Crowston's excellent monograph, *Fabricating Women. The Seamstresses of Old Regime France, 1675–1791* (Durham, NC, 2001), which demonstrates how the rise of the absolutist state in France actually increased women's economic, social and legal opportunities.

10

Gender and history in a post-poststructuralist world

At the end of chapter 7, I suggested that, if the move towards a more discursive understanding of gender has allowed historians to demonstrate the omnipresence of gender, to expose 'the often silent and hidden operations of gender' that shape and define social organization and relations of power, it has nonetheless posed acutely the problem of explaining how gendered identities manage to change over time.[1] This problem is particularly evident in radically constructivist analyses, which disconnect the discursive and cultural aspects of identity from social experience and from relations of domination and inequality. The radical constructivist position is most famously associated with Judith Butler's *Gender Trouble*, in which the author argues that identities and differences are not the spontaneous outcome of a group's 'objective' location in social, political and economic hierarchies. Rather, such identities are discursively constructed by individuals who 'perform' those identities (including gender) through pre-existing cultural processes.[2] Butler elaborated her understanding of how it is that discursively constructed identities can change in a subsequent book, *Bodies that Matter* (1993), which argues that subjects, though discursively constructed, nonetheless possess critical capacities (which are also culturally constructed), and that these capacities allow them to engage in novel actions, to 'rewrite the script' and therefore to 'resignify' their own subject position.

By describing subjects as 'sites of resignification' in a discursive matrix, this particular account of subjectivity as performance of a culturally given script does allow for change in those scripts, and hence for some kind of agency on the part of subjects. It nonetheless retains Butler's radical separation of the cultural aspects of identity from those aspects of identity that are produced by social relations, including relations of political and economic inequality/domination. As feminist philosopher 'Nancy Fraser' has observed, this produces a vision of human subjectivity that 'does not theorize the relationship of embodied individuals, with their relatively enduring dispositions (habitus) to the dispersed subject positions they successively occupy. Nor does it theorize intersubjectivity, the relations to one another of such individuals'.[3] Butler's focus on individual performances and rescriptings of gender thus explores the cultural dimension of identity in isolation from those elements that are determined by the individual's social, economic and/or political position, while considering the intrasubjective, or internal, psychological processes of identity apart from intersubjective relations.

The account of change that Butler offers ('rewriting the script') can thus occur at the individual level only. As such, it is of limited use to historians who, in the aftermath of the linguistic turn continue to search for ways to draw upon the advantages that a discursive understanding of gender offers, without relinquishing the capacity to explain change.[4] One feminist historian of early modern Germany, Lyndal Roper, has proposed a rather different approach to this problem in her suggestion that historians look for some way to understand gender as both discursively constructed *and* as corporeal and psychic experience. Now Roper's turn towards body and psyche does not actually 'solve' the issue of reconciling discursive with social/historical approaches to the construction of subjects. Rather, she recasts the terms in which the question is posed by remapping the question of identity, culture, social experience and the discursive construction of subjects onto a somewhat differently configured analytic matrix, one in which psychoanalytic concepts of subjectivity and sexual identity (especially Lacanian but also Kleinian) play a key role. For Lacan, subjectivity and sexual identity are acquired simultaneously, through an unconscious process of differentiation, division and splitting that begins when the infant enters language. It is a process that is always in the making; it is never definitively accomplished or complete. And this means that subjectivity and sexual identity are unstable and shifting entities, that the coherent individual self is a work in progress that is constantly vulnerable to disruption by the unconscious.[5] The introduction of a more psychoanalytic understanding of subjectivity allows Roper to sidestep the issue of whether gender is purely discursive or purely social (a binary opposition whose terms Roper simply refuses) in favour of a more radical proposition: gendered subjectivities, which are both socially *and* discursively constructed, also contain aspects that are, in some sense, ahistorical, as they are linked to the deep and unchanging structures of the human psyche.

I would therefore like to close the 'post-poststructuralist' section of this book with a brief look at Lyndal Roper's work, focusing in particular on her *Oedipus and the Devil* (1994); a most suggestive set of essays that plays off many of the debates around poststructuralism without ever really becoming entangled in their philosophical snares. Rather, Roper hews closely to her historical object, and uses to great effect a broad range of theoretical insights in order to develop fruitful and imaginative approaches to the very new questions that she poses of her material. In so doing, she raises some searching questions about the capacity of gender, in its purely constructivist incarnation, to serve as a tool of historical analysis.

Subjectivity, sexual difference and psychoanalysis: towards a gendered history of body and identity in early modern Europe

> The challenge of the history of the body to discourse theory is that it confronts discursive creationism with the physical, a reality that is only in part a matter of words ... In this book, I want to argue against an excessive emphasis on the cultural creation of subjectivity, and to argue that witchcraft and exorcism, those most alien of early modern social phenomena, or courtship and ritual, those seemingly irreducibly collective early modern social events, cannot be understood without reference to their psychic dimension.[6]

With these challenging words Lyndal Roper opens her book, *Oedipus and the Devil*, a series of articles on witchcraft, religion and sexuality in early modern Germany that were written durng the period 1988–93. When read together, these essays offer a sustained meditation on the role of the irrational and the unconscious in history, on the importance of the body, and on the relation of these two to sexual difference. They do so through a series of case studies drawn from Reformation and Counter-Reformation Augsburg that involve motherhood, witchcraft, possession, masculinity and sexuality – 'all fields in which gender is at issue, and where the relation of psyche and the body are at stake'.[7] Roper thus proposes no less than a cultural history of that age-old conundrum – the mind–body conjunction, as it was experienced and understood by early modern Germans – but viewed from a startlingly new perspective, one in which gender is not simply an additional line of analysis, but rather lies at the heart of the matter. For as Roper points out, sexual difference, as physiological and psychological fact, and as social construction, is a central and constitutive aspect of human culture. Issues of sexual difference must therefore stand at the heart of cultural history.

Yet central as sexual difference is to conceiving of culture, Roper found that she could no longer simply apply the tools that she had acquired from feminist history to the study of early modern Europe.[8] For the more she meditated on her documents – transcripts from witchcraft trials (including interrogations, whose results were often arrived at through the 'scientific' application of torture), eyewitness accounts of exorcisms, complete with fearsome bodily distortions on the part of the victim, discipline ordinances that sought to impose new levels of bodily self-restraint on subjects – the more Roper came to believe that feminist history, as she and others had practised it, 'rested on a denial of the body'. Roper thus sees each of her essays as part of a larger project – 'often not fully articulated – to think out a different route towards understanding the body, culture and subjectivity'.[9]

Oedipus and the Devil was conceived and written during the period when the 'theory wars' associated with the cultural and linguistic turns in history were at their very height. As such, it represents a sustained and deeply reflective effort to come to grips with what purely discursive and cultural approaches can and cannot deliver to historical understanding. Though profoundly marked by social history's cultural turn, which seemed to offer a more refined set of tools for understanding such phenomena as witchcraft or religious experience, Roper was nonetheless frustrated by the limits of cultural analysis when confronted with such difficult facts as the apparent collaboration of women accused of witchcraft with those who persecuted them in the production of an intelligible narrative of their alleged crimes. How could the states of mind that allowed for such collaboration be explained without recourse to some kind of psychoanalytic explanation? By her own account, the nine essays gathered in her book 'document' Roper's own intellectual journey, 'away from the conviction that gender is a product of cultural and linguistic practice, towards the view that sexual difference has its own physiological and psychological reality, and that recognition of this must affect the way we write history.'[10]

Roper thus frames her methodological exploration in terms of her encounters with social history, cultural history and feminist history, and of her frustration at the inability of these three approaches (even when combined) to address satisfactorily central aspects of early modern social and cultural history: the shape of individual subjectivity, the place of the irrational in social life, the interconnection between the psychic and the somatic. Hence, in Roper's view, historians are too quick to bracket the very thing that demands explanation, namely the question of how social change affects individual psyche, claiming that the latter lies outside the historian's brief, that it is not accessible to historical analysis per se. It is understandable, concedes Roper, that historians should pause before a theory that makes universalist claims for its model of human psychological functioning, claims that seem utterly irreconcilable with the study of history.[11] But as Sally Alexander observed in her influential article, 'Women, Class and Sexual Differences in the 1830s and 1840s',

> the subjectivity of psychoanalysis does not... imply a universal human nature, it suggests that some forms of mental functioning – the unconscious, phantasy, memory, etc. – seem to be so. Subjectivity in this account is neither universal nor ahistorical. First structured through

> relations of absence and loss, pleasure and unpleasure, difference and division, these are simultaneous with the social naming and placing among kin, community, school, class which are always historically specific.

Alexander thus uses the Lacanian proposition that the acquisition of subjectivity and sexual identity occur as the infant enters language (and hence society) to assert that psychic and social process are in fact inextricably bound together.[12]

The claim that historical and psychoanalytic approaches are incompatible is, in this view, a false one, and historians should 'refuse this apparent dilemma' and focus instead on seeking to distinguish that which is historical about subjectivity, such as particular ways of conceptualizing the relationship of mind and body, from those psychic structures that seem more permanent, universal: 'the importance of fantasy, the unconscious, the centrality of parental figures to psychic life'.[13] Indeed, remarks Roper, using psychoanalytic theory to specify what is historical about subjectivity can reveal the historically constructed nature of even so fundamental-seeming a cognitive fact as our contemporary understanding of the mind/body relation:

> An engagement with pre-modern society, with its magical world-view and its belief in the demonic, with its assumption that emotions can cause harm in others or its conviction that sanctity can be seen and felt in the uncorrupted body of the saint itself, offers us a chance of rethinking our own habitual classifications of mental and corporeal.[14]

If the preoccupations expressed here seem to echo those of Caroline Bynum, reflecting an equal concern with questions of body and identity, the methodological solution proposed diverges sharply from the approach adopted in *Holy Feast and Holy Fast*. For if Roper retains a certain scholarly prudence before the universalist claims of psychoanalysis, she is nonetheless convinced that our only way into the study of subjectivities past entails taking seriously the explanatory claims of psychoanalysis, 'so that it provides a way of accounting for meaningful behaviour and individual subjectivity in particular historical circumstances'.[15]

Given her concern to grasp both the psychic and the corporeal as historical phenomena, it is not surprising that Roper should have begun her methodological search in a review of the work of Max Weber, Charles Taylor and, especially, Norbert Elias, for all three scholars strive to link psychoanalytic insight with a historically informed sociology. Hence, *The Protestant Ethic and the Spirit of Capitalism*, *The Sources of the Self* and *The Civilising Process* seek to explain how large-scale historical processes (the rise of capitalism, the Reformation, the development of the modern state) have altered individual self-understandings, and perhaps the very shape of subjectivity itself. The central agent in each story is the state (Elias) or a large social process like the rise of capitalism (Weber), and the drama unfolds around the power of this central agent (state, capitalism) to constrain individual drives in a modernizing movement whose ultimate outcome was the creation of rational individuals.

Yet Roper, who is interested in penetrating the secrets of individual subjectivity, ultimately finds these works unsatisfactory precisely because each offers a 'developmental' narrative of collective subjectivities, 'which turns individuals into mere exemplars of a narrative of collective historical progression'.[16] Moreover, (as Roper underscores) any account of subjectivity where the rational individual constitutes the end-product is at best a partial account, one that fails to address the role of the irrational in shaping individual and social life. The work of Michel Foucault, with its emphasis on the power of language and the role of discourse in constituting individual subjects, answers some of Roper's objections. For example, his analysis of discourses of prohibition shows how such discourses, which contain elements of the irrational and the suppressed, create their own compulsions and transgressive possibilities, suggesting new and delicious forms of perversion with each repressive ordinance.

Nonetheless, Foucault, like Elias and Weber before him, also offers a determinedly collective concept of subjectivity, in which collective rituals, performances, habits of work and sociability are simply 'inscribed' on the individual psyche.[17] This insistence on the collective nature of subjectivities past is further reinforced by the Foucauldian suspicion of psychoanalytic narratives as just one more regulatory discourse, disciplining the refractory force of human sexuality through that modern form of confession that is the talking cure. Early modern historians who have adopted Foucault's perspectives have thus embraced the conviction that the late nineteenth-century invention that is psychoanalysis can have nothing to say about a pre-Freudian world. And this is a real problem in a field where, Roper tells us, the 'otherness' of early modern Europeans is thought to reside precisely in their predilection for collective action, thinking, modes of being, in other words, in their *lack* of a sense of individual subjectivity. Hence, Steven Greenblatt has argued that psychoanalysis proposes a notion of the self that is 'simply foreign to Renaissance culture'; indeed, the very existence of psychoanalysis itself testifies to the unbridgeable gap of difference that separates us from early modern understandings of the self.[18]

There is a certain circularity in this proposition, for the point of departure – the proposition that psychoanalysis depends on a notion of the self which was only in the process of creation in the early modern period – determines the conclusion: we therefore cannot apply psychoanalytic concepts to people who conceived of the subject in a radically different fashion. As Roper forcefully argues, this position allows scholars to

> shunt off all that puzzles them about early modern society into the realm of the 'pre-modern' while using the very concept of the peculiarity of the early modern to deny the usefulness of psychic categories. As a result, early modern people can threaten to become dancing marionettes, tricked out in ruffs and codpieces, whose subjectivities can neither surprise nor unsettle.[19]

Foucault and Greenblatt thus reproduce that same binary division between early modern and modern that structures the 'how we became modern' narratives of Elias, Weber and Taylor. Indeed, early modern subjectivity, entirely submerged in the collective, becomes the absolute other against which the modern world of individuals defines itself: 'It is striking that it is the distinctive nature of early modern people to which historians point when ruling psychoanalysis out of court,' remarks Roper, 'so that what is modern is defined by a change in the notion of the self; a radical imputation of otherness which, however, is parasitic on our own determination to historicize subjectivity by providing a strong narrative of the birth of the self'.[20] And so Roper finally turns to Freud and his disciples, especially to the work of Melanie Klein, in hopes of finding (or forging) tools that will allow her to gain some sense of individual subjectivity in the past. Inextricably linked with this psychoanalytic investigation, Roper tells us, must be some kind of history of the body, for if we are ready (thanks to Elias) to accept the idea that culture shapes how we experience bodily events, we are far less comfortable with the idea that such bodily experiences might themselves influence culture and subjectivity.[21]

It is here, in her effort to explain how the physical 'flows back into the psychic', that Roper finds the tools of Freudian analysis potentially useful, for Freud was centrally concerned with understanding the interconnections between the psychic and the somatic.[22] By adopting a more psychoanalytic approach, Roper hopes to find a way past both the early modern field's aversion to investigating the individual subjectivities of early modern people and feminist historians' reticence about the body. For 'gender cannot be understood as the social acquisition of an unproblematic sexual identity,' concludes Roper. 'Sexual difference has a bodily dimension. Sexual identity can never be satisfactorily understood if we conceive it as a set of discourses about masculinity or femininity. Nor can the individual subject be adequately understood as a container of discourse – a conception which evacuates the subject of psychology'.[23] If the understanding of gender identity as the pure product of discourse can never capture the full, bodily dimensions of gendered subjectivity, perhaps an engagement with psychoanalytic theory can begin to unlock those doors.

Roper's ambition, then, is to use the tools of psychoanalysis in order to grasp the subjectivities of early modern women and men across the period of the Reformation, subjectivities that, in her words, are 'recognizable, evincing patterns with which we are familiar'.[24] Through a series of very precise investigations, based on specific kinds of archives that the cultural revolution of religious reform produced in abundance (witchcraft trials, ordinances of discipline), she seeks to illuminate such questions as: How did early modern understandings of the body shift in the context of struggles between a Catholic theology of the body as a vessel of divine (or diabolic) possession, and a Protestant theology that sundered the link between the physical and the spiritual?[25] How did the magical capacities associated with female bodies differ from those associated with male bodies? How did the dilemmas surrounding the psychic identity of womanhood express themselves in accusations of witchcraft? Gender and matters of sexual difference weave themselves through the fabric of the stories she tells, of the deep antagonisms among women that emerged in the trial of a lying-in maid accused by her (female) clients of harming their young infants through sorcery, or of the generational conflicts among men that expressed themselves in ordinances of discipline intended to control the drunken brawling of village youth. In each case, the dark side of subjectivity comes to the fore: the powerful enmities that can arise when a young mother, anxious about her child's fate and her own ability to nourish it, projects her anxieties onto the person of the older, post-menopausal lying-in maid trusted with its care, when the infant in question fails to thrive; or the political threat that the raw fighting energy of rowdy young men could present to a stable, patriarchal village order. On the one hand, such brute energy, properly channelled, provided the military force necessary to defend the city. But when young (and sometimes not so young) men went marauding through tavern and street, beating one another (and at times their own wives) within an inch of their lives, the village council was forced to intervene in order to control the disruptive impact of such excesses of virility. In the end, Roper concludes, 'sixteenth-century masculinity drew its psychic strength not from the dignity of the mean but from the rumbustious energy which such discipline was supposedly designed to check'.[26] The uncivilized wildness of 'manly' men was thus the product of civilized society's carefully structured rules.

Throughout the nine essays that make up *Oedipus and the Devil*, Roper strives to maintain a tension between certain universal aspects of human psychic process, evoked in her working assumption that early modern subjectivities are 'recognizable' to us, and attention to that which changes in time, namely the particular content with which the categories 'masculine' and 'feminine' are invested. She thus invites us to see gendered subjectivities as the product of a dialectic relationship between those more labile, socially constructed elements and some notion of an essential self that is located in the fact of having a sexed body. On the one hand, therefore, sexuality comprises elements that run deep and are difficult to change. At another level, we find that 'glittering profusion of sexual identities' that historians have discerned in discourse. In between the two, notes Roper, lies the realm of individual subjectivity, a meeting ground for the social and the psychic that lies at the core of each individual. In order to explore the realm of the psychic, however, historians need a theory of subjectivity that will allow them to account for the tenacious hold of sexual stereotypes (in the present or the past), while explaining the attraction of 'particular rhetorics of gender' at a given historical moment. Moreover, historians need to specify the kind of connections that arise between social and psychic phenomena, so that they can distinguish that which is historical about our gendered subjectivities from their trans-historical psychic elements. For so long as it lacks an account of the links between the social and the psychic, gender cannot adequately conceptualize change. By linking gender to the social via individual subjectivity, Roper proposes to endow gender with a historical dimension that it necessarily lacks when it is understood as a discursive creation alone.

Roper thus takes her distance from a long-established article of feminist faith, namely the radical constructivist conviction that gender is the pure product of social, cultural and linguistic practices, asserting, rather that 'sexual difference has its own physiological and psychological reality, and that recognition of this fact must affect the way we write history'.[27] Hence, she astutely identifies one of the fundamental difficulties with both social and linguistic constructionism, namely that each 'short-circuits' the gap between language and subjectivity, as if there were no space there to be bridged. In the constructivist universe, then, language, by means of its social character, simply 'impresses a social construction of gender upon the wax of the individual psyche'. But bodies are not solely creations of discourse. And if we already have plenty of histories of discourses about the body, what is sorely lacking is a history that can problematize the relationship between the psychic and the physical (since bodily experience must of necessity be connected with mental life).

Roper attributes the determined constructivism of feminist historians to their longstanding tendency to 'deny' the importance of the body.[28] Though deeply sympathetic to the desire to escape the snares of femininity by fleeing from their bodies and retreating to the 'rational reaches of discourse', Roper is nonetheless convinced that the costs of such flight are too high. After all,

> sexual difference is not purely discursive nor merely social. It is also physical. The cost of the flight from the body and from sexual difference is evident in what much feminist historical writing has found it impossible to speak about; or indeed, in the passionate tone of the theoretical work which insists on the radically constructed nature of sexual difference... We need an understanding of sexual difference which will incorporate, not fight against, the corporeal.[29]

So experience seems to be entering into the equation once again, though this time through the rather different door of bodily and psychic phenomena.[30]

Roper thus asks us to consider how it is we might link discursive constructs like gender to social and psychic experience. It is a question that was hardly posed in the thick of the theory wars. But the epistemological difficulties that a purely constructivist concept of gender present (namely that gender, conceived as a purely discursive construct, cannot in and of itself explain change) force us to consider this question very seriously. Here, Roper joins Barbara Taylor and Sally Alexander in what Colin Jones and Dror Wahrman have called an 'anticonstructionist backlash: wondering... whether historians have overemphasized the cultural construction of subjectivity to the preclusion of deep historical mechanisms that are a precondition to becoming human'.[31] For Alexander, Taylor and Roper, psychoanalysis is one obvious place to look for a way forward through this dilemma, allowing gender historians to come to terms with that which changes in time (the precise content of fantasies of maleness and femaleness) and that which, perhaps, does not (the basic psychic process, 'those mechanisms of fantasy formation, particularly identification, that are the precondition of having any sexed subjectivity at all').[32]

In order to put some flesh on these rather abstract and speculative bones, let us take a closer look at how Roper actually puts history and psychoanalysis into play as complementary tools of analysis.

The devil made me do it

The nine essays collected in *Oedipus and the Devil* all deal in various ways with changing notions of masculinity and femininity across the sixteenth and seventeenth centuries, and with the various social conflicts that arose around issues of gender and sexuality, religion and witchcraft. In most of these essays, psychoanalytic concepts play a secondary role at best, taking a back seat to more traditional forms of social and cultural analysis: her Foucauldian observation that the patriarchal effort to discipline young men seemed to create the very wildness it sought to control, or her nuanced analysis of the shifting and gendered meanings of 'will' and 'honour' in sixteenth-century Augsburg, and what this language might tell us about how people understood their own (hetero)sexual relations. After the author's forceful call for a more psychoanalytically informed history in the introduction, the relative soft-pedalling of psychoanalytic theory in the historical essays might come as something of a surprise. But in fact, Roper admits, psychoanalysis cannot be deployed on its own in historical research; rather it must be deployed alongside other forms of analysis, for the full range of human behaviour cannot be reduced to basic psychic mechanisms.[33] The analysis offered in most of her essays is thus multi-causal, with historical circumstances and contingency playing at least as great a role as psychic conflict. But in the final two essays of *Oedipus* – 'Witchcraft and Fantasy' and 'Oedipus and the Devil' – psychoanalytic understandings play a more visible role in the overall analysis. Let us take a closer look at the first of these two articles and see precisely how this is so.

Roper's interest in witch trials finds its origins in her desire to hear the voices of early modern women, to understand how women saw and experienced the cultural upheaval that religious reform trailed in its wake. 'But when we pose this question in an oral culture, where the written sources we have are nearly always by men, we draw a blank,' notes Roper.[34] Not even the most determined effort to read these sources 'against the grain' (that is, against their intended meaning) can hope to conjure up the absent voices of women. And so she turned to the transcripts of witch trials, from interrogation to final condemnation (or pardon). For despite the fact that these documents, too, are the products of male interrogation, the voices of the accused are nonetheless audible in the dialogue between male authorities and the accused witch, if for no other reason than that the actions of the former were driven by a logic of discovering the 'truth' of the matter. Witnesses were thus summoned to confirm details, and the witch's tale of her dealings with the devil, often extracted under torture, was then combed through in a punctilious search for any inconsistencies in the narrative. This mania for arriving at the truth meant that 'willing or not, witchcraft trials are the one context in which women "speak" at greater length and receive more attention than perhaps any other'.[35]

Much of the recent historical literature on these trials has treated the persecution of witches as the simple outcome of a raging early modern misogyny, with the trials reflecting nothing more than the 'projections' of a male-dominated society onto the hated female object. While Roper finds plenty of evidence of early modern misogyny in her documents, she nonetheless finds this interpretation of witch persecution lacking, precisely because it 'ignores the creative work which the witch herself carried out, translating her own life experiences into the language of the diabolic, performing her own diabolic theatre'. Witches thus participated actively in the social process whereby they were constructed as such. Far from being 'mere consumers of male discourse, providing witchcraft fantasy on order', witches 'used the elements of their culture to create narratives which made sense of their lives: of their unbearable hatreds, agonies, jealousies'.[36] In other words, participation in the crafting of a personal history as a witch may have served some kind of individual psychological agenda. And this in turn implies that witches exercised some kind of agency in their own narrative production.

When she delved more deeply into the trials themselves, Roper was initially quite taken aback by what she found therein. For her previous research had led her to expect a 'culmination' of the sexual antagonism that pervaded sixteenth- and seventeenth-century German culture:

> The idea of flight astride a broomstick or pitchfork, the notions of a pact with the Devil sealed by intercourse, the sexual abandonment of the dance at the witches' sabbath, all seemed to suggest that witchcraft had to do with sexual guilt and attraction between men and women, and that its explanation might lie in the moralism of the Reformation and Counter-Reformation years, when Catholics and Protestants sought to root out prostitution and adultery, shame women who became pregnant before marriage and impose a rigorous sexual code which cast the women as Eve, the temptress who was to blame for mankind's fall.[37]

But the cases that Roper examined tell quite a different story, a story of deep antagonisms among women, of 'enmities so intense that neighbours could testify against a woman they had known for years in full knowledge that they were sending her to a "blood bath".'[38] Not only were accusers and accused generally female, but the accusations all turned around themes of motherhood and early infancy: childbirth, suckling, food and feeding, the vulnerability of newborn infants, the quasi-magical capacities of parturient women's bodies. As her article 'Witchcraft and Fantasy' argues, it would seem that witchcraft accusation was largely a story of women.

In January 1669, 67-year-old Anna Ebeler found herself accused of murdering the woman for whom she had worked as lying-in maid, by slipping poison into a bowl of soup that was meant to restore the childbirth-weary young mother. As Roper explains, lying-in maids were the frequent objects of such accusations, and their accusers were, overwhelmingly, other women, including the young mothers who had hired them. Lying-in maids were generally older, childless women who moved from house to house, caring for young mothers and their newborns during the six weeks after birth. 'For the six to eight weeks after the mother had given birth, she alone carried on the duties of the mother, dandling, washing and swaddling the baby, and caring for its mother, giving her nourishing soups.'[39] These experts in infant care thus took over the mother's role while she lay confined to her bed, recovering from the birth. They arrived at their clients' doors armed with recipes for an array of strengthening soups that were meant to restore the recently parturient woman while, indirectly, feeding the newborn, who enjoyed the benefit of these soups via the mother's milk. And despite the fact that these were generally older, post-menopausal women, they were at times accused of stepping into the mother's wifely role as well.

The lying-in maid thus occupied an ambiguous and highly charged position in the early modern household, where, during the difficult months after childbirth, when both mother and newborn were at greatest risk, she played a maternal role *vis-à-vis* both mother and child. When things went well, as they did in the vast majority of cases, the childbed ended happily and the lying-in maid was dismissed in an atmosphere of mutual good feeling. But if things went wrong, if the child grew sickly and wasted, or if the mother felt more threatened than cared for by her lying-in maid, the latter was in an extremely vulnerable position, not only because of her social position (an older woman without resources, living alone, from one job to the next), but also because of the way that the anxieties of the post-partum period could be projected on to her ersatz-maternal figure.

Roper's fine analysis of this case, and of several others like it, draws out the themes of dependency and danger that swirled around the figure of the lying-in maid. Hired to care for, and especially to feed and restore the weakened mother, the lying-in maid could easily slide from the role of caregiver to the role of devil's handmaiden in the eyes of her client, one who perverted her knowledge of restorative foods and early infant care to bring harm to both mother and child. Lacking both family and financial resources, the lying-in maid had scant means of defending herself should the dynamic between her and her employer take a dark turn. At the same time, Roper reminds us, the first six weeks after birth were a dangerous period for both mother and child, a time of extreme, if temporary, dependency on this unknown older woman. It is easy to see how this potentially charged situation could take a sudden and sinister turn, particularly if the child ailed or died while under the maid's care.

But Roper's analysis goes beyond the careful treatment of the social and cultural forces at work, and peers into the psychological dynamic that might have arisen between the two women. On the one hand, fear on the part of the young mother, whose role had been temporarily usurped, who depended on this maternal figure for her own nourishment, who may have harboured unacceptable, hence inexpressible ambivalent feelings toward her own child, which feelings she then efficiently deflected away from the child by projecting them on to the lying-in maid. On the other hand, envy on the part of the lying-in maid, who had no stable home, no family, no child, and whose lot in life was to serve those who were blessed with all three. Alas for the lying-in maids of this world, envy was understood to be a primary drive among witches, the very stuff of which the witchly vocation was born. For in a world where emotions were understood to have real impact in the world, to feel envy for a woman was in fact to wish to harm her. In the understanding of witchcraft that both accusers and accused would have shared, the moment where a poor lying-in maid first felt envy for her employer was the moment where the devil slipped in and whispered words of vengeance in her ear.

The social organization of mothering practices thus provided a ready figure who could receive the feelings of ambivalence and distress that often attend childbirth. For

> at a time when the new mother's experience of giving birth and caring for an infant might raise memories of her own infancy, recalling the terrifying

> dependence on the maternal figure for whom she may well have experienced unadmitted, intolerable feelings of hatred as well as love, there was another person playing the maternal role to hand.[40]

One hears the echoes of Melanie Klein here, particularly her concept of splitting, which allows intolerable feelings of hostility to be projected onto another person. Hence the early modern mother, who projected the evil feelings on to the 'other' mother, and recognized only benevolence in herself.[41] At the same time, one cannot help but notice that the heart of the analysis remains social rather than psychoanalytic, with much of the argumentative force of the article deriving from Roper's sensitive account of the social and cultural location of young mother and lying-in maid, and of the available narratives of witchcraft on which both parties drew. The speculations about pre-Oedipal feelings, or mechanisms of splitting and projection, remain just that: speculations. They enrich the article tremendously, for they allow the author to speak of individual actions, motivations, hatreds, jealousies. But they make no direct contribution to the explanatory logic of the article, which rests, in the end, on more traditional forms of social and cultural analysis. This strikes me as an excellent example of how historians creatively use theory – not as some closed explanatory grid that gets pressed downward on to the evidence but rather as a way to open out new avenues of investigation, in this case to bring a sense of individual subjectivity into a field that has too long been animated by collective rite and identity.[42]

Oedipus and the Devil thus offers a searching engagement with certain of the epistemological questions that the poststructuralist turn to pure constructivism left hanging in the balance, notably the status of gender as a tool of historical analysis, but also the question of whether gender, on its own, acts as a motor for historical change. One may have reservations about a solution that rests on positing continuity in the underlying structures of the human psyche across time. Indeed, Roper herself would point out just a few years later that psychoanalysis 'raises, but cannot yet convincingly answer the question of how the psyche varies over time and in different cultures'.[43] Nonetheless, the questions that Roper's work raises about the role of subjectivity and experience in the shaping of gender identity are exactly the questions that need exploring, for it is precisely this kind of inquiry that poststructuralists pushed to one side in their haste to demonstrate the discursive construction of both subjectivity and experience.

Endnotes

1 Joan Scott, 'Women's History', in Joan W. Scott (ed.), *Gender and the Politics of History* (New York, 1988), 27.

2 Judith Butler, *Gender Trouble: Feminism and the Subversion of Identity* (New York, 1990). From a somewhat different point of view, Joan Scott also argues for the completely discursive nature of subjectivity in her article 'The Evidence of Experience'. Joan W. Scott, 'The Evidence of Experience', *Critical Inquiry*, 17:4 (1991), 773–97.

3 Nancy Fraser, 'False Antithesis', in Nancy Fraser (ed.), *Justice Interruptus. Critical Reflections on the 'Postsocialist' Condition* (London, 1997), 215.

4 Mary Louise Roberts' marvellous study *Disruptive Acts: The New Woman in Fin-de-Siècle France* (Chicago, 2002) is the sole work of historical analysis of which I'm aware that manages to translate Butler's theories into historical practice. In this elegant and theoretically sophisticated book, Roberts analyses how seven well-known French women (artists, journalists, writers and one actress) 'performed' their femininity, and so disrupted the sense of masculine and feminine as natural and stable categories in *fin-de-siècle* France.

5 Or as Roper puts it, 'human behaviour is not solely determined by conscious consideration, and identity is not a secure possession but a piecemeal process of identifications and separations'. Roper, *Oedipus and the Devil. Witchcraft, Sexuality and Religion in Early Modern Europe* (London, 1994), 5. My capsule account of Lacan is drawn principally from Sally Alexander, 'Women, Class and Sexual Differences in the 1830s and 1840s: Some Reflections on the Writing of Feminist History', *History Workshop Journal*, 17 (1984), 125–49. See also Juliet Mitchell and Jacqueline Rose, *Feminine Sexuality, Jacques Lacan and the Ecole Freudienne* (London, 1983).

6 Roper, *Oedipus and the Devil*, 17, 3.

7 Roper, *Oedipus and the Devil*, 3.

8 Roper, *Oedipus and the Devil*, 4.

9 Roper, *Oedipus and the Devil*, 4.

10 Roper, *Oedipus and the Devil*, 3.

11 Roper, *Oedipus and the Devil*, 13. Not to mention the well-known problem of applying to an entire society a model designed to uncover the unconscious psychic process of the individual.

12 Sally Alexander, 'Women, Class and Sexual Differences', 134. See also Norbert Elias, 'On Human Beings and Their Emotions: A Process-sociological Essay', *Theory, Culture and Society*, 4 (1987), 339–61.

13 Roper, *Oedipus and the Devil*, 4, 228.

14 Roper, *Oedipus and the Devil*, 21.

15 Roper, *Oedipus and the Devil*, 13.

16 Roper, *Oedipus and the Devil*, 13.

17 Roper, *Oedipus and the Devil*, 9.

18 Stephen Greenblatt, *Renaissance Self-Fashioning: From More to Shakespeare* (Chicago, IL, 1980), as rendered by Roper, *Oedipus and the Devil*, 11, 228.

19 Roper, *Oedipus and the Devil*, 11.

20 Roper, *Oedipus and the Devil*, 228.
21 Roper, *Oedipus and the Devil*, 22. See Emily Martin, *The Woman in the Body: A Cultural Analysis of Reproduction* (Boston, MA, 1987) for a pioneering effort to unlock some of these puzzles by a feminist anthropologist.
22 Roper, *Oedipus and the Devil*, 22.
23 Roper, *Oedipus and the Devil*, 26.
24 Roper, *Oedipus and the Devil*, 227.
25 Her sources include the transcripts from witchcraft trials, in which, Roper assures us, the witch contributed actively to the *mise-en-scène*, translating her own life experiences into the language of the diabolic, performing her own diabolic theatre in the fantasies she wove under judicial examination (which, though often forced from her through torture, were nonetheless, Roper tells us, her own condensations of shared cultural preoccupations). She also analyses accounts of exorcisms (which reveal the very different notions that Catholics and Protestants held regarding the relationship of the body to the divine), and the expanding literature of discipline: those ordinances, proclamations and mandates which secular authorities promulgated from the late fifteenth century on; a literature that crosses the Catholic/Protestant divide to reveal new anxieties about the potential disorder of individuals and households across the upheaval of the Reform.
26 Roper, *Oedipus and the Devil*, 119–20.
27 Roper, *Oedipus and the Devil*, 3.
28 Here I think Roper overstates her claim, leaving to one side the work of such feminist historians as Caroline Bynum, whose path-breaking book, *Holy Feast and Holy Fast: The Religious Significance of Food to Medieval Women* (Berkeley, CA, 1987), explores in much the way that Roper does the intersections between religious expression, female subjectivity (particularly in relation to their bodies) and constructions of masculine and feminine in fourteenth- and fifteenth-century Europe.
29 Roper, *Oedipus and the Devil*, 17, 18.
30 Indeed, it proves very difficult to evacuate the concept of experience from historical analysis. See Joan W. Scott, *Only Paradoxes to Offer: French Feminists and the Rights of Man* (Cambridge, MA, 1996) for an example of the curiously ahistoric effect produced by an analysis that expels all trace of experience in favour of an analysis of the (eternally recurring) discourses that produce both subjects and their experiences.
31 Colin Jones and Dror Wahrman, 'Introduction', in Colin Jones and Dror Warhman (eds), *The Age of Cultural Revolutions: Britain and France, 1750–1820* (Berkeley, CA, 2002), 14.
32 Barbara Taylor, 'Misogyny and Feminism: The Case of Mary Wollstonecraft', in Jones and Wahrman, *Age of Cultural Revolutions*, 214; and Roper, *Oedipus and the Devil*, 13. See also Sally Alexander, 'Women,

Class and Sexual Differences', and Alexander, 'Feminist History and Psychoanalysis', *History Workshop Journal*, 32 (1991), 128–33.

33 See Roper, *Oedipus and the Devil*, 218, where the author argues against reductive readings in which 'everything speaks of phallologocentrism, or betrays the Oedipal complex'. Rather, historians need to investigate the historically particular forms that psychic conflicts take: 'It seems to me that there are some primary areas of attachment and conflict – between those in maternal positions and children – which are pretty fundamental to human existence, but the forms those conflicts may take and the attitudes societies adopt to them may change.'

34 Roper, *Oedipus and the Devil*, 19.

35 Roper, *Oedipus and the Devil*, 20.

36 Roper, *Oedipus and the Devil*, 19–20.

37 Roper, *Oedipus and the Devil*, 202–3.

38 Roper, *Oedipus and the Devil*, 202.

39 Roper, *Oedipus and the Devil*, 212.

40 Roper, *Oedipus and the Devil*, 211.

41 Roper, *Oedipus and the Devil*, 211.

42 For a lucid analysis of the issues at stake in historians' adoption of psychoanalytic approaches, see Garthine Walker, 'Psychoanalysis and History', in Stefan Berger, Heiko Feldner and Kevin Passmore (eds), *Writing History: Theory and Practice* (London, 2003), 141–60.

43 Lyndal Roper, 'Witchcraft and Fantasy', *History Workshop Journal*, 45 (Spring 1998), 270.

Conclusion

Women's and gender history as a work-in-progress

'It is difficult to remember now how there could have been such a gust of masculine laughter at the 1969 Ruskin History Workshop when a number of us women asked for a meeting of those present who might be interested in working on "Women's History",' recalled Sally Alexander as she looked back, in 1984, across the first fifteen years of 'second-wave' scholarship on women's and gender history. 'I do remember the bewilderment and indignation we felt as we walked away from the conference to plan another of our own. It seemed to be the word – Woman – which produced the laughter. Why?' Those plans, Alexander tells us, would become the first National Women's Liberation Conference, held at Ruskin College, Oxford in early 1970.[1] As we have seen, the field of women's history (and, by extension, its more ambitious daughter, gender history) was born out of a hundred such experiences, a hundred such enraging, yet enlightening encounters with male resistance to women's perfectly reasonable, yet somehow terribly threatening suggestion that women, too, have a history, and that the leftist circles of socialist and people's history were surely the first place that that this history should have a hearing. Greeted time and again with mocking laughter and angry denials, even (or perhaps especially) in the left-wing history workshops that proliferated in the wake of '68, that first generation of women needed thick skins indeed if they were to break through that resistance and give women's history the attention they knew it deserved.

By bringing back to vivid life those first, difficult years when women's historians were struggling to carve out some kind of niche for themselves, Alexander's words remind us of the great gulf that separates the early days of 'second-wave' feminist history from gender history as it is now practiced in the early twenty-first century: '[It was] an event which wiped the smile off the male students' faces,' writes Alexander of that first Women's Conference. 'The television room had been taken over by the crèche (run by men), and the college was swarming with women, women and women. Student Union meetings for weeks afterwards rang with incoherent but passionate antagonism to the Women's Conference, focusing on the violation of students' freedoms it had imposed. The different implications it seems of women's liberation were lived vividly enough, though differently, for some men and hundreds of women that weekend.'[2]

At one level, then, the 1970 Conference (and many others like it) enacted the prefigurative politics of women's liberation, with men running the crèche whilst the women met and talked, theorised and expounded, did politics even as they searched for ways to revolutionise historical scholarship. The sense of having moved instantly (if temporarily) forward from patriarchal Oxford to a post-revolutionary feminist utopia must have been heady stuff indeed. Moreover, the powerful synergy between politics and scholarship in the late 1960s and early 1970s clearly proved both stimulating and productive for many a feminist historian, for as Alexander reminds us, the labour of scholarship was suddenly imbued with immediate personal and political significance: 'Women and labour, sex and class, feminism and socialism [became] the intimate inhabitants of both my psyche and my intellectual work... In the early 1970s socialist-feminists struggled to transform those dichotomies into political and theoretical relationships through campaigns and study groups. We diligently appraised and attempted to secure for our own purposes some of the traditions of marxist thought, appropriating the concepts of political economy, historical and dialectical materialism and assessing their revolutionary practices through a feminist lens.'[3] Yet there can be little doubt that working in such a highly-charged atmosphere, in which the simple desire to hold a women's history conference could – and did – provoke both ridicule and fury in male students, placed additional and often quite heavy burdens on the women who chose to embark on the adventure.

The generations who have acceded to the legacy of those early difficult years have been able to work under circumstances of far greater intellectual legitimacy (hence greater institutional security) than the first generation of fighters ever enjoyed. And this has been to the great benefit of history. For as our survey of the past forty years of women's and gender history suggests, scholarship seems to cook best over the slow flame of reflection. Sheltered from the storms of political passion, scholars are able to do that which society asks them to do, namely, step back from the immediacy of contemporary events and reflect on the complexity of the social, cultural, economic and political forces that come together to make history and shape destinies in sometimes curious and unexpected ways. As we have seen, such quiet reflection can produce results that are not always pretty or empowering: Young women who starved themselves not because they were victims of anorexia but rather because they were striving for transcendent holiness in a socio-religious context where such ambitions were both understandable and venerated; witches whose collaboration with their interrogators in the production of the 'fantasy of witch-hood' may have gratified deep and troublingly self-destructive psychic needs on the part of the witch.[4]

Yet within fifteen years of those first women's history conferences and workshops, such engaged, yet dispassionate scholarship had already become the norm in the young sub-discipline, as feminist scholars progressively stepped back from the immediate concerns of their own lives the better to meet women of the past on their own terms and territory. Theories of universal patriarchy, conceived in the urgent and very present-oriented need to understand women's oppression in the here and now soon gave way to more nuanced explorations of particular patriarchal formations. An emphasis on particularity and difference – across the various and differently-located structures of patriarchal oppression, and among the women who experience such uneven forms of male domination – increasingly characterised the work of feminist scholars who were quietly letting go of the dreary homogeneity that had marked the imaginative and political landscapes of universal patriarchy in 1970s North America and Europe.

What is most remarkable in the story of women's and gender history since the late 1960s, then, is not the derisive, angry jeering of those male students and scholars who shut their ears to women's demands and stubbornly defended their right to study their sex and only their sex, dressed up in the clothing of universal human experience. What is remarkable is that today, a mere 40 years later, we live in a world where such sneering dismissal is hardly thinkable. And this alone testifies to how rapidly women's and gender history have carved a central place for themselves on the broader disciplinary landscape. Clearly the move from women's to gender history has played a crucial role here, displacing the accent from the history of a specific (albeit large) social group – women – to a more all-encompassing history of the social relations of the sexes, and the social/historical construction of male and female identities in relation to one another.

But there can be little doubt that the subsequent shift toward a more discursive conception of gender, understood as a 'constitutive element of social relationships' and as a 'primary field within which or by means of which power is articulated' has broadened still further the impact of gender analysis within the historical discipline.[5] As a key axis along which power is both distributed and justified, gender underwrites unequal distributions of power among all kinds of social groups, including, but not limited to the hierarchical relations that have defined the relations of men and women. Hence, as Jacqueline Jones has demonstrated, gender was critical in defining the difference between the (black) slave and (white) planter classes in the nineteenth-century American south. It was equally vital in defining and justifying the domination of European colonizers over a whole host of colonial societies whose inferiority was marked above all by 'defective' gender relations (that is, by a different organisation of male-female relations from that obtaining in the metropole), even by 'degenerate' forms of masculinity, as in Mrinalini Sinha's fin-de-siècle Bengal.

Joan Scott's plea that historians recognise the inherently political dimension of gender has thus clearly been heard, and it has, moreover, encouraged scholars to 'dissolve' the distinctions that, in historical analysis have traditionally separated state from family, public from private, work from sexuality, politics from culture.[6] By reconnecting these falsely separated realms of life and social organisation, feminist scholars have been able to do exactly what Scott called for in 1983: to write 'histories that focus on women's experiences *and* analyse the ways in which politics construct gender and gender constructs politics.'[7] In this fashion, gender has swiftly made its way outward from the particular realm of women's history and into broader histories of human society, where the divisions and orderings of gender constitute a key axis of analysis and insight.

What has it meant for feminist historians that the hopes that Scott (and many others like her) first articulated some twenty-five years ago, have since been realized across a broad range of geographical and chronological fields? After all, few would contest today the proposition that gender and politics are intimately entwined, or that the terms of male and female identity are in large part culturally determined. Moreover, any survey of recent titles in history will show that over the past fifteen years historians *outside* the fields of women's and gender history have increasingly incorporated gender into their analyses, often as a prime category of analysis. All this suggests that in a remarkably short period of time, scholars (in the Anglo-american world, at least) have come to agree that it is no longer possible to write history – whether of the military, political, economic, social or intellectual varieties – without taking gender into account.[8] What has the impact of this indubitable success been on a discipline so much of whose early identity was built on struggle? On the struggle to recover the voices and figures of women in history, on the struggle against sexism both inside the academy and in the larger society around it, on the struggle to valorise and make visible the experiences of women as well as men, on the struggle to uncover those 'silent' operations of gender that shape both individual subjectivity and the organisation of social and political life?

As we have seen, the passage from margin to centre has been lived with regret by some feminists like Joan Hoff, who mourn the loss of an original, mythical 'purity' that, in her view, is innately bound up with the position of constant struggle. But most feminist historians have turned their faces to the future and used their increased intellectual legitimacy to strike out in a number of new and different directions. I have tried to give a sense of several of these new directions in the final chapters of this book, which follow gender history across the period of its greatest visibility, from the late 1980s onward, when it moved from the margins to the centre of scholarly preoccupations within the historical discipline.

Hence, I have argued that gender history owes its increased visibility in large part to the vanguard position of feminist theory in an era when the discipline as a whole was deeply divided over matters of theory and epistemology. During those years, feminist scholars were among the most vocal, creative and imaginative participants in the often-fierce debates that erupted over the status of the subject, over matters of agency, and issues of discursive versus historical or social construction. That feminist scholars should have found themselves in the forefront of such debates during the famous 'theory wars' should not really surprise us, for already in the 1970s, feminist refusal to 'give up the wish to speak in the name of women' had made feminism one of the main 'detonators of crisis' in macro-structural social analysis (including, though not limited to Marxist thought and practice.). Hence, frustrated by social historians' lack of attention to issues of sexual division and sexual difference, feminist scholars articulated one of the earliest, most coherent and most consequent critiques of social history's conceptualisation of social being and how it is experienced by women and by men.[9] As the entire conceptual edifice on which Marxist and other macro-structural forms of social analysis crumbled in the face of their inability to speak meaningfully about individual subjectivity, or about workers whose consciousness of class fails to line up with the politically approved forms, or about those differences that time and again cleave the working-class along ethnic, religious or gendered lines, feminist theory secured its avant-garde role in the tireless search to find a more satisfactory way of understanding the various differences that render class such a fragile category of analysis (and of political action). Not surprisingly, feminist scholars were among the earliest and most resolute upholders of discursive analysis, using the work of Foucault and Derrida (among others) to reveal the deep inadequacies that dog the old categories of social analysis, a move that pressed historians in general toward more cultural and linguistic modes of analysis. Moreover, as these modes of analysis gained force within the discipline at the turn of the 1990s, feminist historians were equally at the forefront of those who found the new approaches still wanting, who asked if there were not something besides mere 'discursive positioning' that might explain that elusive phenomenon we call individual subjectivity.

In the wake of the struggles that attended history's famous linguistic and cultural turn, then, women's and gender history can no longer be said to be shaped by one or two dominant approaches, but is, rather, characterised by a kind of theoretical eclecticism in which scholars deploy a range of tools and approaches so that they might better understand the ways that gender, as social/discursive category and as lived experience, has shaped human history.

After so much struggle and upheaval, one might reasonably ask where women's and gender history are headed from here? While historians are notoriously bad at predicting future outcomes, I would nonetheless hazard a guess that in the short run, at least, work in the field will continue to be characterised by a great diversity of methodological approaches. I say this in part because there is no way to reconcile the deep epistemological differences that divide poststructuralist from anti-poststructuralist but also because the arrival of gender as a tool of historical analysis has not displaced the felt need for a specific history of women.

This is perhaps most obvious in the case of the emerging fields of Eastern European and Russian women's history, where the institutional precarity of the field, combined with a not-yet-fully-attained sense of legitimacy in public discourse creates a situation that in some ways recalls the battles women's history fought simply to have a hearing in 1960s and 70s Western Europe and North America, though one should be wary of pressing the analogy too far. After all, Eastern Europe in the early twenty-first century is not America or Western Europe of yesteryear. An insistence on the centrality of women's history is thus often combined with poststructuralist and postcolonial approaches, for example when studying particular societies within the multi-ethnic empires that for centuries organised these regions politically.[10] Moreover, there is evidence that the history of women may also be making a come-back among a younger generation of students and scholars in North America and Western Europe; scholars who, in the words of Ruth Harris, are 'inspired by an undying interest in the lives of women in the past.'[11]

Perhaps we would do best, then, to consider the 'return' of women's history in both East and West as participating in a broader 'return of the social' that historians like Lynn Hunt, Victoria Bonnell and William Sewell Jr. have called for over the past ten years.[12] Not the social of the too-often-determinist macro-social analyses of the 1960s and 70s but a more culturally-situated social that operates on the 'richer and more supple epistemological terrain' opened up by the cultural turn and that seems to be finding an echo in recent historical practice.[13]

If the return of 'herstory' is indeed part and parcel of a larger return of the social then this provides a salutary reminder that in the early 21st century it will not do to draw hard and fast distinctions between women's and gender history, for the forms of women's history that are now developing in formerly inhospitable environments such as Russia or East Central Europe, or among a new generation of students and scholars in Western Europe and North America are inevitably influenced by the scholarship on gender. In this context, women's history and gender history are not easily uncoupled, nor should we wish for them to be. For as I have argued throughout this book, the considerable methodological gains that the cultural and linguistic turns have brought to historical practice are nowhere more visible than in the field of gender history. Indeed, gender has been at the forefront of scholarly debate for the past thirty years precisely because it is a tool of critical thinking that allows us to interrogate some of the discipline's most cherished categories of analysis.[14] If this vanguard role seems less obvious today than it did five to ten years ago I think that is because of the way that gender has become increasingly central to historical analysis, a phenomenon that is beautifully illustrated by Isabel Hull's book on sexuality and state formation in eighteenth and nineteenth century Germany. It has done so through its attentiveness to the role of language in shaping subjectivity, its far-reaching critique of traditional notions of agency, its insistence that understandings of sexual difference are key in shaping hierarchies of power, its pioneering use of the idea of social construction – an idea that has since been taken up to great effect by scholars across a broad range of domains: race, nationalism, empire, ethnicity, etc. Most importantly, gender has, from the outset, shown its capacity to effectively critique and unsettle the meta-narratives of determinist macro-social analysis.

It is precisely its force as a tool of critical thinking, its demonstrated capacity to refine historical method, that gives gender ongoing relevance in historical scholarship well beyond the fields of women's and gender history. This is perhaps most evident in the importance of gender to historical epistemology in two of the discipline's most cutting-edge fields: trans-national history and histories of empire. These are fields in which feminist scholars have played a key role, using gender not only to write women back in to the story but also to transform the approach more broadly. Hence, the feminist insight that gender is a relational concept, and that men and women, masculinity and femininity are historically and discursively constructed in relation to each other, has deeply influenced the way scholars of empire think about the construction of categories like race, sexuality, nation, ethnicity and religion. Similarly, gender history has informed and enriched historians' understanding of the ways in which such categories are constructed and reconstructed not only in relation to each other but also with respect to the dominant formations of the social and political spheres.[15] Let us pause briefly to examine more closely the ways that gender is shaping current work in imperial and trans-national history. In so doing we may be able to glean some clues as to where gender history might be headed from here.

Feminist scholars have been extremely active in the fields of imperial, post-colonial and trans-national history, and I could easily cite many excellent works here; let me confine myself to three that have been particularly important in shaping the field. First, Ann Laura Stoler's pioneering study *Carnal Knowledge and Imperial Power: Race and the Intimate in Colonial Rule* (2002), which demonstrates the centrality of gender and sexuality to the maintenance of a racially-stratified colonial order in the multiracial Dutch Indies. Taking as her point of departure the feminist insight that the personal is political, Stoler explores the key role that appropriate domestic arrangements and the proper management of sexuality played in shaping racialized colonial worlds and in producing those (white, masculine) subjectivities necessary to upholding the colonial political order. 'Prescriptions for bathing, breastfeeding, cooking, and sleeping arrangements tied anxieties over personhood, race, and what it meant to be Dutch to the choreography of the everyday' writes Stoler in a luminous passage that reminds us that comportment, affiliation and sentiment – the question of how and with whom one lived – were at least as important as somatics and biology in defining the distinctions of race that ordered colonial society.[16] Pursuing the implications of Foucault's notion that sexuality is a 'charged transfer point of power,' Stoler compellingly demonstrates how European supremacy lodged its most powerful arguments in the tissues of everyday domestic life, grounding those arguments in an often subliminal set of associations about European manliness, racial membership, sexual morality and the management of empire.[17]

A similar concern with the construction of colonial subjectivities animates Catherine Hall's *Civilising Subjects: Metropole and colony in the English imagination, 1830–1867.* More specifically, Hall seeks to elucidate the role of empire (in this case the island of Jamaica) in the 'making' of colonising subjects and 'of racialised and gendered selves, both in the Empire and at home.'[18] In pursuit of this goal, Hall re-frames the British Empire as a trans-national space, treating it as a singular, if differentiated space of moral and political argument in order to explore the circulation of individuals (travellers, missionaries) and the consolidation and re-working of ideas about racial difference within that space. At the heart of her story are the nonconformist (principally Baptist) women and men of Birmingham who, as militants in the antislavery movement at home and as missionaries, eager to 'civilise' the African Jamaicans, 'constituted themselves as colonisers' in both Jamaica and at home.[19] Taking the missionary movement as a formative moment in the emergence of modern racial thinking, Hall explores the connections between the abolitionists' paternalist racial discourse, centred on the social and cultural 'uplift' of their black sisters and brothers, with the discourses of 'scientific' racism, organised around the idea of fixed and immutable differences. But she is also concerned with the importance of race and gender, empire and family in constructing new, colonially-refracted forms of subjectivity in those (white) Englishmen and women who never left metropolitan soil, travelling to Jamaica in their imaginations only.

In this vein, Hall's elegant analysis of stay-at-home colonial femininity is particularly illuminating, drawing as it does on recent scholarship (including her own *Family Fortunes*) on the role of religion and social action in constituting arenas of female agency. 'The civilising of others had to take place on multiple fronts, from the civilising work which women did on men in the drawing-room or the parlour, to the work with servants in the back kitchen, fallen women in the city, or the enslaved women of their imaginations' writes Hall in a passage that reveals how, in the imperial context, 'home' came to carry a dual sense, signifying at one and the same time the private and domestic sphere of individual women and that of social action, undertaken collectively on behalf of the metropole's poor and downtrodden.[20] Moreover, and thanks in part to the civilising efforts of Baptist missionaries, the public and political meanings of 'home' radiated further still, beyond England's poor and out toward the shores of Jamaica. Here, the conviction that 'civilisation' rested on a particular gender order founded on separate spheres for men and women, and that any other means of organising sexuality and domestic life was self-evidently 'savage,' acquired new political significance, providing a central criterion for judging Afro-Jamaicans' fitness (or lack thereof) for full membership in the imperial polity. Hence, in the 'heady days' leading up to and following the emancipation (1834), Baptist evangelicals sought to bring the virtues of British domesticity to their Afro-Jamaican 'brethren,' thereby ensuring their cultural uplift and ultimate integration into the imperial polity. Twenty years and several rebellions later, a new generation of colonial officials and metropolitan politicians would come to see in Afro-Jamaicans' refusal to fully adopt a 'proper' domestic and gender order the cultural marker of indelible racial inferiority and the justification for a hardening of racial hierarchies.

Hall's investigation of the gendered construction of racial categories in relation to the imperial social and political formation, though sharing important ground with Stoler's analysis, differs somewhat in the emphasis she places on understanding the specific kinds of political agency that the continual reworking of such categories both enabled and constrained: 'At moments, in certain conjunctures, particular representations won wide enough consent to become hegemonic and legitimate political consequences. But these binaries were just as continuously being dissolved, the "essential" characteristics of different peoples slipping away... '[21] In both works, one is struck by the deep insights that gender analysis gives into the various ways that the state-society relationship was reformulated over the *longue durée* of colonial rule.

It is precisely the question of the state-society relationship that lies at the heart of Mrinalini Sinha's fine-grained study *Specters of Mother India: The Global Restructuring of an Empire* (2006), which explores the gendered re-configuration of agency and citizenship in late-colonial India. Sinha takes as her point of departure the massive international controversy that was set off by the publication (in 1927) of American journalist Katherine Mayo's *Mother India*. This was a sizzling exposé of various grisly social ills in India, often involving women, girls and matters of sexuality that Mayo laid at the door of an irremediably backward Hindu culture. *Mother India* was written to demonstrate the folly of Britain's ever implementing a gradual devolution of political power in colonial India, given the socially and culturally 'degenerate' Indians' evident unfitness for self-rule. But members of the Indian nationalist movement, though highly critical of Mayo's conclusions, nonetheless seized on her dire portrait of Indian society to argue that the social backwardness Mayo had identified was a product not of defective Hindu culture but rather of the political condition of colonial rule. In particular, they fingered the colonial state as an obstacle to progressive social reform in India.

Sinha argues persuasively that the ensuing debate over the inability of the colonial state to effectively intervene in civil society snowballed rapidly, constituting a 'moment of rupture in the reconstitution of the interwar imperial social formation.'[22] Indeed, notes Sinha, the trans-national controversy unleashed by *Mother India,* which erupted in an era of global restructuring in colonial rule, both provoked and enabled an (ultimately short-lived) re-thinking of the state-society relationship in nationalist circles. The occasion for the emergence of this alternative understanding was the campaign, undertaken in reaction to Mayo's book, to pass a new law against child marriage, one that would operate at the national level and so supersede the collective rights of the various religious communities with whom the colonial state traditionally negotiated. Under ordinary circumstances, women's lives were ruled by the mediating power of these communities, which fiercely defended their right to define and control the lives of 'their' women.[23] Yet the campaign surrounding this new law interpellated women directly as a collective public identity, one that cut across the traditional religious communities, and women's organisations responded eagerly to the call.

By prising women from the 'tight embrace' of the communities while legitimating a new language of individual rights 'beyond the collective rights of communities,' the Child Marriage Restraint Act set in motion a temporary shift in the way state and society were aligned.[24] This in turn provided the potential for an alternative understanding of the relationship between women and the state, one that operated independently of the mediation of the collective identities of the communities. The Mayo controversy thus had an extraordinary and unexpected political outcome as, for a brief moment at the end of the 1920s the state-society relationship was re-imagined around individual, versus communal rights, with women as the 'paradigmatic citizen-subjects of a nation-state-in-the-making.'[25]

I have paused here to reflect a bit more deeply on the recent work of Stoler, Hall and Sinha because I believe that these three books have a great deal to tell us about where gender history might be headed in the near future. Hence, much of the power of this work derives from the fact that gender informs the way each has conceptualised and gone about a research project that reaches far beyond the classic domains of women's history to analyse national and trans-national political orders, and understandings of race, sexuality and citizenship. By using gender to critically reflect on the categories and concepts that organise research in imperial and trans-national history, then, feminist scholars have been able to make a vital and pioneering contribution to historical analysis more broadly, re-casting the political in far larger terms, and, in so doing, re-thinking state-society relations in new and broader terms.[26]

I think that in the future we can expect that more and excellent work will continue to be done along these lines by gender historians and by a host of others who might not identify themselves as such but whose thinking may be no less deeply marked by the force of gender as a tool of critical analysis. At the same time, it is worth pointing out that the very centrality of gender to so much recent historical scholarship has resulted in a paradox. For if now more than ever gender informs how historians go about their work, such work nonetheless tends to deploy gender alongside other tools and categories, a fact which might lead one to conclude that gender has as its vocation to disappear. Paradoxically, then, the operations of gender as a tool of critical analysis have become less visible even as it is being incorporated into ever-wider realms of research. This has led some scholars to worry that gender, rendered banal through overuse, has lost its critical edge.[27] But as I hope my discussion of Stoler, Hall and Sinha makes clear, the success of gender does not necessarily imply that its has 'lost' its critical edge; far from it. A widely-diffused tool of historical analysis can always become banal or routine in the hands of scholars who choose to treat gender as an interpretive device that permits the re-discovery of the same old binary oppositions. But scholars who do such a thing are precisely refusing to use gender for explicitly critical purposes, preferring to turn it to normative ends rather than to deploy gender's undimmed power to unsettle comfortable binaries. Such a refusal may tell us much about the scholars in question but says nothing at all about the critical force of gender.

Finally, I think that the highly political orientation of so much recent work in gender history (as opposed, for example, to focusing on labour and material culture) points to the ongoing importance of Joan Scott's influential formulation of gender as foundational to political and social order. As Ruth Harris has observed, this way of thinking about gender actually 'accepts' the categories and periodisation of conventional political history, 'rejecting in a stroke the study of material culture – be it Marxist or *Annalist* in style – in which patterns of social evolution, often continuous rather than disruptive, stand outside the textbook dates of revolution and regime change.'[28] Scott's hope, of course, was that analysing gender in conjunction with race and class would open up new, transformative dimensions to historical analysis. As is clear from the work of numerous gender historians (including Isabel Hull, Catherine Hall, Ann Stoler and Mrinalini Sinha), this has indeed proven to be the case. But this way of thinking about gender, with its emphasis on discursive construction and its rigorous exclusion of experience, has also tended to privilege political history over histories of material culture, histories of discourses about the body rather than histories that seek to explore the corporeal reality of the body and its centrality to the construction of gender identity.[29] It is, moreover, an understanding of gender that has tended to link gender to a set of presentist concerns and categories (such as race and socio-political transformation) that are not easily transferable to the study of the past.[30]

Ruth Harris is far from alone in her concern with the overwhelmingly political-and-cultural-history orientation of so much recent gender history. Michael Roper has pursued this same point from a somewhat different perspective – that of a historian who is interested in the formation of gendered subjectivities but deeply dissatisfied with the limits of current approaches that understand masculinity and femininity as the products of social or cultural construction rather than as aspects of personality. As Roper astutely observes, this way of thinking about subjectivity 'elides' the psychic into the cultural without ever stopping to analyze the mechanisms that mediate between individual subjects and cultural formations.[31] Roper attributes this limitation to the particular way that Joan Scott defined gender as a tool of historical analysis in her widely-read – and widely-cited – 'Gender: A Useful Category of Analysis,' which famously argues that gender is a key aspect of how power is structured and symbolized. Clearly, this way of conceiving gender gave Scott's formulation 'imperial reach', allowing her to argue that gender was present even when women were not. But it did so at the cost of prising gender from the realm of experience and re-directing our attention from the familiar breeding grounds of gender/sexual identity, such as the family or kinship structures, to more public and institutional sources of such identity: labour markets, education, the polity, all of which, Scott argues persuasively, are structured by sexual difference.

One can easily understand why Scott might have privileged focusing on the wider social and institutional bases of sexual identity. For in the mid-1980s, when women's history had trouble liberating itself from the history of the family, such an approach promised to give gender a broader purchase on historical analysis in its many guises – political, social, intellectual, economic. Nonetheless, this way of defining gender has tended to produce work that, in Roper's view, 'looks down from political discourse through to the subject.' Subjects are thus reduced to mere 'after-effects' of political discourse and people are treated as 'subject positions' defined entirely within a discursive web.[32]

If Scott's discursive notion of gender, with its implicit orientation of historical research toward political and cultural history, has anchored gender history solidly within the discipline, this conceptualisation has nonetheless left historians who are interested in subjectivity faced with a new challenge: that of finding ways to write about bodily and emotional experiences that do not treat such experiences as wholly composed by and through ideological formations. In Roper's view, this means going back to analyse the very family structures that Scott recommended we flee in favour of broader, social and political sources of identity, so that we might explore those 'primitive emotional investments' that underpin the social scripts of gender. For at the end of the day, 'familial relationships might have a more foundational significance for subjectivity than others – such as political discourse.' After all, as Leonore Davidoff has observed, it is within the family – 'however it has been constituted – that formation of both body and psyche, literally and symbolically, first takes place.'[33] To persist in conceiving of subjectivity primarily in terms of representation is to endorse a 'profoundly lifeless notion of human existence,' concludes Roper in words that remind us that much of the current dissatisfaction with the cultural and political (i.e., discursive) understanding of gender stems from its inability to capture (as did E.P. Thompson for the notion of class) its profound anchoring in human relationships.

Scott herself has expressed considerable concern of late with the limits of gender in this very political and discursive formulation, and has proposed that feminist scholars shift their attention to the body-culture link, using (among other things) the tools of psychoanalysis.[34] Of course, feminist historians have been working with psychoanalytic understandings of sexual difference for some time now, reflecting on the ways in which gendered identities are produced not by discursive positioning but rather by internal processes of splitting and identification. In these processes, female and male are produced as absolute opposites, but the binarism is unstable and threatens constantly to collapse, as elements of suppressed femininity surface in men and vice-versa. Lyndal Roper, Sally Alexander, Carolyn Steedman and, more recently Barbara Taylor (to name but four) have all worked with psychoanalytically informed notions of subjectivity, struggling in particular to understand the different temporalities involved in the constitution of sexed subjectivities, the long-term processes of fantasy and identification that constitute 'enduring' aspects of human nature versus more culturally and historically specific aspects of self:[35] 'Repetitions in the constitution of human subjectivity – among which sexual difference is the most insistent and irresolute – are structured historically through law, kinship, the economy, for example; they are grounded in the body, figured in space and speech,' writes Sally Alexander in a passage that reminds us of the fascination that such approaches hold, but also of the epistemological difficulties entailed in marrying psychoanalytic insights with social analysis. 'The human subject is formed through fantasy and identification, processes as historically resonant as Fernand Braudel's *longue durée* and as slow to change... '[36]

More recently, Barbara Taylor has suggested that these different temporalities can be arrayed in terms of that which endures (mental structures, that is, psychic processes such as identification, repression or sublimation) and that which changes over time (the particular contents of mental life - beliefs, feelings, fantasies, dreams - which are shaped in part by culturally-available materials).

'Inasmuch as the functioning of the human mind remains constant over time, analysing its mechanisms with concepts like repression, identification, sublimation seems entirely legitimate' writes Taylor. 'However, another criticism of psychoanalytic-historical interpretations – that they ignore the historicity of mental *contents*, the transformations that beliefs, feelings and fantasies undergo over time... is more difficult to rebut...'[37] Now this formulation, which is very close to that proposed by Lyndal Roper (above, p 169), rests on a distinction between psychic process and psychic contents that may in fact be impossible to make.[38] But assuming that it is legitimate to distinguish structure from content in this way, to posit that mental processes have functioned similarly across time despite continuous transformations in mental contents, the question still remains: can historians work simultaneously within the two temporalities, retaining (in Taylor's words) 'a sense of the historicity of psychic life while at the same time exploring its deepest, continuous features? The question, far from resolved here, seems to me one of the most compelling confronting modern historians.'[39]

If those feminist historians who are working with psychoanalytic concepts are offering more questions than answers at this point, there is no denying the profound interest for historians (and challenge to the canons of historical method) that those questions pose. So I think that alongside more and excellent work that uses gender to enrich studies of politics, empire and trans-national history, we can also expect to see gender historians continuing to work at the multiple points where bodies and culture intersect, wrestling with the question of sexual difference, and of the role of corporeal and psychic experiences in the constitution of gendered subjectivities. Ultimately, however, the question 'whither women's and gender history' can never be answered in the abstract; indeed, such a question will only be resolved by history's practitioners, rather than by those who merely speculate about how history can and cannot be written.

Endnotes

1 Sally Alexander, 'Women, Class and Sexual Differences in the 1830s and 1840s. Some reflections on the writing of feminist history,' *History Workshop Journal 17* (1984) 127.

2 Alexander, 'Women, Class and Sexual Differences,' 127.

3 Alexander, 'Women, Class and Sexual Differences,' 127.

4 Lyndal Roper, *Oedipus and the Devil: Witchcraft, Sexuality and Religion in Early Modern Europe* (London, 1994) 227.

5 Joan Scott, 'Gender: A Useful Category of Historical Analysis', in Joan Scott, *Gender and the Politics of History* (New York, 1988) 43, 45.

6 Scott, 'Women in History,' *Past and Present: A Journal of Historical Studies, 101* (1983), 141–57.

7 Scott, 'Women's History,' 156.
8 For some reflections on the more arduous road gender has followed in France, see Laura Lee Downs, 'French History Without Gender?,' Robert Gildea and Anne Simonin, eds., *Writing Contemporary History* (London, 2008) 76–94.
9 Alexander, 'Women, Class and Sexual Differences,' 127, 131.
10 For a recent example, see Maria Bucur and Nancy Wingfield, eds., *Gender and War in Twentieth Century Eastern Europe* (Bloomington, IN, 2006). In Western Europe and North America, where the need for a specifically women's history also continues to make itself felt, this need has taken the form of maintaining specific journals that keep the focus on women as a matter of political and intellectual militancy, or of maintaining courses on the particular history of women within the programs on women's and gender history that have proliferated in universities since the 1970s.
11 Ruth Harris, 'Is Gender Dead?' in Gildea and Simonin, eds., *Op. cit.*, 75.
12 Bonnell and Hunt, *Beyond the Cultural Turn: New Directions in the Study of Society and Culture (Berkeley, CA, 1999)*, 11; William Sewell Jr., *Logics of History: Social Theory and Social Transformation* (Chicago, IL, 2005).
13 Sewell, 80. See, for example, Silvia Evangelisti, 'Rooms to share: convent cells and social relations in early-modern Italy', in *The Art of Survival: Gender and History in Europe, 1450–2000 (Past & Present* Supplement 1, Oxford, 2005).
14 Bonnie Smith, *The Gender of History: Men, Women and Historical Practice*, (Cambridge, MA, 1998)
15 Mrinalini Sinha, *Specters of Mother India: The Global Restructuring of an Empire* (Durham, NC, 2006), 13.
16 Ann Laura Stoler, *Carnal Knowledge and Imperial Power: Race and the Intimate in Colonial Rule* (Berkeley, CA, 2002), 17.
17 Ibid, 16
18 Catherine Hall, *Civilising Subjects: Metropole and Colony in the English Imagination, 1830–1867* (London, 2002), 13.
19 Ibid, 12.
20 Ibid, 18.
21 Ibid, 276.
22 Mrinalini Sinha, *Specters of Mother India,*. 253.
23 Ibid, 9.
24 Ibid, 10.
25 Ibid, 10.
26 I have already mentioned Isabel Hull's work in this regard, but one might also cite Claudia Koonz's classic *Mothers in the Fatherland: Women, the Family and Nazi Politics* (New York, 1987) as well as more recent work that continues to use gender to re-think the political: Tara Zahra, *Kidnapped Souls: National Indifference and the Battle for Children in the Bohemian Lands* (Ithaca, NY, 2008); Kevin Passmore, 'The Gendered Genealogy of Political Religions Theory,' *Gender & History 20:3*, (2008), 644–68; Laura

Lee Downs, '"Each and every one of you must become a *chef:*" Towards a social politics of working-class childhood on the extreme right in 1930s France,' *Journal of Modern History* (March 2009), 1–44.

27 Joan Scott, 'Feminism's History,' *Journal of Women's History16/2* (2004); and Scott, *Gender and the Politics of History*, Introduction to the Second Edition (New York, 1999).

28 Harris, *Op. cit.,* 71.

29 Here one might cite Carolyn Bynum's *Holy Feast and Holy Fast*, Lyndal Roper's *Oedipus and the Devil,* or her more recent *Witch Craze: Terror and Fantasy in Baroque Germany* (London, 2004). Kathleen Canning's very useful essay 'The Body as Method? Reflections on the Place of the Body in Gender History,' in Canning, *Gender History in Practice: Historical Perspectives on Bodies, Class and Citizenship* (Ithaca, NY, 2006), 168–89, underscores the fact that, while vigorously debated by scholars outside history (Judith Butler, Donna Haraway), the body remains a 'largely unexplicated and undertheorized *historical* concept.' (169). I think her otherwise very useful essay tends to underestimate the contributions of psychoanalytically-informed historians, particularly Kleinians (Lyndal Roper, Sally Alexander, Barbara Taylor), to understanding gender identity as embodied process.

30 Harris, *Op. cit.,* 71.

31 Michael Roper, 'Slipping Out of View: Subjectivity and emotion in gender history,' *History Workshop Journal 59*, Spring 2005, 58.

32 *Ibid*, 58, 59, 60.

33 *Ibid*, 67; Leonore Davidoff, *Worlds Between. Historical Perspectives on Gender and Class*, Cambridge, 1995, 229, quoted in Roper, 'Slipping Out of View', 67.

34 Joan W. Scott, 'Millenial Fantasies: the future of "gender" in the 21st century,' in Claudia Honegger and Caroline Arni, eds., *Gender – die Tücken einer Kategorie* (Zurich, 2001), 19–37. As Michèle Barrett has pointed out, efforts to hitch psychoanalytic understandings of subjectivity to social analysis turn on the relative weight that different psychoanalytic theories attach to the biological, the psychic and the social. Michèle Barrett, 'The Concept of "Difference"', *Imagination in Theory* (London, 1999), 120.

35 Sally Alexander, *Becoming a Woman and Other Essays in Nineteenth and Twentieth Century Feminist History*, (New York, 1995); Barbara Taylor *Mary Wollstonecraft and the Feminist Imagination* (Cambridge, 2003); Carolyn Steedman, *Landscape for a Good Woman;* Lyndal Roper, *Op cit.*

36 Sally Alexander, *Becoming a Woman*, 247. See also Roper, *Oedipus and the Devil*, 13.

37 Taylor, *Mary Wollstonecraft*, 258.

38 See my discussion of Roper's *Oedipus and the Devil,* above, 169.

39 Taylor, *Mary Wollstonecraft*, 259.

Suggestions for further reading

Alberti, Johanna, *Gender and the Historian* (London, 2002).

Appleby, Joyce, Hunt, Lynn and Jacob, Margaret, *Telling the Truth About History* (New York, 1994).

Boureau, Alain, *The Myth of Pope Joan*, trans. Lydia Cochrane (Chicago, IL, 2001).

Bridenthal, Renate, Grossman, Atina and Kaplan, Marion, *When Biology Became Destiny: Women in Weimar and Nazi Germany* (New York, 1984).

Browne, Jude (ed.), *The Future of Gender* (Cambridge, 2007).

Butler, Judith, *Undoing Gender* (New York, 2004).

Canning, Kathleen, 'Feminist History After the Linguistic Turn: Historicizing Discourse and Experience', *Signs*, 19:2 (1994), 368–404.

Cooper, Frederick and Stoler, Ann Laura (eds), *The Tensions of Empire: Colonial Cultures in a Bourgeois World* (Berkeley, CA, 1997).

Cott, Nancy, *The Bonds of Womanhood* (New Haven, CT, 1977).

The Grounding of Modern Feminism (New Haven, CT, 1987).

Davidoff, Leonore, *Worlds Between: Historical Perspectives on Gender and Class* (Cambridge, 1995).

Davis, Natalie Zemon, 'Women on Top', in Davis (ed.), *Society and Culture in Early Modern France* (Stanford, CA, 1975).

de Beauvoir, Simone, *The Second Sex* (Harmondsworth, 1975).

de Grazia, Victoria and Furlough, Ellen (eds), *The Sex of Things: Gender and Consumption in Historical Perspective* (Berkeley, CA, 1996).

Duby, Georges and Perrot, Michelle, *Histoire des femmes en Occident*, 5 vols (Paris, 1991).

Gender & History, 20:3, special 20th anniversary issue (November, 2008).

Gordon, Linda, *Woman's Body, Woman's Right* (New York, 1976).

Groppi, Angela, 'Dot et institutions: la conquête d'un "patrimoine"', *Clio, Histoire, Femmes et Sociétés*, 7 (1998).

Herlihy, David and Klapisch-Zuber, Christiane, *Les Toscans et leurs familles. Une étude du catasto florentin de 1427* (Paris, 1978).

Hesse, Carl, *The Other Enlightenment: How French Women Became Modern* (Princeton, NJ, 2001).

Hufton, Olwen, *The Prospect Before Her: A History of Women in Western Europe, 1500–1800* (London, 1995).

Hunt, Lynn, 'The Challenge of Gender', in Hans Medick and Anne-Charlotte Trepp, *Geschlectergeschichte und Allgemeine Geschichte* (Goettingen, 1998), 59–97.

Jordanova, Ludmilla, *Sexual Visions: Images of Gender in Science and Medicine between the Eighteenth and Twentieth Centuries* (Madison, WI, 1989).

Juster, Susan, *Disorderly Women: Sexual Politics and Evangelicalism in Revolutionary New England* (Ithaca, NY, 1994).

Kent, Susan Kingsley, *Sex and Suffrage in Britain, 1860–1914* (Princeton, NJ, 1987).

Klapisch-Zuber, Christiane, 'La bourse ou les boules de saint Nicolas. De quelques représentations des biens féminins en Italie', *Clio, Histoire, Femmes et Sociétés, 7* (1998).

L'Ombre des ancêtres. Essai sur l'imaginaire médiéval de la parenté (Paris, 2000).

Le Doeuff, Michèle, *Hipparchia's Choice: An Essay Concerning Women, Philosophy, etc.* (trans. Trista Selous. Oxford, Blackwell, 1991)

Levine, Philippa (ed.), *Gender and Empire* (Oxford, 2004).

Michel, Koven and Michel, Sonya, 'Womanly Duties: Maternalist Politics and the Origins of Welfare States in France, Germany, Great Britain, and the United States, 1880–1920', *American Historical Review*, 95 (October 1990), 1076–108.

Midgeley, Clare, *Gender and Imperialism* (Manchester, 1997).

Nussbaum, Martha Craven, *Women and Human Development: The Capabilities Approach* (Cambridge, 2000).

Okin, Susan Moller, *Gender, Justice and the Family* (New York, 1989).

Pedersen, Susan, *Eleanor Rathbone and the Politics of Conscience* (New Haven, CT, 2004).

Pollard, Miranda, *Reign of Virtue: Mobilizing Gender in Vichy France* (Chicago, IL, 1998).

Poovey, Mary, 'Feminism and Deconstruction', *Feminist Studies*, 14:1 (Spring 1988), 52–65.

Purkiss, Diane, *The Witch in History. Early Modern and Twentieth-Century Representations* (London, 1996).

Steedman, Carolyn, *Landscape for a Good Woman. A Story of Two Lives* (London, 1986).

Walker, Garthine, *Crime, Gender and Social Order in Early Modern England* (Cambridge, 2003).

White, Luise, *Speaking with Vampires. Rumor and History in Colonial Africa* (Berkeley, CA, 2000).

Woolf, Virginia, *A Room of One's Own* (New York, 1929).

Woolf, Virginia, *Three Guineas* (New York 1966) .

Bibliography

Abensour, Léon, *Histoire générale du féminisme des origines à nos jours* (Paris, 1921).

Alexander, Sally, 'Women's Work in Nineteenth Century London: A Study of the Years 1820–50', in Anne Oakley and Juliet Mitchell (eds), *The Rights and Wrongs of Women* (London, 1976).

'Women, Class and Sexual Differences in the 1830s and 1840s: Some Reflections on the Writing of Feminist History', *History Workshop Journal*, 17 (1984), 125–49.

Becoming a Woman and Other Essays in Nineteenth and Twentieth Century Feminist History (New York, 1995).

Amos, Valerie and Parmar, Pratibha, 'Challenging Imperial Feminism', *Feminist Review*, 17 (1984), 3–19.

Anagol, Padma, 'The Age of Consent Act [1891] Reconsidered: Women's Perspectives and Participation in the Child-Marriage Controversy in India', *South Asia Research*, 12:2 (November 1992), 100–18.

'The Emergence of the Female Criminal in India: Infanticide and Survival Under the Raj', *History Workshop*, 53 (2002).

The Emergence of Feminism in India, 1850–1920 (London, 2006)

Applewhite, Harriet B. and Levy, Darlene Gay, *Women and Politics in the Age of the Democratic Revolution* (Ann Arbor, MI, 1990).

Arnold, David, *The Congress in Tamilnadu: National Politics in South Asia, 1919–1937* (New Delhi, 1977).

Assiter, Alison, *Enlightened Women: Modernist Feminism in a Postmodern Age* (London, 1995).

Bakhtin, Mikhail, *The Dialogic Imagination* (Austin, TX, 1981).

Bard, Christine, 'Review of Mary Louise Roberts, *Civilization Without Sexes: Reconstructing Gender in Postwar France, 1917–1927*', *Journal of Modern History*, 69:2 (June 1997), 365–8.

Barrett, Michèle, *Women's Oppression Today: Problems in Marxist-Feminist Analysis* (London, 1980).

'The Concept of Difference', in Michèle Barrett, *Imagination in Theory. Essays on Writing and Culture* (London, 1999), 111–23.

Basu, Aparna, 'Women's History in India: An Historiographical Survey', in Karen Offen, Ruth R. Pierson and Jane Rendall (eds), *Writing Women's History: International Perspectives* (Bloomington, IN, 1991), 181–209.

Beard, Mary, *Woman as a Force in History: A Study in Tradition and Realities* (New York, 1946).

Beechey, Veronica, *Unequal Work* (London, 1987).

Benhabib, Seyla and Cornell, Drucilla, (eds), *Feminism as Critique: On the Politics of Gender* (Minneapolis, MN, 1987).

Bennett, Judith, 'Feminism and History', *Gender & History*, 1:3 (Autumn 1989), 251–71.

Berg, Maxine, *A Woman in History: Eileen Power, 1889–1940* (Cambridge, 1996).

Bock, Gisela, 'Women's History and Gender History: Aspects of an International Debate', *Gender & History*, 1:1 (Spring 1989), 7–30.

Bonnell, Victoria and Hunt, Lynn, *Beyond the Cultural Turn: New Directions in the Study of Society and Culture* (Berkeley, CA, 1999).

Bonnet, Marie-Jo, *Un choix sans équivoque. Recherches historiques sur les relations amoureuses entre les femmes, XVIe–XXe siècles* (Paris, 1981).

Boswell, John, *Christianity, Social Tolerance and Homosexuality: Gay People in Western Europe from the Beginning of the Christian Era to the Fourteenth Century* (Chicago, IL, 1980).

Bourdieu, Pierre, *The Logic of Practice*, trans. Richard Nice (Stanford, CA, 1990).

Brod, H., *The Making of Masculinities: The New Men's Studies* (London, 1987).

Bucur, Maria and Wingfield, Nancy (eds), *Gender and War in Twentieth Century Eastern Europe* (Bloomington, IN, 2006).

Buer, Mabel, *Health, Wealth and Population in the Early Days of the Industrial Revolution* (London, 1926).

Burton, Antoinette, *The Burdens of History* (Chapel Hill, NC, 1994).

'Thinking Beyond the Boundaries: Empire, Feminism and the Domains of History', *Social History*, 26:1 (January 2001), 60–71.

Butler, Judith, *Gender Trouble: Feminism and the Subversion of Identity* (New York, 1990).

Bodies that Matter: On the Discursive Limits of Sex (New York, 1997).

Butler, Judith and Scott, Joan W. (eds), *Feminists Theorize the Political* (London, 1992).

Bynum, Caroline, *Holy Feast and Holy Fast: The Religious Significance of Food to Medieval Women* (Berkeley, CA, 1987).

'Why All the Fuss About the Body? A Medievalist's Perspective', *Critical Inquiry*, 22 (1995), 1–33.

Canning, Kathleen, *Gender History in Practice: Historical Perspectives on Bodies, Class and Citizenship* (Ithaca, NY, 2006).

Carby, Hazel, 'White Women Listen. Black Feminism and the Boundaries of Sisterhood', in Center for Contemporary Cultural Studies (ed.), *The Empire Strikes Back* (London, 1982); Echols, Alice, *Daring to be Bad: Radical Feminism in America, 1967–1975* (Minneapolis, MN, 1989).

Chakrabarty, Dipesh, 'A Small History of Subaltern Studies', in Henry Schwartz and Sangeeta Ray (eds), *A Companion to Postcolonial Studies* (Oxford, 2000), 467–85.

Chandra, Bipan, *The Rise and Growth of Economic Nationalism in India: Economic Policies of Indian National Leadership, 1880–1905* (Delhi, 1969).

Chartier, Roger, 'Intellectual History or Sociocultural History? The French Trajectories', in Dominick LaCapra and Steven L. Kaplan (eds), *Intellectual History: Reappraisals and New Perspectives* (Ithaca, NY, 1982).

On the Edge of the Cliff. History, Language, and Practice (Baltimore, MD, 1997).

Clark, Alice, *The Working Life of Women in the Seventeenth Century* (London, 1919).

Corbin, Alain, *Les filles de noce. Misère sexuelle et prostitution aux XIX*[e] *et XX*[e] *siècles* (Paris, 1978).

'Le "sexe en deuil" et l'histoire des femmes au XIXe siècle', in Michelle Perrot (ed.), *Une histoire des femmes, est-elle possible?* (Marseille, 1984), 142–54.

'Des hommes, des femmes, des genres', interview with Alain Corbin and Michelle Perrot, *Vingtième siècle*, 75 (juillet–septembre, 2002), 167–76.

Crowston, Clare Haru, *Fabricating Women. The Seamstresses of Old Regime France, 1675–1791* (Durham, NC, 2001).

Dauphin, Cécile, *et al*. 'Women's Culture and Women's Power: Issues in French Women's History', *Journal of Women's History*, 1:1 (Spring 1989), 63–88 (originally published in *Les Annales, E.S.C.*, mars–avril, 1986, 271–93).

Davidoff, Leonore, 'Class and Gender in Victorian Society: The Diaries of Arthur Munby and Hannah Cullwick', in J.L. Newton, M. Ryan and J. Walkowitz (eds), *Sex and Class in Women's History* (London, 1983).

'Mastered for Life: Servant and Wife in Victorian and Edwardian England', in A. Sutcliffe and P. Thane (eds), *Essays in Social History* (Oxford, 1986).

Davidoff, Leonore and Hall, Catherine, *Family Fortunes: Men and Women of the English Middle Class, 1780–1850* (London, 1987).

Davin, Anna, 'Imperialism and Motherhood', *History Workshop*, 5 (Spring 1978), 9–65.

Davis, Angela, 'Reflections on the Black Woman's Role in the Community of Slaves', *Black Scholar*, 3 (December 1971), 2–15.

Women, Race and Class (New York, 1981).

Davis, Belinda, *Home Fires Burning: Food, Politics and Everyday Life in World War I Berlin* (Chapel Hill, NC, 2000).

Davis, Natalie Zemon, 'Women's History in Transition: The European Case', *Feminist Studies*, 3:3/4 (Spring/Summer 1976), 83–103, reprinted in Joan W. Scott (ed.), *Feminism and History* (Oxford, 1996), 79–104.

Delphy, Christine, *L'Ennemi principale: I L'Economie politique du patriarcat; II Penser le genre* (Paris, 1998, 2001).

d'Emilio, John, *Sexual Politics, Sexual Communities: The Making of a Homosexual Minority in the United States, 1940–1970* (Chicago, IL, 1983).

Derrida, Jacques *Of Grammatology*, trans. G. Spivak (Baltimore, MD, 1976).

Desai, A.R., *Social Background of Indian Nationalism* (Bombay, 1966, first published in 1948).

Dill, Bonnie Thornton, 'Race, Class, and Gender: Prospects for an All-inclusive Sisterhood', *Feminist Studies,* 9 (Spring 1983), 131–50.

Downs, Laura Lee, 'If "Woman" is Just an Empty Category, Then Why Am I Afraid to Walk Alone at Night? Identity Politics Meets the Postmodern Subject', *Comparative Studies in Society and History* (April 1993), 414–37.

Manufacturing Inequality: Gender Division in the French and British Metalworking Industries, 1914–1939 (Ithaca, NY, 1995).

'French History Without Gender?', in Robert Gildea and Anne Simonin (eds), *Writing Contemporary History* (London, 2008), 76–94.

'"Each and every one of you must become a *chef:*" Towards a Social Politics of Working-Class Childhood on the Extreme Right in 1930s France,' *Journal of Modern History* (March 2009), 1–44.

Dubesset, Mathilde, Thébaud, Françoise and Vincent, Catherine, 'Quand les femmes entrent à l'usine. Les ouvrières des usines de guerre de la Seine, 1914–1918', masters' thesis (Université de Paris VII, 1974).

Dyhouse, Carol, *Girls Growing Up in Late Victorian and Edwardian England* (London, 1981).

Feminism and the Family in England, 1880–1939 (Oxford, 1989).

Eisenstein, Zillah (ed.), *Capitalist Patriarchy and the Case for Socialist Feminism* (New York, 1978).

Elias, Norbert, 'On Human Beings and Their Emotions: A Process-sociological Essay', *Theory, Culture and Society*, 4 (1987), 339–61.

Engels, Friedrich, *On the Origins of the Family, Private Property and the State,* ed. Eleanor Leacock (New York, 1972).

Evangelisti, Silvia, 'Rooms to Share: Convent Cells and Social Relations in Early-Modern Italy, in *The Art of Survival: Gender and History in Europe, 1450–2000* (*Past & Present* Supplement 1, Oxford, 2005).

Evans, Richard, *In Defence of History* (London, 1997).

Faderman, Lillian, *Surpassing the Love of Men: Romantic Friendships and Love Between Women from the Renaissance to the Present* (New York, 1981).

Febvre, Lucien, *Le Problème de l'incroyance au XVIe siècle. La religion de Rabelais* (Saint-Amand, Cher, 1942).

Flandrin, Jean-Louis, *Les Amours paysannes. Amour et sexualité dans les campagnes de l'ancienne France, XVIe–XIXe siècles* (Paris, 1975).

Foucault, Michel, 'Nietzsche, Genealogy, History', in D.F. Bouchard and S. Simon (eds and trans.), *Language, Counter-memory, Practice; Selected Essays and Interviews* (Ithaca, NY, 1977).

The History of Sexuality. An Introduction, trans. Robert Hurley, vol. I (New York, 1980).

Fraisse, Geneviève, *La Raison des femmes* (Paris, 1992).

Fraser, Nancy, 'Rethinking the Public Sphere. A Contribution to the Critique of Actually Existing Democracy', in Nancy Fraser, *Justice Interruptus. Critical Reflections on the 'Postsocialist' Condition* (London, 1997), 69–98.

'False Antithesis', in Nancy Fraser (ed.), *Justice Interruptus. Critical Reflections on the 'Postsocialist' Condition* (London, 1997), 207–23.

Garton, Stephen, 'The Scales of Suffering: Love, Death and Victorian Masculinity', *Social History*, 27:1 (January 2002), 40–58.

Gay, Peter, *The Bourgeois Experience: Victoria to Freud*, vol. I, *The Education of the Senses* (New York, 1984).

Geertz, Clifford, *The Interpretation of Cultures: Selected Essays* (New York, 1973).

George, Dorothy, *London Life in the Eighteenth Century* (London, 1925).

England in Transition (London, 1931).

Gilmore, David, *Manhood in the Making. Cultural Concepts of Masculinity* (New Haven, CT, 1990).

Glucksmann, Miriam, *Women Assemble: Women Workers and the New Industries in Interwar Britain* (London, 1990).

Gouda, Frances and Clancy-Smith, Julia (eds), *Domesticating the Empire. Race, Gender and Family Life in French and Dutch Colonialism* (Charlottesville, VA, 1998).

Grayzel, Susan, *Women's Identities at War: Gender, Motherhood, and Politics in Britain and France During the First World War* (Chapel Hill, NC, 1999).

Greenblatt, Stephen, *Renaissance Self-Fashioning: From More to Shakespeare* (Chicago, IL, 1980).

Guha, Ranajit, 'On Some Aspects of the Historiography of Colonial India', *Subaltern Studies I: Writings on South Asian History and Society* (Delhi, 1982), 1–7.

Elementary Aspects of Peasant Insurgency in Colonial India (Delhi, 1983).

Guha, Ranajit and Spivak, Gayatri Chakravorty (eds), *Selected Subaltern Studies* (New York, 1988).

Hall, Catherine, *White, Male and Middle-Class: Explorations in Feminism and History* (Oxford, 1992).

Civilising Subjects: Metropole and Colony in the English Imagination, 1830–1867 (London, 2002).

Halperin, David, *One Hundred Years of Homosexuality: And Other Essays on Greek Love* (New York, 1990).

Hardiman, David, *Peasant Nationalists of Gujarat: Kkeda District* (Delhi, 1981).

Harris, Ruth, 'Is Gender Dead?', in Robert Gildea and Anne Simonin (eds), *Writing Contemporary History* (London, 2008), 69–76.

Hartmann, Heidi, 'Capitalism, Patriarchy and Job Segregation by Sex', in Zillah Eisenstein (ed.), *Capitalist Patriarchy and the Case for Socialist Feminism* (New York, 1979), 206–47.

'The Unhappy Marriage of Marxism and Feminism: Towards a More Progressive Union', in Lydia Sargent (ed.), *Women and Revolution* (Boston, MA, 1981).

Helly, Dorothy, and Reverby, Susan, 'Introduction', in Dorothy Helly and Susan Reverby (eds), *Gendered Domains. Rethinking Public and Private in Women's History. Essays from the Seventh Berkshire Conference on the History of Women* (Ithaca, NY, 1992).

Hewitt, Nancy, 'Beyond the Search for Sisterhood: American Women's History in the 1980s', *Social History,* 10:3 (1985).

Higginbotham, Evelyn Brooks, 'Beyond the Sound of Silence: Afro-American Women in History', *Gender & History,* 1:1 (Spring 1989), 50–67.

Hobsbawm, Eric, *Primitive Rebels: Studies in Archaic Forms of Social Movement in the 19th and 20th Centuries* (Manchester, 1978).

Hobsbawn, Eric and Ranger, Terence, *The Invention of Tradition* (Cambridge, 1983).

Hoff, Joan, 'Gender as a Postmodern Category of Paralysis', *Women's History Review,* 3:2 (1994), 149-68.

hooks, bell, *Feminist Theory: From Margin to Center* (Boston, MA, 1984).

Houbre, Gabrielle, *La Discipline de l'amour. L'éducation sentimentale des filles et des garçons à l'âge du romantisme* (Paris, 1997).

Hufton, Olwen, 'Femmes/hommes: une question subversive', *Passés recomposés. Champs et chantiers d'histoire* (Paris, 1995), 235–42.

Hull, Gloria T., Scott, Patricia Bell and Smith, Barbara (eds), *All the Women Are White, All the Blacks Are Men, But Some of Us Are Brave: Black Women's Studies* (Old Westbury, CT, 1982).

Hull, Isabel, *Sexuality, State and Civil Society in Germany, 1700–1815* (Ithaca, NY, 1996).

Hunt, Lynn, *The Family Romance of the French Revolution* (Berkeley, CA, 1992).

Hunt, Nancy, 'Introduction', in Nancy Hunt (ed.), *Gendered Colonialisms* (Oxford, 1998).

Hutchins, Bessie L., 'The Working Life of Women', Fabian Women's Group Series, *Fabian Tracts,* 157 (London, 1911).

Women in Modern Industry (London, 1915).

Jayawardena, Kumari, *The White Woman's Other Burden: Western Women and South Asia During British Rule* (New York, 1995).

Jones, Gareth Stedman, *Outcast London: A Study in the Relationship Between Classes in Victorian Society* (Oxford, 1971).

Languages of Class: Studies in English Working-Class History, 1832–1982 (Cambridge, 1983).
'The Determinist Fix: Some Obstacles to the Further Development of the Linguistic Approach to History in the 1990s', *History Workshop Journal*, 42 (Autumn 1996), 19–35.
'The New Social History in France', in Colin Jones and Dror Warhman (eds), *The Age of Cultural Revolutions: Britain and France, 1750–1820* (Berkeley, CA, 2002).
Jones, Jacqueline, *Labor of Love, Labor of Sorrow. Black Women, Work and the Family from Slavery to the Present* (New York, 1985).
Jordanova, Ludmilla, *History in Practice* (London, 2000).
Joyce, Patrick, 'History and Postmodernism', *Past and Present*, 133 (November 1991).
'The End of Social History?', *Social History*, 20 (1995).
Kelly, Joan, 'Did Women have a Renaissance?' in Catherine Stimpson (ed.), *Women, History and Theory. The Essays of Joan Kelly* (Chicago, IL, 1984), 19–50, first published in Renate Bridenthal and Claudia Koonz (eds.), *Becoming Visible. Women in European History* (Boston, MA, 1977).
'Family and Society', in Catherine Stimpson (ed.), *Women, History and Theory: The Essays of Joan Kelly* (Chicago, 1984), 110–55.
Kerber, Linda, 'Separate Spheres, Female Worlds, Woman's Place: The Rhetoric of Women's History', *Journal of American History*, 75 (June 1988), 9–39.
Knowles, Lilian, *The Industrial and Commercial Revolutions in Great Britain during the Nineteenth Century* (London, 1921).
Koonz, Claudia, *Mothers in the Fatherland: Women, the Family and Nazi Politics* (New York, 1987).
Krishnamurty, J. (ed.), *Women in Colonial India: Essays on Survival, Work and the State* (Delhi, 1989).
Kumar, Kapil, *Peasants in Revolt: Tenants, Landlords, Congress and the Raj in Oudh, 1866–1922* (New Delhi, 1984).
Kumar, Radha *The History of Doing: An Illustrated Account of Movements for Women's Rights and Feminism in India, 1800–1990* (London, 1993).
Lal, Maneesha, 'Sexe, genre et l'historiographie féministe contemporaine: l'exemple de l'Inde coloniale', *Cahiers de genre,* 34 (2003), 149–69.
Lambert, Peter, 'The Professionalization and Institutionalization of History', in Stefan Berger, Heiko Feldner and Kevin Passmore (eds), *Writing History: Theory and Practice* (London, 2003), 42–60.
Landes, Joan, *Women and the Public Sphere in the Age of the French Revolution* (Ithaca, NY, 1988).
Le Doeuff, Michèle, *The Sex of Knowing* (trans. Kathryn Hamer and Lorrain Code, London, Routledge, 2003)

Lewis, Jane, 'Women Lost and Found: The Impact of Feminism on History', in Dale Spender (ed.), *Men's Studies Modified: The Impact of Feminism on the Academic Disciplines* (Oxford, 1981).

Women in England, 1870–1950: Sexual Divisions and Social Change (Brighton, 1984).

Liddington, Jill and Norris, Jill, *'One Hand Tied Behind Us': The Rise of the Women's Suffrage Movement* (London, 1978).

Lodge, David, *After Bakhtin: Essays on Fiction and Criticism* (London, 1990).

Lorde, Audre, 'The Master's Tools Will Never Dismantle the Master's House', in Cherrie Moraga and Gloria Anzaldua (eds), *This Bridge Called My Back: Writings by Radical Women of Color* (New York, 1981).

Marcuzzo, Maria Cristina and Rossi-Doria, Anna (eds), *La Ricerca della donne* (Torino, 1987).

Martin, Emily, *The Woman in the Body: A Cultural Analysis of Reproduction* (Boston, MA, 1987).

Masselos, Jim, 'The Dis/Appearance of Subalterns: A Reading of a Decade of Subaltern Studies', *South Asia*, 15:1 (1992), 105–25.

Maugue, Annelise, *L'Identité masculine en crise au tournant du siècle* (Marseille, 1987).

Melman, Billie, *Women's Orients. Englishwomen and the Middle East, 1718–1918* (Ann Arbor, MI, 1995).

'Under the Western Historian's Eyes: Eileen Power and the Early Feminist Encounter with Colonialism', *History Workshop Journal*, 42 (1996), 147–68.

Midgley, Mary, 'On Not Being Afraid of Natural Sex Difference', in Morwenna Griffiths and Margaret Whitford (eds), *Feminist Perspectives in Philosophy* (London, 1988).

Mill, John Stuart, *On Liberty, with the Subjection of Women and Chapters on Socialism* (Cambridge, 1989).

Mitchell, Juliet, and Rose, Jacqueline, *Feminine Sexuality, Jacques Lacan and the Ecole Freudienne* (London, 1983).

Mohanty, Chandra Talpade, 'Under Western Eyes: Feminist Scholarship and Colonial Discourses', reprinted in Chandra Talpade Mohanty, *Feminism Without Borders. Decolonizing Theory, Practicing Solidarity* (Durham, NC, 2003), 17–42.

Moraga, Cherrie and Anzaldua, Gloria (eds) *This Bridge Called My Back: Writings by Radical Women of Color* (New York, 1981).

Mosse, George, *Nationalism and Sexuality. Respectable and Abnormal Sexuality in Modern Europe* (New York, 1985).

Newton, Judith, Ryan, Mary and Walkowitz, Judith, *Sex and Class in Women's History* (London, 1983).

Nicholson, Linda (ed.), *Feminism/Postmodernism* (London, 1990).

Nussbaum, Martha, *Sex and Social Justice* (Oxford, 1999).

Nye, Robert, *Masculinity and Male Codes of Honor in France* (Berkeley, CA, 1992).

Oakley, Annie, *Sex, Gender and Society* (London, 1972).

O'Brien, Patricia, 'Michel Foucault's History of Culture', in Lynn Hunt (ed.), *The New Cultural History* (Berkeley, CA, 1989).

O'Hanlon, Rosalind, 'Recovering the Subject: Subaltern Studies and Histories of Resistance in Colonial South Asia', *Modern Asian Studies*, 22:1 (1988), 189–224.

O'Hanlon, Rosalind and David Washbrook, 'Histories in Transition: Approaches to the Study of Colonialism and Culture in India', *History Workshop Journal* (Autumn 1991), 110–27.

Ortner, Sherry, 'Is Female to Male as Nature is to Culture?' in Michelle Rosaldo and Louise Lamphere (eds), *Women, Culture and Society* (Stanford, CA, 1974), 67–87.

Outram, Dorinda, *The Body and the French Revolution. Sex, Class and Political Culture* (New Haven, CT, 1989).

Pandy, Gyanendra, *The Ascendancy of the Congress in Uttar Pradesh, 1926–1934: A Study in Imperfect Mobilisation* (Delhi, 1978).

Pankhurst, Sylvia, *The Suffragette* (New York, 1911).

Passmore, Kevin, '"Planting the Tricolour in the Citadels of Communism": Women's Social Action in the Croix de feu and Parti social français', *Journal of Modern History*, 71 (1999), 814–51

'Postructuralism and History', in Stefan Berger, Heiko Feldner and Kevin Passmore (eds), *Writing History: Theory and Practice* (London, 2003), 118–40.

'Introduction', in Kevin Passmore (ed.), *Women, Gender and Fascism in Europe, 1919–45* (Manchester, 2003).

'The Gendered Genealogy of Political Religions Theory', *Gender & History*, 20:3 (2008), 644–68.

Pateman, Carole, 'The Fraternal Social Contract', in Carol Pateman, *The Disorder of Women* (Stanford, CA, 1989), 33–57.

Pedersen, Susan, 'National Bodies, Unspeakable Acts: The Sexual Politics of Colonial Policy-Making', *Journal of Modern History*, 63 (December 1991), 647–80.

Perrot, Michelle, 'Les femmes, le pouvoir, l'histoire', in Michelle Perrot (ed.), *Une histoire des femmes, est-elle possible?* (Marseille, 1984), 206–22.

Les Femmes ou les silences de l'histoire (Paris, 1998).

Pinchbeck, Ivy, *Women Workers and the Industrial Revolution, 1750–1850* (London, 1930, reprinted by Virago, 1981).

Poovey, Mary, *Uneven Developments: The Ideological Work of Gender in Mid-Victorian England* (Chicago, IL, 1988).

Pomata, Gianna, 'History, Particular and Universal: On Reading Some Recent Women's History Textbooks', *Feminist Studies*, 19:1 (Spring 1993), 7–50.

'Close-ups and Long Shots: Combining Particular and General in Writing the Histories of Women and Men', in Hans Medick and Anne-Charlotte

Trepp, *Geschlectergeschichte und Allgemeine Geschichte* (Goettingen, 1998), 101–124.

Power, Eileen, *Medieval English Nunneries* (Cambridge, 1922).

Prakash, Gyan, 'Writing Post-Orientalist Histories of the Third World: Perspectives from Indian Historiography', *Comparative Studies in Society and History*, 32:2 (April 1990).

Ramusack, Barbara, 'From Symbol to Diversity: The Historical Literature on Women in India', *South Asia Research*, 10:2 (November 1990), 139–57.

Rendall, Jane, 'Review Article: Women's History: Beyond the Cage?', *History*, 75 (1990), 63–72.

'Uneven Developments: Women's History, Feminist History and Gender History in Great Britain', in Karen Offen, Ruth Roach Pierson and Jane Rendall (eds), *Writing Women's History: International Perspectives* (Bloomington, IN, 1991), 45–57.

Rigby, S.H., *Chaucer in Context* (Manchester, 1996).

Riley, Denise, *War in the Nursery: Theories of the Child and Mother* (London, 1983).

'Am I that Name?' Feminism and the Category of 'Women' in History (Minneapolis, MN, 1988).

Roberts, Mary Louise, *Disruptive Acts: The New Woman in Fin-de-Siècle France* (Chicago, 2002).

Roper, Lyndal, *Oedipus and the Devil: Witchcraft, Sexuality and Religion in Early Modern Europe* (London, 1994).

'Witchcraft and Fantasy', *History Workshop Journal*, 45 (Spring 1998), 265–71.

Witch Craze: Terror and Fantasy in Baroque Germany (London, 2004).

Roper, Michael and Tosh, John (eds), *Manful Assertions: Masculinities in Britain Since 1800* (London, 1991).

Rosaldo, Michelle, 'A Theoretical Overview', in Michelle Rosaldo and Louise Lamphere (eds), *Women, Culture and Society* (Stanford, CA, 1974).

'The Use and Abuse of Anthropology', *Signs*, 5:3 (1980).

Rose, Sonya, *Limited Livelihoods: Gender and Class in Nineteenth-Century England* (Berkeley, CA, 1992).

Rousseau, Jean-Jacques, *Emile*, Book V, 'Sophie, or the Education of Woman', trans. William Payne (London, 1893).

Rubin, Gayle, 'The Traffic in Women: Notes on the Political Economy of Sex', in Rayna Reiter (ed.), *Towards an Anthropology of Women* (New York, 1975), 157–210.

Said, Edward, *Orientalism* (New York, 1978).

'Orientalism Reconsidered', in Frances Barker *et al.* (eds), *Europe and its Others*, 2 vols (Colchester, 1985), vol. I.

Samuel, Raphaël, *People's History and Socialist Theory* (London, 1981).

Sangari, Kumkum and Vaid, Sudesh, *Recasting Indian Women. Essays in Colonial History* (New Delhi, 1989).

Sarkar, Sumit, 'Orientalism Revisited: Saidian Frameworks in the Writing of Indian History', *Oxford Literary Review*, 16 (1994).

Writing Social History (Delhi, 1997).

Sarkar, Tanika, 'The Hindu Wife and the Hindu Nation: Domesticity and Nationalism in Nineteenth-century Bengal', *Studies in History*, 8:2 (1992), 213–35.

Schreiner, Olive, *Women and Labour* (London, 1911).

Schweitzer, Sylvie, *Les Femmes ont toujours travaillé. Une histoire du travail des femmes au XIXe et XXe siècles* (Paris, 2002).

Scott, Joan W., 'Women in History: The Modern Period', *Past and Present: A Journal of Historical Studies*, 101 (1983), 141–57.

'Gender: A Useful Category of Analysis', in Joan W. Scott, *Gender and the Politics of History* (New York, 1988).

'Women in *The Making of the English Working Class'*, in Joan W. Scott, *Gender and the Politics of History* (New York, 1988), 68–90.

'A Statistical Representation of Work: La Statistique de l'Industrie à Paris, 1847–1848', in Joan W. Scott, *Gender and the Politics of History* (New York, 1988), 113–38.

'Women's History: The Emergence of a New Field', in Peter Burke (ed.), *New Perspectives in Historical Writing* (University Park, PA, 1989).

'The Evidence of Experience', *Critical Inquiry*, 17:4 (1991), 773–97.

Only Paradoxes to Offer: French Feminists and the Rights of Man (Cambridge, MA, 1996).

Gender and the Politics of History, 2nd edition (New York, 1999).

'Millenial Fantasies: The Future of "Gender" in the 21st Century', in Claudia Honegger and Caroline Arni (eds), *Gender – die Tücken einer Kategorie* (Zurich, 2001), 19–37.

'Feminism's History', *Journal of Women's History*, 16:2 (2004).

Seeley, Paul, 'O Sainte Mère: Liberalism and the Socialization of Catholic Men in Nineteenth-Century France', *Journal of Modern History*, 70 (December 1998), 862–91.

Sewell Jr., William, *Logics of History: Social Theory and Social Transformation* (Chicago, 2005).

Sharma, Ursula, *Women, Work and Property in North-West India* (London, 1980).

Sinha, Mrinalini, *Colonial Masculinity: The 'Manly Englishman' and the 'Effeminate Bengali' in the Late Nineteenth Century* (New Delhi, 1997; first published Manchester, 1995).

'Giving Masculinity a History', *Gender & History*, 11 (1999), 445–60.

Specters of Mother India: The Global Restructuring of an Empire (Durham, NC, 2006).

Smith, Barbara (ed.), *Home Girls: A Black Feminist Anthology* (New York, 1983).

Smith, Bonnie, *Ladies of the Leisure Class: The Bourgeoises of Northern France in the Nineteenth Century* (Princeton, NJ, 1981).

The Gender of History: Men, Women and Historical Practice (Cambridge, MA, 1998).

Smith-Rosenberg, Carroll, 'The Female World of Love and Ritual', *Signs*, 1 (Autumn 1975), 1–30.

'Hearing Women's Words: A Feminist Reconstruction of History', *Disorderly Conduct: Visions of Gender in American History* (Oxford, 1985).

Sneal, Anil, *The Emergence of Indian Nationalism: Competition and Collaboration in the Later Nineteenth Century* (Cambridge, 1968).

Spelman, Elizabeth, *Inessential Woman. Problems of Exclusion in Feminist Thought* (Boston, MA, 1988).

Spiegel, Gabrielle, 'History, Historicism and the Social Logic of the Text in the Middle Ages', *Speculum*, 65 (1990).

Spivak, Gayatri Chakravorty, 'Deconstructing Colonial History', *Subaltern Studies*, IV (1985).

'Can the Subaltern Speak?', in Cary Nelson and Lawrence Grossberg (eds), *Marxism and the Interpretation of Culture* (Urbana, IL, 1988).

Steedman, Carolyn, *Landscape for a Good Woman: A Story of Two Lives* (London, 1986).

Childhood, Culture and Class in Britain. Margaret McMillan, 1860–1931 (New Brunswick, NJ, 1990).

'"Public" and "private" in women's lives', *Journal of Historical Sociology*, 3:3 (1990).

'La Théorie qui n'en est pas une, or, why Clio doesn't care', *History and Theory* (1992), 33–50.

'Bimbos from Hell', *Social History*, 19:1 (January 1994), 57–66.

Stoler, Ann Laura, 'Carnal Knowledge and Imperial Power: Gender, Race and Morality in Colonial Asia', in Micaela di Leonardo (ed.), *Gender at the Crossroads of Knowledge: Feminist Anthropology in the Postmodern Era* (Berkeley, CA, 1991), 51–101.

Carnal Knowledge and Imperial Power: Race and the Intimate in Colonial Rule (Berkeley, CA, 2002).

Strachey, Rachel, *The Cause* (London, 1978, first published 1928).

Strobel, Margaret, *European Women and the Second British Empire* (Bloomington, IN, 1991).

Summerfield, Penny, *Women Workers in the Second World War: Production and Patriarchy in Conflict* (London, 1984).

Taylor, Barbara, 'Misogyny and Feminism: The Case of Mary Wollstonecraft', in Colin Jones and Dror Wahrman, *The Age of Cultural Revolutions: Britain and France, 1750–1820* (Berkeley, CA, 2002), 203–17.

Mary Wollstonecraft and the Feminist Imagination (Cambridge, 2003).

Thane, Pat and Bock, Gisela (eds), *Maternity and Gender Politics: Women and the Rise of the European Welfare States, 1880s–1950s* (London, 1991).

Thébaud, Françoise, *Ecrire l'histoire des femmes* (Fontenay-St-Cloud, 1998).

Ecrire l'histoire des femmes et du genre, 2nd edition (Saint-Cloud, 2007).

Thompson, Edward, *The Making of the English Working Class* (London, 1988, first published 1963).

Tosh, John, 'What Should Historians do with Masculinity? Reflections on Nineteenth Century Britain', *History Workshop Journal*, 38 (1994), 179–202.

A Man's Place: Masculinity and the Middle-class Home in Victorian England (New Haven, CT, 1999).

Trimberger, Ellen Kay, 'E.P. Thompson: Understanding the Process of History', in Theda Skocpol (ed.), *Vision and Method in Historical Sociology* (Cambridge, 1984).

Turner, Victor and Turner, Edith, *Image and Pilgrimage in Christian Culture: Anthropological Perspectives* (Oxford, 1978).

Vansina, Jan, *Living With Africa* (Madison, WI, 1994).

Vickery, Amanda, 'Golden Age to Separate Spheres? A Review of the Categories and Chronology of English Women's History', *Historical Journal,* 36:2 (1993), 383–414.

Walby, Sylvia, *Patriarchy at Work* (Minneapolis, MN, 1986).

Walker, Garthine, 'Psychoanalysis and History', in Stefan Berger, Heiko Feldner and Kevin Passmore (eds), *Writing History: Theory & Practice* (London, 2003), 141–60.

Walkowitz, Judith R., *City of Dreadful Delight: Narratives of Sexual Danger in Late Victorian London* (Chicago, IL, 1992).

Weigman, Robin, 'Object Lessons: Men, Masculinity, and the Sign *Women*', *Signs*, 26:2 (2001), 355–88.

White, Deborah G., 'Female Slaves: Sex Roles and Status in the Antebellum Plantation South', *Journal of Family History* (Autumn 1983), 248–61.

Whitehead, Harriet, 'The Bow and the Burden Strap: A New Look at Institutionalized Homosexuality in Native North America', in Sherry Ortner and Harriet Whitehead (eds), *Sexual Meanings, The Cultural Construction of Gender and Sexuality* (Cambridge, 1981).

Wildenthal, Lora, *German Women for Empire, 1884–1945* (Durham, NC, 2001).

Young, Robert, *White Mythologies. Writing History and the West* (New York, 1990).

Zahra, Tara, *Kidnapped Souls: National Indifference and the Battle for Children in the Bohemian Lands* (Ithaca, NY, 2008).

Index

Abensour, Léon 9
Ackroyd-Beveridge, Annette 124
adult education 40, 313
Age of Consent Controversy 120, 125–8
Agency 30, 40, 49–52, 91, 93–4, 101, 113, 186, 188, 190
Alexander, Sally 23, 27, 28, 168–9, 169, 174, 180–1, 182–3, 194, 195, 196, 197
Alexander, William 18
Amos, Valerie 115, 142
Anagol, Padma 127–8, 138, 140, 141, 144
anthropology 4, 43–54, 89–90
  and feminist theory 4, 43–4
Anzaldua, Gloria 28, 53
Applewhite, Harriet B. 162
Arni, Caroline 197
Arnold, David 139
Assiter, Alison 101

Bachofen, J.J. 18
Bakhtin, Mikhail 102
Banerjee, Nirmala 141
Bard, Christine 99, 105
Barker, Frances 141
Barrett, Michèle 7, 137, 142, 145, 197
Basu, Aparna 140
Baudrillard, Jean 89
Beard, Mary 9, 17
Beechey, Veronica 41
Benhabib, Seyla 101
Bennett, Judith 7, 54
Berg, Maxine 8, 10, 18–19
Berger, Stefan 138, 181
Berkshire Conference of Women Historians 29
Bernard Shaw, Mrs 18
Bhabha, Homi 109, 140
Birdwood, Sir George 144
Bismarck, Otto von 129
Board of Trade, Report of the Departmental Committee (1918) 42
Bock, Gisela 41, 74, 85
body, history of 46–54, 73–87, 165–81, 193, 194, 197
Bonnell, Victoria 99, 101, 105, 187, 196
Bonnet, Marie-Jo 85
Boswell, John 85
Bourdieu, Pierre 78–9, 80, 83, 87
Bowlby, Rachel 6
Braudel, Fernand 194
Bridenthal, Renate 27
Brod, H. 85
Bucur, Maria 196
Buer, Mabel 10, 18
Bülow, Frieda von 130–1, 144–5
Burke, Peter 7
Burton, Antoinette 87
Butler, Judith 7, 101, 105, 165–6, 179, 197
Bynum, Caroline 25, 47–52, 54, 79, 169, 180, 197

Canning, Kathleen 197
Carby, Hazel 28
Catherine of Sienna 49
Catholicism in late medieval Europe 47–54
Cauer, Minna 134
Chakrabarty, Dipesh 108, 138, 139

Chandra, Bipan 139
Chartier, Roger 86, 96, 105
Chatterjee, Partha 139
Chew, Doris 32
Child Marriage Restraint Act 191
citizenship, gendering of 47, 147–64
Clancy-Smith, Julia 106–7, 138, 142, 144
Clark, Alice 9, 10, 11, 17, 19, 27
Code, Lorraine 105
Cooper, Selina 32
Corbin, Alain 75–8, 78, 85, 86, 163
Cornell, Drucilla 101
Crowston, Clare Haru 164
cultural turn *see* linguistic turn

Dauphin, Cécile 53
Davidoff, Leonore 26, 32, 40, 41, 56, 68–9, 72, 93, 194, 197
Davidson, Hannah 58
Davin, Anna 87
Davis, Angela 70
Davis, Belinda 105
Davis, Natalie Zemon 17, 19, 26–7, 73, 74, 84
d'Elmio, John 85
Delphy, Christine 41
Derrida, Jacques 90, 91, 101, 186
Desai, A.R. 139
di Leonardo, Micaela 145
difference among women 23–4, 27–9, 45–6, 59–60, 136–7
Dill, Bonnie Thornton 45, 53
Downs, Laura Lee 25, 35–39, 41, 42, 196, 197
Drake, Barbara 40
Drieu la Rochelle, Pierre 97, 105
Dubesset, Mathilde 42
Dyhouse, Carol 32, 41

East India Trading Company 113–14, 119
Ebeler, Anna 176–8
Echols, Alice 26–8, 53
Eisenstein, Zillah 28, 41
Eley, Geoff 148
Elias, Norbert 80–1, 169–71, 179
Elshtain, Jean Bethke 46
Empire, history of 187–90, 195
Engels, Friedrich 18, 53
Engineering Employers' Federation of Great Btitain 38
Enlightenment 150–64
Evans, Richard 104

Fabian Socialist Women's Group 18, 40
Faderman, Lillian 85
Febvre, Lucien 86
Feldner, Heiko 138, 181
feminism 1–95
  first wave 20–1, 32–3
  second wave 1–8, 20–34, 56
  Socialist 24–6, 31–4, 43
  Third-World 114–17
Feminist Archive (Bath) 31
Fichte, J.G. 160
Firestone, Shulamith 29
Flandrin, Jean-Louis 86
Foucault, Michel 27, 83, 87, 91, 93, 102, 103, 104, 109, 142, 146, 170, 171, 186
Fraser, Nancy 162, 165–6, 179
Freud, Sigmund 86, 155, 171
Friedrich II of Prussia 129

Garton, Stephen 86
Gay, Peter 86
Geertz, Clifford 90, 101
George, Dorothy 10, 18
German Colonial Association 129
German Women's Association for Nursing 130
German-National Women's League 131
Gildea, Robert 196
Gilmore, David 87
Girdler, J.S., 'Observations of the Pernicious Consequences of Forestalling, Regrating and Engrossing' 19
Glucksmann, Miriam 41
Gouda, Frances 106–7, 138, 142, 144
Gramsci, Antonio 139
Grayzel, Susan 105
Greenblatt, Steven 170
Griffiths, Morwena 7
Grossberg, Lawrence 140
Guha, Ranajit 108–9, 139, 141

Habermas, Jurgen 147–50, 152
Hall, Catherine 20, 24, 26, 28, 31, 40, 56, 68–9, 72, 93, 96, 104, 189–90, 192, 196
Halperin, David 85

Hamer, Kathryn 105
Hamilton, Kerry 17, 19
Haraway, Donna 197
Hardiman, David 139
Harris, Ruth 187, 193, 196, 197
Hartmann, Heidi 33, 41
Hawkes, Terence 101, 142
Helly, Dorothy 54
Hewitt, Nancy 44, 52
Higginbotham, Evelyn Brooks 28, 148
Hill, Christopher 139
Hill, Georgina 18
Hippel, Theodore Gottlieb von 159, 160
historical construction *see* social construction
Hobbes, Thomas 162–3
Hobsbawm, Eric 40, 139
Hoff, Joan 7, 54, 73, 84–5, 102, 185
Honegger, Claudia 197
hooks, bell 28
Houbre, Gabrielle 85
Hufton, Olwen 19
Hull, Gloria T. 53, 70
Hull, Isabel 148, 150–64, 188, 192, 196
Hunt, Lynn 99, 101, 105, 187, 196
Hunt, Nancy 138
Hunter, W.W. 144
Hurley, Robert 87
Hutchins, Bessie 10, 18

Ibert Bill (1883/4) 119, 122–5
Ibert, C.P. 122
imperialism 106–46, 188, 190–3
  in Africa 129–36
  in India 108–29, 190–1
industrial development 9–19, 35–42, 56–70
  agricultural revolution 9–19
  and changing sexual division of labour 13–17, 58–67, 70–2
  during World War One 35–42
  industrial revolution 11–17, 19, 56, 68–70
  and mass production 35–42
International Federation for Research Women's History (IFRWH) 29

Jayawardena, Kumari 145
Jones, Colin 105, 174, 180
Jones, Gareth Stedman 40, 102–5
Jones, Jacqueline 45, 53, 55–67, 70–2, 135, 184–5
Jordanova, Ludmilla 27
Joyce, Patrick 96, 104

Kant, Immanuel 159, 160, 163
Kaplan, Steven L. 86
Kelly, Joan 22, 27, 28
Kerber, Linda 52, 53
Klein, Melanie 41, 166, 178, 197
Knowles, Lilian 10, 18
Koonz, Claudia 27, 196
Krishnamurty, J. 140
Kumar, Kapil 139
Kumar, Radha 140

Lacan, Jacques 94, 162, 166, 169, 179
LaCapra, Dominick 86
Lal, Maneesha 140
Lambert, Peter 138
Lamphere, Louise 52
Landes, Joan 46, 148, 150, 162
Le Doeuff, Michele 105
Leacock, Eleanor 53
Lesbian Archive (Manchester) 31
Lévi-Strauss, Claude 89–90, 101
Levy, Darlene Gay 162
Lewis, Jane 32, 41
Liddington, Jill 25, 32–3, 41
linguistic turn 2, 5, 88, 88–105, 107, 109, 168, 186–7
Lodge, David 102
London School of Economics (LSE) 10, 18
Lorde, Audre 23, 24, 27–8

Macaulay, Thomas Babington 120, 143
macro-structural analysis 2, 5, 56
Mani, Lata 141
Marcuzzo, Maria Cristina 26, 54
Martin, Emily 180
Marx, Karl 103, 109, 148
Marxist historiography 5, 25, 30–4, 103–4, 107–10, 112
masculinity 4, 73–87, 117–29, 131–3, 167, 172, 174
Masselos, Jim 139
Maugue, Annelise 86
Mayo, Katherine, Mother India 190–1
Medick, Hans 8
Melman, Billie 114, 141, 142
Men's Studies 4, 73

Michel, Andrée 3
microhistory 5, 56
Midgley, Mary 7
Mill, John Stuart 117, 141
Millett, Kate 29
Mitchell, Juliet 27, 174
Mohanty, Chandra Talpade 114–17, 142
Moraga, Cherrie 28, 53
Mosse, George 85
Moynihan, Daniel, 'The Negro Family: The Case for National Action' 66

National Women's Liberation Conference (Oxford University, 1970) 182–3
Native Volunteer Movement (1885/6) 119, 120–2, 143
Nelson, Cary 140
Newton, Judith 41, 52
Nicholson, Linda 101
Norris, Jill 25, 32–3, 41
Nussbaum, Martha 164
Nye, Robert 76, 78–84, 86, 87

Oakley, Anne 7, 27
O'Brien, Patricia 78, 87
Offen, Karen 84
O'Hanlon, Rosalind 113–14, 141, 142
Okin, Susan Moeller 46
oral history 32–3
Ortner, Sherry 52
Outram, Dorinda 162
Owen, Robert 33

Pandy, Gayanendra 139
Pankhurst, Sylvia 33, 41
Parliamentary Commission on Women and Children in Agriculture (1843) 14
Passmore, Kevin 28, 88, 101, 102, 104, 138, 181, 196
Pateman, Carole 46, 148, 150, 162
patriarchy 5, 24–6, 28, 43–72, 94, 110–11, 115, 124–6
  and capitalism 25–6, 33–4, 39, 41
Payne, William 87
Pedersen, Susan 144–5
Perrot, Michelle 3, 7, 46, 53, 73, 85
Peters, Carl 129, 131, 144
Pierson, Ruth Roach 84, 140
Pinchbeck, Ivy 9–19, 27, 40
Pomata, Gianna 8, 17, 22, 26, 54
Poovey, Mary 72
possession 167, 172, 180
postmodernism *see* poststructuralism
poststructuralism 5–6, 28, 73, 79, 88–105, 136–7, 146–7, 162, 166, 187
Power, Eileen 9, 17, 18, 141
Prakash, Gyan 141
Pratibha Parmar 115, 142
psychoanalysis and history 5, 94, 101, 103, 194–5, 197
Public Service Commission (1886/7) 119–20, 125

race 55–67, 117–46
  and colonialism 117–46, 188–91, 196
  and gender 55–67, 106–46, 189–92
  and post-emancipation society in the United States 60–7
  and slavery in the United States 55–60
racist categories and social order 55–67, 117–46
Rageot, Gaston 37
Ramusack, Barbara 140
Ranger, Terence 141
Ray, Sangeeta 138
Reiter, Rayna 7, 52
Rendall, Jane 7, 54, 84, 87, 140
Reverby, Susan 54
Riley, Denise 28, 92, 103, 145
Roberts, Mary Louise 97–9, 105, 179
Robespierre, Maximilien 162
Roper, Lyndal 145, 166–81, 193, 194, 195, 197
Roper, Michael 85, 193, 194, 197
Rosaldo, Michelle 43–4, 52, 53
Rose, Jacqueline 179
Rose, Sonya 41, 103
Rossi-Doria, Anna 26, 54
Rousseau, Jean-Jacques 84, 87, 159, 162
Rubin, Gayle 7, 52
Ryan, Mary 41, 52

Said, Edward 109–10, 112–15, 117–18, 140–2
Samuel, Raphaël 40
Sangari, KumKum 110–11, 115, 140, 141
Sargent, Lydia 41
Sarkar, Sumit 127, 139–40
Sarkar, Tanika 127, 143
Saussure, Ferdinand de 28, 89, 136

Schreiner, Olive 9, 17
Schwantz, Henry 138
Schweitzer, Sylvie 19
Scott, Joan Wallach 6, 7, 8, 17–18, 27, 40, 92–4, 101–5, 162, 178, 179, 180, 185, 193, 196, 197
Scott, Patricia Bell 53, 70
Second Sex Conference (New York University, 1979) 23–4
Seeley, Paul 86
separate spheres 24–6, 43–72, 81–2
Sewell Jr, William 187, 196
sex, gender distinction 3–4, 79–80, 87, 165–6, 179
sexuality, history of 27, 75–7, 78–87, 111, 185, 188–92
Sharma, Ursula 140
Simonin, Anne 196
Sinha, Mrinalini 85, 117–28, 143, 144, 185, 190, 191, 192, 196
Skocpol, Theda 86
Smith, Barbara 53, 70
Smith, Bonnie 11, 18, 45, 53, 196
Smith-Rosenberg, Carroll 21, 26, 45, 53
Sneal, Anil 139
Snitow, Ann 27
social history 5, 9–19, 27, 99–101, 104, 107–12, 138, 168, 186
  Annales school 5, 30, 72–8, 86
  labour history 5, 30–42, 64
  social/cultural construction 5, 44–5, 66–7, 69–70, 74, 83, 88, 91
Society for German Colonization 129, 131
Spelman, Elizabeth 28
Spender, Dale 41
Spivak, Gayatri Chakravorty 101, 110, 140, 141, 142
Steedman, Carolyn 18, 72, 137, 145, 146, 194, 197
Stimpson, 28
Stoler, Ann Laura 145, 188–9, 190, 192, 196
Strachey, Rachel 33, 41
Strobel, Margaret 145
subaltern studies 8, 108–13, 138–40, 144
subjectivity/identity 6, 23–4, 51–2, 68, 94–6, 98–9, 100–1, 115–17, 155, 165–81, 188, 189, 193–4, 195
Summerfield, Penny 32, 41
Sutcliffe, A. 40
Taylor, Barbara 25, 33, 41, 174, 180, 194, 195, 197
Taylor, Charles 169, 171
Thane, Patricia 32, 40, 41
Thébaud, Françoise 22, 26, 42
Thompson, Edward Palmer 30–1, 39–40, 86–7, 139, 194
Tosh, John 83–7, 143
Toulouse Conference 'L'histoire des femmes est-elle possible?' (1982) 7, 29
trans-national history 188–92, 195
Trepp, Anne-Charlotte 8
Trimberger, Ellen Kay 86
Turner, Edith 54
Turner, Victor 54

Vaid, Sudesh 110–11, 115, 140, 141
Vansina, Jan 138
Vickery, Amanda 72
Villard, Léonie 6
Vincent, Catherine 42
Virago Press 31, 40

Wahrman, Dror 105, 174, 180
Walby, Sylvia 41
Walker, Garthine 181
Walkowitz, Judith 41, 52, 143
Washbrook, David 113–14, 141, 142
Washington, Georgia 63
Weber, Max 169, 170, 171
Weigman, Robin 85
White, Deborah G. 70–1
White, Jerry 40
Whitehead, Harriet 45, 52
Whitford, Margaret 7
Wildenthal, Lora 127, 128–9, 131–6, 144, 145
Wingfield, Nancy 196
witchcraft 167–81, 184
Women's Research and Resources Centre (later the Feminist Library, London) 31
Woolf, Virginia 1, 6, 9
Worpole, Ken 40

Yeo, Stephen 40
Young, Robert 117, 142

Zahra, Tara 196
Ziemann, Grete 134, 145